ALLE ZEIT WACH 1842

Günter Fandel (Ed.)

Management Problems in Health Care

With 29 Figures and 43 Tables

Springer-Verlag
Berlin Heidelberg New York
London Paris Tokyo

Professor Dr. Günter Fandel
Lehrstuhl für Betriebswirtschaft
Fernuniversität Hagen
Feithstraße 140
5800 Hagen 1, FRG

ISBN 978-3-642-73672-8 **ISBN 978-3-642-73670-4 (eBook)**
DOI 10.1007/978-3-642-73670-4

Softcover reprint of the hardcover 1st edition 1988

2142/7130-543210

Preface

The treatment and the solution of health economic problems by using management concepts is a permanent challenge; the question of controlling the costs or the efficiency of the supply of medical services is concerned. The articles in this book hope to make a concrete contribution to this subject by reporting on the latest research the authors have made in this area.

The medical services involved can either be part of the general provision of medical care and treatment to the population or can be provided by hospitals which are complex systems of public health care. The division of the contents of this book reflects this distinction. The four articles in Part A are concerned with problems of general health care. Part B is dedicated to particular problems relating to hospital planning and contains five articles.

In Part A the first article by Heidenberger deals with 'Optimal Resource Allocation in Horizontally and Vertically Disaggregated Health Programs' Using corresponding model formulations and linear programming the problem is solved of how a fixed budget should be distributed among the measures of a social health program so that the control of an illness is as effective as possible. In the case in question the illness to be controlled is high blood pressure. The possibilities for using this type of approach in health programs to combat other illnesses are obvious. The generalized approach developed by the author makes it easier to handle these problem situations and to solve them with less restrictive assumptions than forerunners of this approach. Feucht and Ostheimer examine 'Micro-Economic Aspects of Magnetic Resonance Tomography'. MR tomographic scanners belong to the high technology of medical equipments, and can discover and recognize particular illnesses faster and more reliable than ever before. At the same time they are also very complex systems with a great demand for personnel and space, cause considerable investment costs, and are subject to rapid technological changes given the present medical-technical progress. The purchase of an MR tomographic scanner by a doctor or a hospital is so bound up with high amortization risks. Questions on the most favourable configuration, on the development of the numbers of patients and cases for examination, on costs and proceeds and even on the break-even-point of such an investment practically suggest themselves. The authors attempt to offer suitable answers to the many different questions in this area. 'Regional Location and Capacity Planning for ESW Lithotripters and CT Scanners' is the subject of Bach's article. Using renal lithotripters and CT scanners as examples the author shows how a model of operating and transportation costs can be used to support decisions as to the purchasing and operation of machines for advanced medical technology. The model can be used to support the systematic compilation of the planning options which can be found with AMT machines or should be taken into account. Furthermore, the consequent effects of an AMT machine as regards costs, and in medical and spatial respects, can be illustrated with the model. Starting point for the considerations is the assumption that within this context single AMT machines must be observed in relation to other AMT machines in a metropolitan area of a region or in a Federal State. Fandel and Prasiswa's analysis of 'Planning and Organization of Economic Units in the Field of Out-Patient Medical Care' is concerned with the problem of optimal unit size, organization forms and inputstructure for a doctor's practice depending on the number of patients to be treated. A linear output-oriented production model with various procedural possibilities is discussed as an approach to the solution. The methodical considerations are then applied to an ophthalmologist's practice and the results shown.

Part B begins with an article from Hansen on 'Outcome Based Hospital Financing and Decision Oriented Hospital Management',in order to provide hospital services on an optimal cost basis while simultaneously maximizing the profit of the hospital. This conflict situation seems to be solved best by formulating a convex programming problem with a saddle point as optimal solution. A second concern of Hansen's work are the flows of information between the wards and the functional areas. The traditional organizations make considerable mistakes in data transmission, which a computer-based system of information processing can greatly reduce. In Fandel's contribution 'Special Problems of Recource Planning in Hospitals' three different problem areas are discussed on the basis of corresponding literature surveys. These are: location planning for different functional areas in a hospital, personnel scheduling in wards and departments on a minimum cost basis, and the stocking of easily perishable goods such as X-ray materials and blood plasma. The article from Fandel and Schmidt deals with 'Approaches to the Planning of the Optimal Supply of Beds in Hospitals'. Almost 90% of total costs in a hospital can be interpreted as fixed costs in that, given existing

capacity, they are directly determined by the number of available beds and accrue independently of how many patients are actually treated. Because of this, examination as to the numbers of beds on offer in existing hospitals and the optimal organization of their supply are of great importance. The article gives first a survey of the approaches in the literature on this subject. An important aspect here is how the hospital's admission policy treats urgent and non-urgent cases. The non-admittance rate for urgent cases and the waiting times for non-urgent cases are fundamental determinants of an optimal bed supply. A new recommendation for a solution is developed from the criticism of the approaches in the literature in order to determine the optimal numbers of regular and emergency beds in a hospital. The solution principle and the algorithm used are illustrated by means of a practical case. Fandel and Hegemann's work 'On Capacity Planning of Diagnosis Systems in Hospitals' shows how the queueing theory, extended by elements of the stochastic network technique, can be used in the capacity and process planning of complex diagnosis systems in hospitals. The model developed is, in contrast to approaches used up to now in the literature, a generalization on two patient flow systems, inpatients and outpatients, which run through the diagnostic system for examination purposes. The methodical considerations are supplemented by a study of a practical case in which the attempt is made to use the analytical considerations for the purpose of improving capacity utilization and patient flow in the diagnostic areas of the Hagen General Hospital.
In the final contribution in Part B from Stähly the theme is 'Simulation Models for the Analysis of Hospitals with Regard to their Emergency Infrastructure'. A hospital model is presented which allows the simulation of the actual reaction of a hospital service in extreme emergencies, such as natural or technical catastrophes, in regard to optimal capacity utilization. With the help of suitable choice of parameters small, medium sized and large hospitals can be studied in such situations. The importan point is to organize the hospital's stand-by services and the reactions of its management in such a way that in extreme cases no capacity is wasted. The analysis of the results of the simulations forms the basis for the derivation of rules for decision-making and for emergency plans as to how problems in hospitals during catastrophes should be mastered.

Finally, I would like to take the opportunity of thanking all those who supported and assisted in the publication of this book. I would like to thank the authors for their articles and for their generous cooperation. I would particularly like to thank the Fernuniversität for its considerable support. I would like to thank Gabriele Dahl, Christiane Kocherscheidt, Manuela Kutschinski, Lioba Lanwer, Thomas Giersiepen and Frank Reh for their extreme patience in preparing the manuscripts for printing.

Hagen, March 1988 Günter Fandel

Table of Contents

Part A: Problems of General Provision with Medical Services

Optimal Resource Allocation in Horizontally and Vertically Disaggregated Health Programs

Kurt Heidenberger

1 Introduction

A health program can be disaggregated horizontally and vertically. A program is called horizontally disaggregated if different diseases or different measures for the same disease are considered for disjoint populations or population strata. Stratification criteria may be e. g. age, sex, social class or geographical area. Within each stratum we allow for a vertical program disaggregation, i. e. each stratum-specific activity is split up into a stochastic sequence of steps. Given a fixed amount of resources the policy question is how to allocate them between the strata and within each stratum between the successive stages of the stochastic decision tree in order to maximize overall program effectiveness. Program effectiveness is usually measured in terms of "additional health"; we don't discuss the measurement problems involved but refer to the literature (Brooks 1986).

Among the worldwide most well-known health programs are the hypertension detection and reduction programs in the United States of America. Hypertension, i. e. high blood pressure, there affects about one in six adults. It is the single most important risk factor in cardiovascular disease, the leading cause of death in the United States as well as in several other industrialized countries, e. g., in the Federal Republic of Germany which has a hypertension prevalence of 17 % too. The causes

of hypertension are unknown in most cases. However, high blood pressure can be lowered by various therapeutic regimens. Several studies have shown that adequate (not necessarily medical) treatment reduces morbidity and mortality risks for hypertensives (Fraser 1986, Nichols/Weinstein 1978). The American Heart Association, the federal government and other public and private organizations stimulated and sponsored hundreds of hypertension programs which now are in operation at the community, city, regional, and state levels. Many of these programs asked the central agencies' managerial advice in allocating their scarce resources. One of these agencies, the Community Development Service of the National High Blood Pressure Education Program in the Department of Health, Education and Welfare considered a nonseparable mathematical programming model of Nichols and Weinstein (1978) in this regard. Ahmed (1978) supplemented this model by a variant. The model's central issue is how to allocate a given budget to the links of an intervention chain in order to maximize the number of adequately treated hypertensives via their reaching the final link. This model for the first time not only looks at screening (first link) and therapy but also adequately considers the compliance, or drop-out problem in hypertension management.
Our paper now proceeds as follows: After a description of this concrete and problem-oriented model we first point to its limits. Then we generalize the underlying abstract problem structure in several respects and construct a linear programming model, which is easier to handle and requires less restrictive assumptions than its predecessors. Finally we provide a numerical example by applying our model to the data of the Nichols/Weinstein/Ahmed-problem.

2 The Nichols/Weinstein-model

2.1 The problem

Nichols and Weinstein (1978) model the process of screening, diagnosis, treatment and follow-up of hypertensives as an n-component series system. In such a system each single component must work in order for the system as a whole to be successful.

Each step i either "functions" with probability p_i, thus sending the individual to the next stage, or "fails" with probability $1-p_i$ and sends the individual to an uncontrolled state. Each stage i incurs certain per capita cost C_i. It comprises the basic cost of caring for the individual at that stage as well as, in addition, the cost of intervention measures to increase the probability p_i that the individual will proceed to the next stage.

Figure 1 shows an illustrative eight-stage model (Nichols/Weinstein 1978).

Stage 1 defines the target population, especially its size N. Selection of the target population in the Nichols/Weinstein-model, however, is not part of the optimization problem involved. The target population may be defined according to criteria related to the prevalence of hypertension or to the effectiveness of intervention. Such criteria are, e. g., age, race, sex and occupation. The probability that a member of the target population will be screened is p_1. This probability may be increased by the following measures (among others): Publicizing the existence of screening sites, door-to-door canvassing, motivating providers (physicians, pharmacists, organizers of fairs, firms etc.) and providing mobile screening units.

Stage 2 relates to primary screening. Primary screening is defined as the initial blood pressure measurement. An individual at stage two has a measured blood pressure level above the specified cut-off level with probability p_2. p_2 depends on the prevalence of hypertension in the target population and on the accuracy of the screening test (see also Weinstein/Fineberg 1980). The unit costs of screening C_2 comprise the cost of the actual blood pressure measurement plus any unit costs of record keeping and administration.

Stage 3 categorizes the individual as having suspected hypertension. At this stage an individual has been screened once and found to have elevated blood pressure. The costs, C_3, incur for efforts necessary to increase the probability, p_3, that the individual reaches secondary screening. One can think of these efforts to range from a verbal recommendation that the individual sees his physician, to making appointments for the patient, to repeated phone or mail reminders, to home visits.

Stage 4 relates to secondary screening. Repeated measurements of blood pressure are usually necessary before a final diagnosis of confirmed hypertension can be made. With probability p_4 the preliminary finding of pathologically elevated blood pressure is true.

Stage 5 models the status "confirmed hypertension". The costs, C_5, here are for interventions aimed at increasing the probability, p_5, that the patient will start receiving treatment.

Stage 6 marks the beginning of treatment. Costs C_6 include the initial examination by a physician, diagnostic tests, medication for six months and any efforts to ensure continued care comprising one or more of the following: patient education, reminders to attend appointments, measures to improve access to care, group therapy sessions and instruction in home care.

Stage 7 categorizes patients who continue treatment for six months. At this stage follow-up and adherence to prescribed regimens has to be ensured. Costs, C_7, here are for lifetime treatment (medications and physician visits) and for increasing compliance with therapeutical regimens, e. g., via patient education or group therapy. p_7 is the probability of long-term success, that is controlled blood pressure.

Stage 8 represents this ideal status. A patient reaching it has permanently reduced his blood pressure to the desired level.

The decision variables here are the transition probabilities p_3, p_6, and p_7. The unit cost at each stage C_i is a convex, twice differentiable function $g_i(p_i)$ of p_i $(i = 3,6,7)$. The health policy goal is to allocate

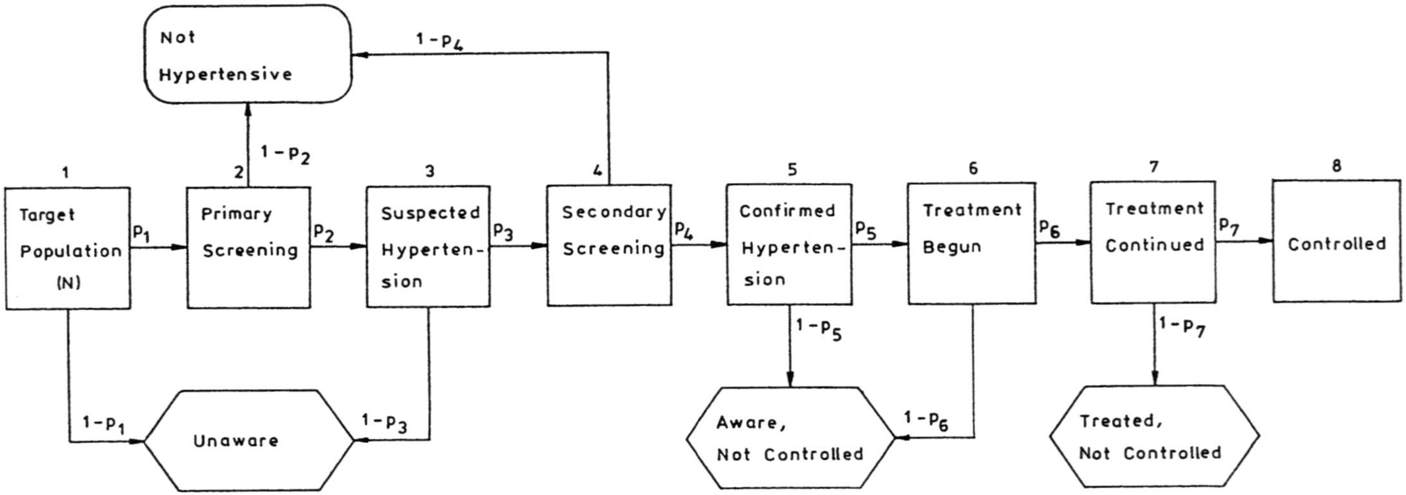

Figure 1: A multistage model of hypertension detection and follow-up ($p_1 \ldots p_7$: probabilities); source: Nichols/Weinstein 1978, p. 1528, modified

the available resources to the seven stages in such a way that the chances of an hypertensive individual to reach stage 8 are maximized. The only resource category considered is a budget B.

Many programs to be implemented before the Nichols/Weinstein-recommendations concentrated resource allocation on screening without special regard to further stages in the above 8-link chain. The resulting loss in efficiency (compared to an optimal allocation) is about 30 % (Nichols/ Weinstein 1978).

2.2 The mathematical model

Nichols and Weinstein consider a hypertension and treatment program with n + 1 stages and n transition probabilities (in the above example n equals 7). They construct the following model:

$$N \cdot \prod_{i=1}^{n} p_i \longrightarrow \max \text{ , subject to} \tag{1}$$

$$N \cdot \sum_{i=1}^{n} \prod_{j=0}^{i-1} p_j g_i(p_i) \leq B \text{ ,} \tag{2}$$

$$0 \leq p_i \leq 1 \text{ ,} \qquad i = 1, \ldots, n \tag{3}$$

$$p_o \equiv 1 \text{ .} \tag{4}$$

In deriving the formal optimality conditions they assume that the cost functions $g_i(p_i)$ have the properties:

$$g_i'(p_i) \geqq 0 \text{ ,} \tag{5}$$

$$g_i''(p_i) \geqq 0 \text{ ,} \tag{6}$$

$$\lim_{p_i \to 1} g_i(p_i) = \infty \text{ .} \tag{7}$$

With these assumptions we obtain the following optimality conditions (using the Lagrangian):

$$\prod_{j=1}^{i} p_j g_i'(p_i) + \sum_{j=i+1}^{n} \prod_{k=1}^{j-1} p_k g_j(p_j) = \prod_{j=1}^{n} p_j / \lambda \text{ ,} \tag{8}$$

$$i = 1, \ldots, n \text{ .}$$

Together with the budget constraint (2) a system of n + 1 non-linear equations results. The optimal values of the variables $p_1, \ldots, p_n, \lambda$ can be found by a numerical-iterative procedure e. g. by the more-dimensional Newton-method (see, e. g., Stoer 1972). Observe that (3) has not been used in deriving the optimality conditions because of premise (7): hence only one Lagrange-multiplier in (8).

The interpretation of the mathematical model is straightforward: the product terms in equation (8) obviously represent the expected per capita cost at stage i (i = 1, ..., 7). The sum of these stage-specific costs is total expected per capita cost.

2.3 The Ahmed variant

Nichols and Weinstein treat the population size N as a constant. Ahmed (1978) extends their model by two features: First, he also treats N as a variable, and second, he allows for the intermediate stages, too, to have a positive health benefit R_i. The corresponding model reads as follows:

$$N \cdot \sum_{i=1}^{n+1} \prod_{j=0}^{i-1} p_j R_i \longrightarrow \max \text{ , subject to} \tag{9}$$

$$N \cdot \sum_{i=1}^{n} \prod_{j=0}^{i-1} p_j g_i(p_i) \leq B \text{ ,} \tag{10}$$

$$0 \leq p_i \leq 1 \text{ ,} \qquad i = 1, \ldots, n \text{ ,}$$

$$N \geq 0 \text{ ,}$$

$$p_o \equiv 1 \text{ .}$$

Ahmed requires for the coefficients: $\sum_{i=1}^{n+1} R_i = 1$. But this is not essential for the algorithmic treatment of the model, if $R_{n+1} \neq 0$. Now Ahmed shows:

The use of N as a variable simplifies the numerical treatment of the system of equations resulting from the optimality conditions. If R_{n+1} is the only nonzero effectiveness coefficient R_i then the system of equations can be solved recursively. If other R_is are not zero as well Ahmed proposes a solution algorithm which takes advantage of a recursive substructure which exists in this case too. In both cases for the respective equations the zeros of a onedimensional function of one variable have to be found, e. g., using the Newton-method. This is a simplification compared to the Nichols/Weinstein-approach as there zeros of a multi-dimensional function of many variables have to be found (see equation (8)).

The mathematical foundation of the Ahmed-algorithms stems from the local Kuhn-Tucker-conditions (introductory see Blum/Oettli 1975, pp. 62-63). We form the Lagrangian

$$L = N \sum_{i=1}^{n+1} \prod_{j=0}^{i-1} p_j R_i - \lambda \left(N \sum_{i=1}^{n} \prod_{j=0}^{i-1} p_j g_i(p_i) - B \right) .$$

For each optimal solution of (9) - (10) we have $N > 0$. Hence $N \frac{\partial L}{\partial N} = 0$ gives us:

$$\sum_{i=1}^{n+1} \prod_{j=0}^{i-1} p_j R_i = \lambda \sum_{i=1}^{n} \prod_{j=0}^{i-1} p_j g_i(p_i) . \tag{11}$$

As a consequence we have $\lambda > 0$.

$\lambda \frac{\partial L}{\partial \lambda} = 0$ implies:

$$N \sum_{i=1}^{n} \prod_{j=0}^{i-1} p_j g_i(p_i) - B = 0 . \tag{12}$$

$p_k \frac{\partial L}{\partial p_k} = 0$ results in

$$\sum_{i=k+1}^{n+1} \prod_{j=1}^{i-1} p_j R_i = \lambda \left(\sum_{i=k+1}^{n} \prod_{j=1}^{i-1} p_j g_i(p_i) + \prod_{j=1}^{k} p_j g_k'(p_k) \right) ,$$

for each $k = 1, \ldots, n - 1$. (13)

$p_n \frac{\partial L}{\partial p_n} = 0$ gives us:

$$\prod_{j=1}^{n} p_j R_{n+1} = \prod_{j=1}^{n} p_j \lambda g_n'(p_n) \tag{13'}$$

If we substract the equations (13) resp. (13') from (11) we obtain for each k = 1, ..., n:

$$\sum_{i=1}^{k} \prod_{j=0}^{i-1} p_j R_i = \lambda \left(\sum_{i=1}^{k} \prod_{j=0}^{i-1} p_j g_i(p_i) - \prod_{j=1}^{k} p_j g_k'(p_k) \right). \tag{14}$$

Obviously equation (14) suggests to look for a recursive solution procedure as it only contains variables p_j with $j \leq k$.

Hence Ahmed (1978) offers the following iterative algorithm:

a) Set p_n to an arbitrary value between 0 and 1.

b) Solve equation (13') for λ (note: equation (13') can be rewritten as $R_{n+1} = \lambda g_n'(p_n)$).

c) Using λ from step b) solve equation (14) recursively for p_1, p_2, ..., p_n^*.

d) If $p_n = p_n^*$ then a solution is found, go to g).

e) Set new $p_n := \frac{1}{2}$ (old $p_n + p_n^*$). Go to step b).

f) Compute N from equation (12).

g) STOP

Observe, the value of each variable p_i in step c) is found by an iterative procedure for determining the zeros of a onedimensional function of one variable. Thus the Ahmed-algorithm has two nested iteration loops.

If only R_{n+1} is not equal zero the outer loop disappears as the left hand side of equation (14) vanishes. Dividing its right hand side by λ leaves a sequentially solvable nonlinear system of equations. In this special case the above algorithm is reduced to the steps c) and f).

The above derivation for the special case makes the relation between the two Ahmed-algorithms more evident than the original paper, which first presents the special case and then separately develops the more general model.

2.4 The model's limits

The power both of the Nichols/Weinstein-model as well as of the Ahmed-variants is limited mainly by their five common characteristics:

- The models cannot deal with horizontal disaggregation; i.e., they are not able to cope with problems involving simultaneous resource allocation for several (horizontally disaggregated) population groups each with its own serial n-component system.

- The models' ability to structure vertical disaggregation is limited too. General tree structures cannot be modelled, only stemlike ones.
- Only one resource constraint can be dealt with.
- The cost functions $g_i(p_i)$ have to fulfill the requirements (5), (6), and (7), i. e. those specific assumptions on differentiability and limit behaviour have to be valid.
- A postoptimal sensitivity analysis is impossible.

Furthermore the Ahmed-algorithm has an Achilles-heel by equation (13'): If $g_n(p_n)$ is constant in a certain subinterval $[0,k]$ of the interval $[0,1]$ then $g_n'(p_n)$ equals zero there and λ cannot be computed any longer. As a consequence in this case one always has to ensure that p_n is greater than k.

3 A more general problem and its model

Accepting the above critique as a starting point we first generalize the basic abstract problem structure of the Nichols/Weinstein/Ahmed-model without respect to algorithmic concerns. In the later paragraphs we then show that the generalized problem can be modelled as a linear program.

3.1 The problem

We consider the following formal problem: For each of M populations a specific health program is given as a stochastic tree structure, see figure 2. Each tree m has a finite number of nodes ($m = 1, \dots, M$).

Each node k different from the starting-node 1_m has a certain (in most practical cases nonnegative) health benefit (i. e. effectiveness) R_k. Note that choosing a measurement scale for the R_ks may have implications for the overall coefficient structure of the R_ks. If, e. g., the R_ks are measured on a bounded scale either only the end nodes are allowed to have nonvanishing effectiveness coefficients or proper standardization of all R_ks is due.

The individuals of population m proceed sequentially through the stochastic tree where each of the policy-dependent branching probabilities depends on its edge-specific piecewise-linear, monotone, convex (and hence continuous) cost function. The size of population m is K_m ($m = 1, \dots, M$), a constant; what part N_m of it will be included is a policy variable, however.

Given the above premises the task now is to maximize the total sum of all health benefits of all population-specific program parts subject to a given quantity of a bundle of resources. From a mathematical point of view the underlying abstract problem is the simultaneous optimization

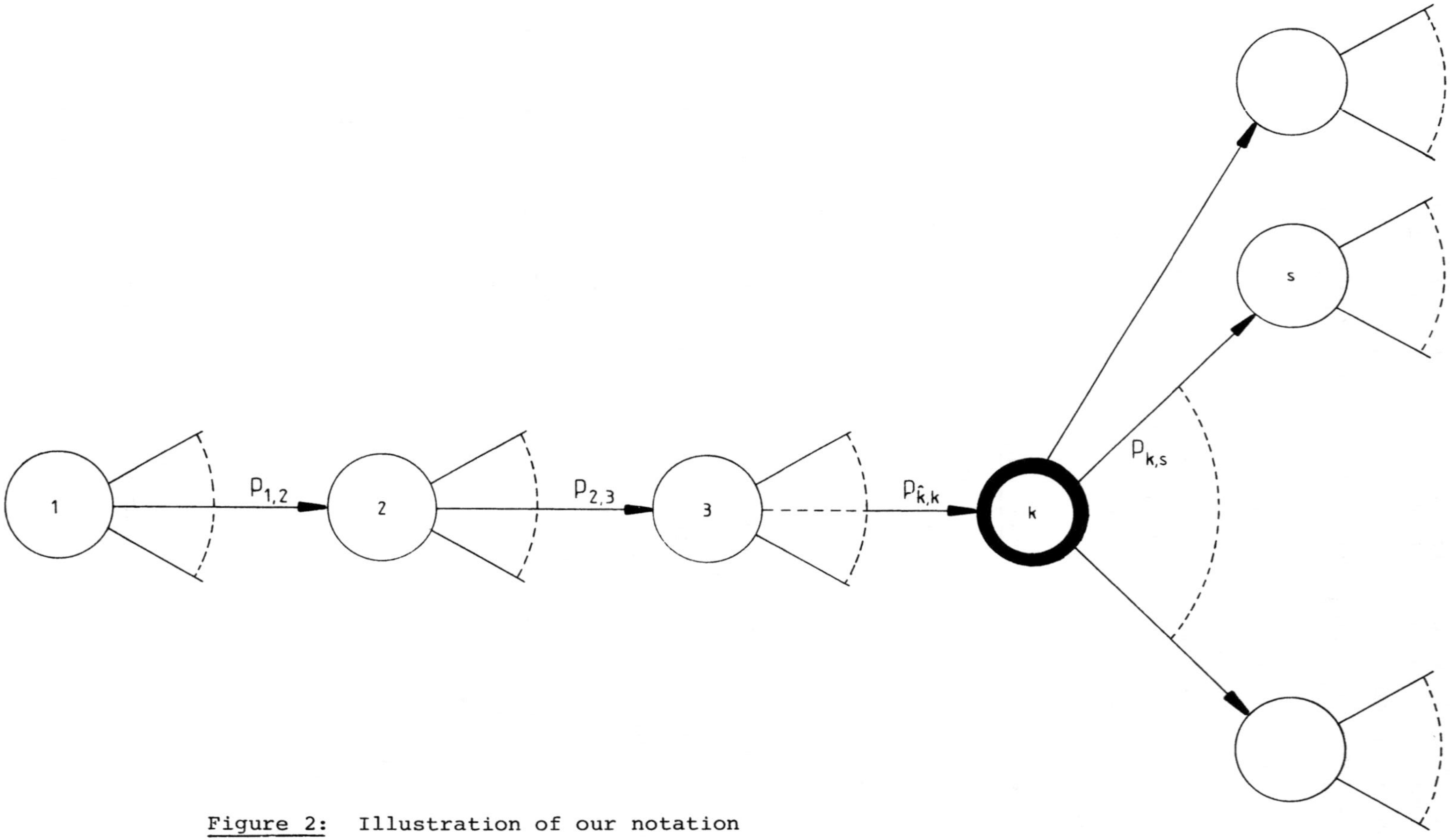

Figure 2: Illustration of our notation

of several finite horizon stochastic decision chains with continuous action space and multiple resource constraints.

The above more general problem extends the Ahmed-variant of the Nichols/Weinstein-model in a canonical way. Observe, that the graph of figure 1, which is also used by Ahmed, does not have a tree-structure. But a trivial modification can change this by simply doubling those nodes which are entered by two arrows.

Our extended problem eliminates all the limits of the Ahmed-variant of the Nichols/Weinstein-model. This is evident for almost all points of critique except for the last one concerning sensitivity analysis. Once we will have developed our LP-model this point will be obvious too.

In the following paragraphs we stepwise build a linear programming model for our extended problem. In order to make the process of model construction transparent we start out from a nonlinear, nonseparable model which easily can be identified as a direct extension of the Ahmed-model ((9) and (10)). Then we show: If we define the decision variables in a suitable way and take advantage of the piecewise linearity of the cost functions we can transform the nonlinear first-step model to a LP-model.

3.2 A nonseparable first-step model

We refer to the extended problem in the previous paragraph and especially to the general tree structure in figure 2. Following the basic idea of the Nichols/Weinstein-model in its Ahmed-variant ((9) and (10)) it suggests itself to first choose this mathematical formulation:

$$\sum_{m=1}^{M} N_m \sum_{k \in A_m} \prod_{j \in I_k} p_{\hat{j},j} R_k \longrightarrow \max \,, \tag{15}$$

subject to

$$\sum_{m=1}^{M} N_m \sum_{\substack{k \in A_m \setminus E_m \\ s \in S_k}} \prod_{j \in I_k} p_{\hat{j},j}\, g^r_{k,s}(p_{k,s}) \leq B^r \,, \tag{16}$$

$$\text{for each } r = 1, \ldots, R \,;$$

$$p_{o_m,1_m} = 1 \,,$$

$$\sum_{s \in S_k} p_{k,s} = 1 \,, \quad \text{for each } k \in A_m \setminus E_m \,;\ m = 1, \ldots, M \,, \tag{17}$$

$$0 \leq N_m \leq K_m \,, \quad \text{for each } m = 1, \ldots, M \,, \tag{18}$$

$$0 \leq p_{\hat{k},k} \,, \quad \text{for each } k \in A_m \,, \; m = 1, \ldots, M \,, \tag{19}$$

where

M	denotes the number of populations,
A_m	denotes the index set of the nodes of tree m (m = 1, ..., M),
E_m	denotes the index set of the end nodes of tree m (m = 1, ..., M),
1_m	denotes the index of the first node of tree m (m = 1, ..., M),
o_m	denotes the index of a fictitious predecessor node of node 1_m (m = 1, ..., M),
$\hat{k}$	denotes the index of the predecessor node of node k, for each $k \in A_m$ (m = 1, ...,M),
$p_{\hat{k},k}$	denotes the decision variable "transition probability between the nodes $\hat{k}$ and k",
$g^r_{\hat{k},k}$	denotes the piecewise linear, monotone convex cost function which quantifies the resource consumption of type r depending on the value of $p_{\hat{k},k}$,
B^r	denotes the available amount of resource type r (r = 1, ..., R),
R	denotes the number of the different resource types,
l_k	denotes the index set of the nodes on the path from the starting node to node k (including k),
S_k	denotes the index set of all nodes immediately following k,
K_m	denotes the size of population m (m = 1, ..., M), it is the upper bound for N_m,
N_m	denotes the decision variable "number of individuals of population m to be included".

The above model is hard to handle from an algorithmic point of view. Therefore, in the next paragraph, we show that it can be transformed to a linear programming model.

3.3 A linear programming model

First a convention: In order to prevent overload of our notation we suppress the index m.

We now define x_k as

$$x_k := N \prod_{j \in l_k} p_{\hat{j},j} \,, \quad \text{for each } k \in A \,. \tag{20}$$

(As $p_{o,1} = 1$ it follows that $x_1 = N$)

This definition implies:

$$p_{\hat{k},k} = \frac{x_k}{x_{\hat{k}}}\ , \text{ for each } k \in A \setminus \{1\}\ . \tag{21}$$

$g^r_{\hat{k},k}(.)$ is convex, monotone and piecewise linear, and, hence, can be written as (see figure 3):

$$g^r_{\hat{k},k}(p_{\hat{k},k}) = c^r_{\hat{k},k} + \sum_{l=1}^{f^r_{\hat{k},k}} c^{r,l}_{\hat{k},k}\, p^{r,l}_{\hat{k},k}\ , \tag{22}$$

for each $k \in A \setminus \{1\}$;

where

$$\sum_{l=1}^{f^r_{\hat{k},k}} p^{r,l}_{\hat{k},k} = p_{\hat{k},k} \quad \text{and} \tag{23}$$

$$0 \leq p^{r,l}_{\hat{k},k} \leq d^{r,l}_{\hat{k},k}\ , \quad \text{for each } k \in A \setminus \{1\}\ ; \tag{24}$$

here one has to ensure that

$$p^{l+1}_{\hat{k},k} = 0 \quad \text{if} \quad d^{r,l}_{\hat{k},k} - p^{r,l}_{\hat{k},k} > 0\ . \tag{25}$$

For the constants $d^{r,l}_{\hat{k},k}$ and $c^{r,l}_{\hat{k},k}$ the following relations holds:

$$\sum_{l=1}^{f^r_{\hat{k},k}} d^{r,l}_{\hat{k},k} = 1 \quad \text{and} \tag{26}$$

$$0 \leq c^{r,l-1}_{\hat{k},k} \leq c^{r,l}_{\hat{k},k}\ , \text{ for each } l = 2, \ldots, f^r_{\hat{k},k}\ . \tag{27}$$

We now define $x^{r,l}_k$ as

$$x^{r,l}_k := p^{r,l}_{\hat{k},k}\, x_{\hat{k}}, \quad \text{for each } k \in A \setminus \{1\}\ . \tag{28}$$

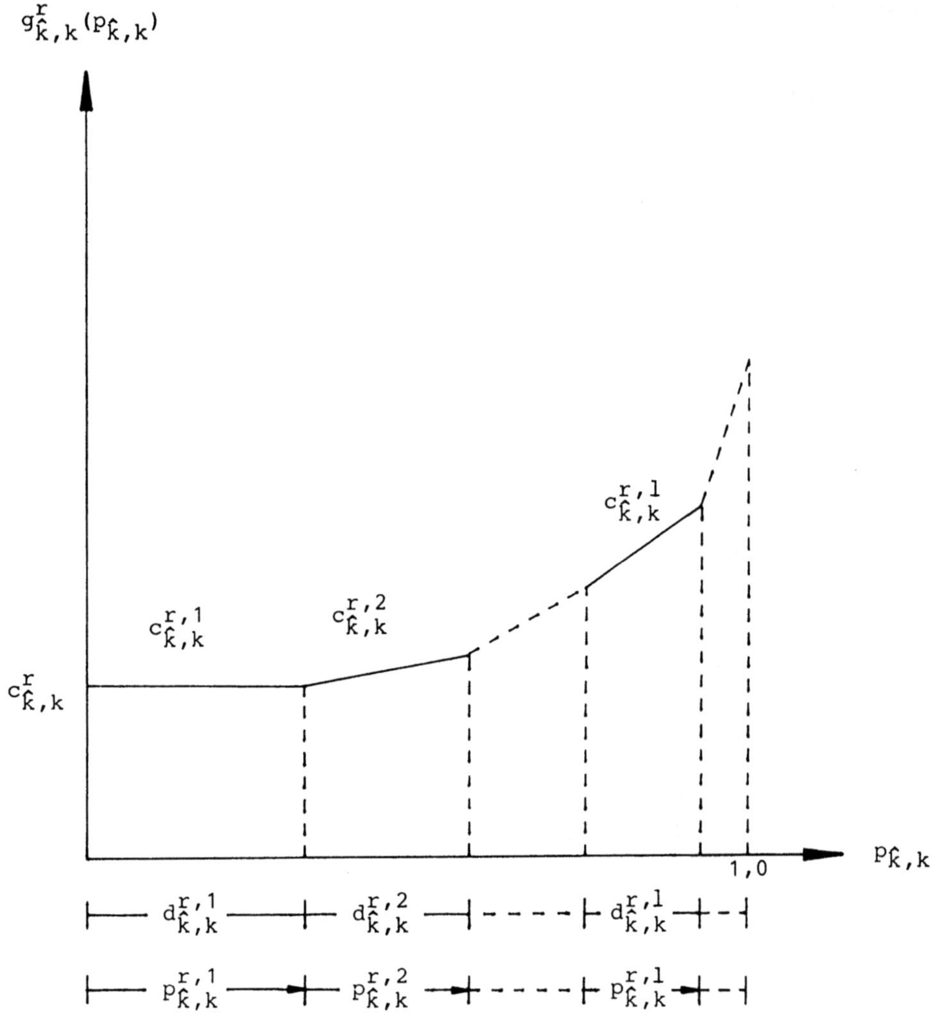

Legend: $c^{r,l}_{\hat{k},k}$: Slope of the respective line segment

$d^{r,l}_{\hat{k},k}$: Interval sizes between points of support

$p^{r,l}_{\hat{k},k}$: Interval specific variable

Figure 3: The piecewise linear convex function $g^r_{\hat{k},k}$

Then because of (23) we have

$$\sum_{l=1}^{f^r_{\hat{k},k}} x_k^{r,l} = x_{\hat{k}} \sum_{l=1}^{f^r_{\hat{k},k}} p_{\hat{k},k}^{r,l} = x_{\hat{k}}\, p_{\hat{k},k} = x_k \quad . \tag{29}$$

Using the relations (20) - (29) for our nonlinear first-step model in the preceding paragraph, we obtain the following LP-model ((30) - (35)):

Objective function (15) and definition (20) imply

$$\sum_{m=1}^{M} \sum_{k \in A} R_k x_k \longrightarrow \max \tag{30}$$

From the relations (16), (22) and (28) it follows that

$$\sum_{m=1}^{M} \sum_{\substack{k \in A \setminus E \\ s \in S_k}} c^r_{k,s}\, x_k + \sum_{l=1}^{f^r_{k,s}} c^{r,l}_{k,s}\, x_s^{r,l} \le B^r , \tag{31}$$

for each $r = 1, \ldots, R$.

In equation (29) we have shown

$$\sum_{l=1}^{f^r_{\hat{k},k}} x_k^{r,l} = x_k , \qquad \text{for each } k \in A \setminus \{1\} . \tag{32}$$

Substituting (28) into (24) we have

$$0 \le x_k^{r,l} \le d^{r,l}_{\hat{k},k}\, x_{\hat{k}} , \tag{33}$$

for each $k \in A \setminus \{1\}, l = 1, \ldots, f^r_{\hat{k},k}$.

Substituting (21) into (17) we obtain

$$\sum_{s \in S_k} x_s = x_k , \qquad \text{for each } k \in A \setminus E . \tag{34}$$

By definition (20) and inequality (18) the following relation holds

$$0 \leq x_1 \leq K . \tag{35}$$

Now the LP-model is complete. Condition (25) is "automatically" satisfied because of the convexity of $g^r_{\hat{k},k}(.)$ and the linearity of the objective function to be maximized. Remember furthermore that by convention all variables as well as A, E and K have a suppressed group specific index m (m = 1, ..., M).

3.4 A "compressed" variant of the LP-model

If the positions of the points of support of the functions $g^r_{\hat{k},k}$ do not depend upon r then the number of variables and constraints of our LP-model can be reduced by substituting the left hand side of equation (32) for x_k. In this case the index r of the variables $x^{r,l}_{\hat{k},k}$ as well as of the constants $f^r_{\hat{k},k}$ and $d^{r,l}_{\hat{k},k}$ is no longer necessary. In order to preserve the uniformity of our notation we furthermore define

$$x^1_1 : = x_1 ,$$

and

$$f_{o,1} = 1 .$$

We obtain the simplified model by the following steps:

Objective function (30) and equation (32) imply

$$\sum_{m=1}^{M} \sum_{k \in A} \sum_{l=1}^{f_{\hat{k},k}} R_k \, x^l_k \longrightarrow \max . \tag{36}$$

Because of (32) and (31) we have

$$\sum_{m=1}^{M} \sum_{\substack{k \in A \setminus E \\ s \in S_k}} \sum_{l=1}^{f_{\hat{k},k}} c^r_{k,s} \, x^l_k + \sum_{l=1}^{f_{k,s}} c^{r,l}_{k,s} \, x^l_s \leq B^r , \tag{37}$$

for each r = 1, ..., R .

Substituting (32) into (33) we obtain

$$0 \leq x^l_k \leq \sum_{\tilde{l}=1}^{f_{\hat{k},k}} d^l_{\hat{k},k} \, x^{\tilde{l}}_{\hat{k}} , \tag{38}$$

for each $k \in A \setminus \{1\}, l = 1, \ldots, f_{\hat{k},k}$.

By (32) and (34) we have

$$\sum_{s\in S_k} \sum_{l=1}^{f_{k,s}} x_s^l = \sum_{l=1}^{f_{\hat{k},k}} x_k^l , \qquad \text{for each } k\in A\setminus E . \tag{39}$$

Relation (35) remains unchanged, hence

$$0 \leq x_1^1 \leq K . \tag{40}$$

4 Sample application of the LP-model to the Nichols/Weinstein/Ahmed-Problem

4.1 The data

For illustration purposes we use the data of the numerical examples of Nichols/ Weinstein (1978) and Ahmed (1978). These data are based on actual pr grams. The step-specific transition probabilities and cost-functions are listed in table 1. In their example Nichols and Weinstein treat $p_{1,2}$ as a variable and keep N constant. Ahmed, however, in his example keeps $p_{1,2}$ fix and conceives N as a variable. Otherwise he uses the same data (see also our paragraph 2.2 and 2.3 above).

Nichols and Weinstein use hyperbolic cost functions for interpolating the discrete empirical baseline data. The choice of this class of functions is relatively arbitrary. Other function classes also satisfy the stringent requirements (5), (6), and (7) for the functions $g_{\hat{k},k}(.)$. Ahmed, e. g., in addition introduces three further function families: the inverse square, the logarithmic and the exponential form.

As a sample budget value Nichols and Weinstein use one million \$ in their example. The values for the health benefit (i. e. effectiveness) coefficient R_k (see table 1) have been taken from the Ahmed-paper. The coefficients R_k here are without dimension. Maximal effectiveness is 1. It is only reached in state 8 as the R_ks sum up to one.

Observe that we use our notation introduced in paragraph 3.2. Hence we write "$p_{i,j}$" instead of the original "p_i" used by Nichols, Weinstein and Ahmed.

4.2 The LP-model

Our LP-model in both variants has piecewise linear cost functions as a prerequisite. To satisfy this premise we approximate the cost-functions

$g_{\hat{k},k}$ of table 2 by continuous, piecewise linear functions $\tilde{g}_{\hat{k},k}$ in the interval [0;0,99] in such a way that

$$\max \{ |g_{\hat{k},k}(p_{\hat{k},k}) - \tilde{g}_{\hat{k},k}(p_{\hat{k},k})| \,\big|\, p_{\hat{k},k} \in [0;0,99] \} < \varepsilon .$$

Note that it will do to consider only the interval [0;0,99] as the functions $g_{\hat{k},k}$ have "very high" values in the remaining interval [0,99;1]. Hence all models automatically force the $p_{\hat{k},k}$-values to be less or equal 0,99.

We now apply the LP-model of paragraph 3.4 to the problem in paragraph 2.1 (see also figure 1). For this special case according to the relations (36) - (40) we obtain the following model:

$$R_1x_1^1 + R_2x_2^1 + R_3x_3^1 + R_4(x_4^1 + \ldots + x_4^{f_{3,4}}) + R_5x_5^1 + R_6x_6^1 +$$

$$+ R_7(x_7^1 + \ldots + x_7^{f_{6,7}}) + R_8(x_8^1 + \ldots + x_8^{f_{7,8}}) \longrightarrow \max \text{ , s. t.} \tag{41}$$

$$c_{1,2}x_1^1 + c_{1,2}^1x_2^1 + c_{2,3}x_2^1 + c_{2,3}^1x_3^1 + c_{3,4}x_3^1 + (c_{3,4}^1x_4^1 + \ldots +$$

$$+ c_{3,4}^{f_{3,4}}x_4^{f_{3,4}}) + c_{4,5}(x_4^1 + \ldots x_4^{f_{3,4}}) + c_{4,5}^1x_5^1 + c_{5,6}x_5^1 + c_{5,6}^1x_6^1 +$$

$$+ c_{6,7}^1x_6^1 + (c_{6,7}^1x_7^1 + \ldots + c_7^{f_{6,7}}x_7^{f_{6,7}}) + c_{7,8}(x_7^1 + \ldots +$$

$$+ x_7^{f_{6,7}}) + (c_{7,8}^1x_8^1 + \ldots + c_{7,8}^{f_{7,8}}x_8^{f_{7,8}}) \leq B , \tag{42}$$

$$\left.\begin{array}{l}
0 \leq x_4^1 \leq d_{3,4}^1x_3^1 , \\
\quad\vdots \qquad\quad \vdots \\
0 \leq x_4^{f_{3,4}} \leq d_{3,4}^{f_{3,4}}x_3^1 , \\
\\
0 \leq x_7^1 \leq d_{6,7}^1x_6^1 , \\
\quad\vdots \qquad\quad \vdots \\
0 \leq x_7^{f_{6,7}} \leq d_{6,7}^{f_{6,7}}x_6^1 ,
\end{array}\right\} \tag{43}$$

$$0 \leq x_8^1 \leq d_{7,8}^1 + \ldots + x_7^{f_{6,7}}) ,$$
$$\vdots \qquad \vdots$$
$$0 \leq x_8^{f_{7,8}} \leq d_{7,8}^{f_{7,8}}(x_7^1 + \ldots + x_7^{f_{6,7}}) ,$$

$$0 \leq x_1^1 \leq K . \tag{44}$$

The above inequalities already take into account the special conditions of our example. Constraint (39), e. g., is superfluous as the tree of figure 1 doesn't have any "real" branches; it essentially only has a "stem". With respect to the data of table 1 only for the functions $\tilde{g}_{3,4}$, $\tilde{g}_{6,7}$ and $\tilde{g}_{7,8}$ we choose to have more than one point of support. For the block of restrictions (43) we have taken advantage of the fact that the seemingly missing constraints are unnecessary as we will immediately see. The a-priori fixation of the variables $p_{1,2}$, $p_{2,3}$, $p_{4,5}$, and $p_{5,6}$ in table 1 of course implies

$$\left.\begin{aligned} x_2^1 &= x_1^1 , \\ x_3^1 &= 0.15\ x_1^1 , \\ x_5^1 &= 0.67\ (x_4^1 + \ldots x_4^{f_{3,4}}) , \\ x_6^1 &= 0.75 \cdot 0.67\ (x_4^1 + \ldots + x_4^{f_{3,4}}) . \end{aligned}\right\} \tag{45}$$

We now substitute x_2^1, x_3^1, x_5^1, and x_6^1 of (41) - (43) by the right hand sides of (45) and we obtain the claimed result.

For the R_k-values of table 2 and $K = \infty$ ("Ahmed"-data) our sample model simplifies in the following way:

$$0.007\ (x_4^1 + \ldots + x_4^{f_{3,4}}) + 0.09\ (x_7^1 + \ldots + x_7^{f_{6,7}}) +$$
$$+ 0.9\ (x_8^1 + \ldots + x_8^{f_{7,8}}) \longrightarrow \max , \quad \text{subject to}$$

$$40\ x_3^1 + (115 + c_{3,4}^1)x_4^1 + \ldots + (115 + c_{3,4}^{f_{3,4}})x_4^{f_{3,4}} +$$
$$+ (2800 + c_{6,7}^1)x_7^1 + \ldots + (2800 + c_{6,7}^{f_{6,7}})x_7^{f_{6,7}} +$$
$$+ c_{7,8}^1 x_8^1 + \ldots + c_{7,8}^{f_{7,8}} x_8^{f_{7,8}} \leq B ,$$

$$\left.\begin{array}{ll}
x_4^1 - d_{3,4}^1 x_3^1 & \leq 0 \,, \\
\vdots & \vdots \\
x_4^{f_{3,4}} - d_{3,4}^{f_{3,4}} x_3^1 & \leq 0 \,, \\
 & \\
x_7^1 - d_{6,7}^1 \cdot 0.5\ (x_4^1 + \ldots + x_4^{f_{3,4}}) & \leq 0 \,, \\
\vdots & \vdots \\
x_7^{f_{6,7}} - d_{6,7}^{f_{6,7}} \cdot 0.5\ (x_4^1 + \ldots + x_4^{f_{3,4}}) & \leq 0 \,, \\
 & \\
x_8^1 - d_{7,8}^1\ (x_7^1 + \ldots + x_7^{f_{6,7}}) & \leq 0 \,, \\
\vdots & \vdots \\
x_8^{f_{7,8}} - d_{7,8}^{f_{7,8}}\ (x_7^1 + \ldots + x_7^{f_{6,7}}) & \leq 0 \,, \\
 & \\
x_k^l \geq 0 \,, \quad \text{for each } k \text{ and } l \,. &
\end{array}\right\} \qquad (46)$$

Depending on the actually chosen linearization $\tilde{g}_{\hat{k},k}$ of $g_{\hat{k},k}$ $(k = 4,7,8)$ which approximates $g_{\hat{k},k}$ within an ε-tube we obtain concrete values for $d_{\hat{k},k}^1$ and $c_{\hat{k},k}^1$ (see also figure 3). The next paragraph presents the results of some sample computations. We used 10^6 for B. We then compare our results with those of the highly specialized Ahmed-method.

4.3 Results of the sample computations

Table 3 shows the results of our sample computations. The values of the variables x_k^l for $l = 3,4,7$, and 8 directly result from model (46) and the data of table 2. The values of the remaining variables x_k^l for $l = 1,2,5$, and 6 follow from (45). Model (46) is a special case of the "compressed" model type in paragraph 3.4. From equation (32) we immediately get the values of the variables x_k of the fuller model type in paragraph 3.3. Finally from (20) and (21) we obtain the values of the variables N, $p_{1,2}, \ldots, p_{7,8}$ by dividing x_k by $x_{\hat{k}}$. Table 3 also compares these values to those produced by the Ahmed-algorithm.

Note that the numerical results of the Ahmed-paper relate to the example presented by Nichols and Weinstein, i. e., R_8 (= 1) is the only nonzero constant R_k there. So his results cannot immediately be used for comparison purposes.

Table 4 for various ε-values compares the results of our LP-model to those of the Ahmed-approach. We not only employ the hyperbolic cost function of table 2 but also three further functions alternatively used by Ahmed to interpolate the underlying discrete data:

$$g_{\hat{k},k}(p_{\hat{k},k}) = a_{\hat{k}} + b_{\hat{k}}/(1-p_{\hat{k},k})^2 \ , \quad \text{(invers-square)},$$

$$g_{\hat{k},k}(p_{\hat{k},k}) = a_{\hat{k}} - b_{\hat{k}} l_n(1-p_{\hat{k},k}) \ , \quad \text{(logarithmic)},$$

$$g_{\hat{k},k}(p_{\hat{k},k}) = a_{\hat{k}} + b_{\hat{k}} \exp(1/1-p_{\hat{k},k}) \ , \quad \text{(exponential)} ,$$

where $a_{\hat{k}}$ and $b_{\hat{k}}$ are suitable constants.

Table 4 does not need any further general comments because of the discussion in paragraph 4.2. The line "# controlled" shows how many hypertensives are under control after the screening and treatment process, i. e., how many have reached stage 8, the final link of the chain. This number is not identical with the value of our objective function because the stages 5 and 7 contribute a, however small, amount to the objective function, even if certain individuals prematurely have the program. If R_k is the only nonvanishing effectiveness constant then objective function and "# controlled" are identical. But this is not the case in our example.

$p_{1,2}$, $p_{2,3}$, and $p_{4,5}$ here are a-priori fixed pseudo-variables (see table 1). $p_{6,7}$ in the LP-models always has a value of 0.67, with two exceptions. This can be explained as follows: the slopes of the linearizations $\tilde{g}_{6,7}$ (see table 2) behind the "boundary value" of 0.67 first are higher than those of the corresponding original functions. For ε = 10 our linearizations of the invers-square and exponential case however underestimate the original slopes in that region.

We see that the maximal relative error of the solutions of our linearizations does not exceed 9 % though ε varies by a factor up to 50. Thus in our LP-model, so to speak as a by-product, we apparently have a relatively robust approximation also for the case that the convex functions $g_{\hat{k},k}$ are twice differentiable. Our conjecture is further supported by these facts: We consider four different function classes and use approximation software in order to largely prevent a bias of "favourable" approximations which may be more present in manual procedures.

5 Discussion

We now want to summarize the features of our LP-model. We are going to point to its algorithmic power as well as to its broad range of application which even extends into the private sector of an economy.

To gain the proper perspective we remind of the characteristics of its predecessors: Nichols and Weinstein(1978)deal with the special case described in our paragraphs 2.1 and 2.2. The authors' starting point are the following assumptions: Only one target population is considered; N, the population size, is a constant; the twice differentiable convex functions $g_k(p_k)$ grow larger without bound if p_k approaches the limit of unity; the stochastic tree essentially only consists of a stem (see figure 1); only the final link of the screening-treatment chain has an associated positive health benefit; only one resource constraint can be handled (see paragraph 2.4). In our terminology of chapter 1 the authors consider the problem of resource allocation in a health program which is vertically disaggregated in a stem-structure and not disaggregated horizontally.

Ahmed (1978) extends the Nichols/Weinstein-model by two features: He conceives N as a variable and furthermore he allows for the intermediate stages to have some positive health benefit as well.

Nichols and Weinstein solve their resulting nonseparable mathematical programming model by standard algorithms of nonlinear optimization (see section 2.2 above). Ahmed proposes a special solution algorithm which exploits the special structure of his still nonseparable model (see section 2.3). The Ahmed-method, however, is not applicable to our more general problem structure. On the other hand if the functions used by Nichols, Weinstein and Ahmed are approximated by piecewise linear ones, our LP-model can map the respective problems in a linear-separable way (see chapter 4).

In addition our LP-approach allows to model more general situations and treat them in an algorithmically simple way:

- The fragmented empirical data can nonparametrically be interpolated by piecewise linear functions g_k. Hence no smoothing interpolation techniques, e. g. nonlinear splines, are any longer necessary.
- The requirement $g_k \to \infty$ for $p_k \to 1$ is superfluous.
- We can model horizontally and vertically disaggregated health programs without restrictions.
- Several resource constraints can be taken into account.
- If more than one objective function is of importance this can be integrated via standard techniques such as goal programming (introductory see Hillier/Lieberman 1986).
- Sensitivity analysis and parametric programming are easily applicable in linear programming and allow to cope with uncertainty in the data (introductory see Hillier/Lieberman 1986).

. Our model easily can be implemented on microcomputers because commercial LP-software is available at reasonable rates (see Sharda 1984).

Hence the LP-model removes all the technical limits of its predeccors listed in section 2.4.

Last but not least we want to point to the different contexts in which our formal model can be helpful as a structuring and an optimization tool.

Its health application spectrum ranges from community oriented health promotion programs to targeted screening and early detection of diseases for populations at risk, to cure, where the regional application intensity of new technologies may be of concern. Not always it is obvious that the model is applicable. Community oriented health promotion programs at first glance are not amenable to such a structure. In considering the various attitudes of the population (laypeople and physicians) towards health habits and these behaviours themselves, however, as stages, we get a notion of how to apply our model. Now we only have to arrange these stages in some sequential order according to their health relevance and to some program dependent logic of stepped attainment. Another point: if we cure talking about populations in general we not necessarily only think of groups of individuals but also allow for groups of institutions such as hospitals.

Two remarks are due at the end: First our model does not make any essential assumptions about the socioeconomic political frame in which our approach is applicable. That is, in a more market oriented health care system as well as in a nationalized health service as well as in all imaginable forms between our model may assist in rational decision making at policy level (see also Blum 1981 for a general introduction).

Second, it follows from the above sketched different problems to be tackled with our model, that similar tasks may be modeled in the private sector of an economy as well. One, e. g., can think of stepped, strata specific marketing intensities in different continents, countries, regions and cities or of the optimal resource allocation between competing divisions or projects in a corporation. An R & D-application is in preparation.

Acknowledgement

The basic concept of this paper was developed while the author was a research fellow with Harvard University, Cambridge, MA. I would like to thank Prof. M. C. Weinstein and Prof. M. Zelen for their invitation and encouragement as well as the German Science Foundation (DFG) for its financial support.

At the University of Erlangen-Nürnberg I have to thank the students L. Langenstein, J. Palupski and U. Raab for computational assistance in preparing the numerical example in chapter 4.

Literature:

Ahmed, R.C.: On optimal resource allocation in community hypertension programs, in: Management Science 24, 1978, pp. 1749-1752.

Blum, E., and Oettli, W.: Mathematische Optimierung, Berlin/Heidelberg/ New York 1975.

Blum, H.: Planning for Health, 2nd ed., New York 1981.

Brooks, R.G.: The Development and Construction of Health Status Measures. An Overview of the Literature, Report 1986: 4, The Swedish Institute for Health Economics, IHE, Lund 1986.

Fraser, G.E.: Preventive Cardiology, New York/Oxford 1986.

Hillier, E.S., and Lieberman, G.J.: Introduction to Operations Research, 4th ed., Oakland/CA 1986.

Nichols, A.L., and Weinstein, M.C.: Optimal resource allocation in community hypertension programs, in: Management Science 24, 1978, pp. 1526-1537.

Sharda, R.: Linear Programming on microcomputers. A survey, in: Interface 14, No. 6, 1984, pp. 27-38.

Stoer, J.: Einführung in die Numerische Mathematik I, Berlin/Heidelberg/ New York 1972.

Weinstein, M.C., and Fineberg, H.V.: Clinical Decision Analysis, Philadelphia/PA 1980.

Step $\hat{k}$	Effective-ness[#] $R_{\hat{k}}$	Cost Function $g_{\hat{k},k}(p_{\hat{k},k})$; (in $)	Transition Probability $p_{\hat{k},k}$
1	0	1	1 ; (fix)[*]
2	0	5	0,15; (fix)
3	0	$- 50 + \frac{25}{1-p_{3,4}}$ for $p_{3,4} \geqq 0,5$	$p_{3,4}$; (variable)
		0 for $p_{3,4} < 0,5$	
4	0	15	0,67; (fix)
5	0,01	0	0,75; (fix)
6	0	$100 + \frac{33,3}{1-p_{6,7}}$ for $p_{6,7} \geqq 0,67$	$p_{6,7}$; (variable)
		200 for $p_{6,7} < 0,67$	
7	0,09	$2450 + \frac{175}{1-p_{7,8}}$ for $p_{7,8} \geqq 0,5$	$p_{7,8}$; (variable)
		2800 for $p_{7,8} < 0,5$	
8	0,9	-	-

Legend: [#]: plausible values used by Ahmed

[*]: Nichols and Weinstein here treat p_1 as a variable; Ahmed uses $p_1 \equiv 1$; see text

Table 1: Step-specific transition probabilities, effectiveness and cost-functions. Source: Nichols/Weinstein 1978, pp. 1532-33 and Ahmed 1978, p. 1751

$\hat{k}$	l	$p_{\hat{k},k}$	$g_{\hat{k},k}(p_{\hat{k},k})$	$d^{1}_{\hat{k},k}$	$c^{1}_{\hat{k},k}$
3	1	0,5	0	0,5	0
	2	0,95	450	0,45	1 000
	3	0,98	1 200	0,03	25 000
	4	0,99	2 450	0,01	125 000
6	1	0,67	200	0,67	0
	2	0,95	725	0,28	1 875
	3	0,98	1 529	0,03	26 785
	4	0,99	2 600	0,01	107 142
7	1	0,5	2 800	0,5	0
	2	0,85	3 617	0,35	2 333
	3	0,93	4 950	0,08	16 667
	4	0,96	6 825	0,03	62 500
	5	0,97	8 283	0,01	145 833
	6	0,98	11 200	0,01	291 667
	7	0,99	19 950	0,01	875 000

Legend: $d^{1}_{\hat{k},k}$, $c^{1}_{\hat{k},k}$ see fig. 3; $l_{\hat{k},k}$, $p_{\hat{k},k}$, $g_{\hat{k},k}(p_{\hat{k},k})$ see text

Table 2: A linearization of the functions $g_{3,4}$, $g_{6,7}$, $g_{7,8}$ of table 1 for $\varepsilon = 250$

Results of model (46), (see 3.4):

$x_3^1 = 1\,428,1$;

$x_4^1 = 714,1$; $x_4^2 = x_4^3 = x_4^4 = 0$;

$x_7^1 = 238$; $x_7^2 = x_7^3 = x_7^4 = 0$;

$x_8^1 = 119$; $x_8^2 = 83,3$; $x_8^3 = x_8^4 = \ldots = x_8^7 = 0$;

Value of the objective function: 208,25

Values of the additional variables x_k in model 3.3:	$\frac{x_k}{x_{\hat{k}}} = p_{\hat{k},k}$:	Ahmed:
$x_1 = 9\,520,9$	$N = 9\,521$	$N = 9\,341$
$x_2 = 9\,520,9$	$p_{1,2} = 1,0$	$p_{1,2} = 1,0$
$x_3 = 1\,428,1$	$p_{2,3} = 0,15$	$p_{2,3} = 0,15$
$x_4 = 714,1$	$p_{3,4} = 0,5$	$p_{3,4} = 0,5$
$x_5 = 476,0$	$p_{4,5} = 0,67$	$p_{4,5} = 0,67$
$x_6 = 357,0$	$p_{5,6} = 0,75$	$p_{5,6} = 0,75$
$x_7 = 238,0$	$p_{6,7} = 0,67$	$p_{6,7} = 0,74$
$x_8 = 202,3$	$p_{7,8} = 0,85$	$p_{7,8} = 0,8$

Table 3: Results of the sample computations for the LP-model (46) with the data of table 2

Function type $g_{\hat{k},k}$	hyperbolic						invers square						logarithmic						exponential					
	LP-model					A	LP-model					A	LP-model					A	LP-model					A
ε	10	50	100	250	500		10	50	100	250	500		10	50	100	250	500		10	50	100	250	500	
Variable																								
N	10112	9842	10444	9521	8648	9341	8941	10180	10710	9814	8764	8957	9640	9411	10019	9138	8324	9236	9593	11307	11017	10248	9530	8143
$p_{1,2}$	1,0	1,0	1,0	1,0	1,0	1,0	1,0	1,0	1,0	1,0	1,0	1,0	1,0	1,0	1,0	1,0	1,0	1,0	1,0	1,0	1,0	1,0	1,0	1,0
$p_{2,3}$	0,15	0,15	0,15	0,15	0,15	0,15	0,15	0,15	0,15	0,15	0,15	0,15	0,15	0,15	0,15	0,15	0,15	0,15	0,15	0,15	0,15	0,15	0,15	0,15
$p_{3,4}$	0,5	0,5	0,5	0,5	0,5	0,5	0,5	0,5	0,5	0,5	0,5	0,53	0,5	0,5	0,5	0,5	0,5	0,5	0,5	0,5	0,5	0,5	0,5	0,59
$p_{4,5}$	0,67	0,67	0,67	0,67	0,67	0,67	0,67	0,67	0,67	0,67	0,67	0,67	0,67	0,67	0,67	0,67	0,67	0,67	0,67	0,67	0,67	0,67	0,67	0,67
$p_{5,6}$	0,75	0,75	0,75	0,75	0,75	0,75	0,75	0,75	0,75	0,75	0,75	0,75	0,75	0,75	0,75	0,75	0,75	0,75	0,75	0,75	0,75	0,75	0,75	0,75
$p_{6,7}$	0,67	0,67	0,67	0,67	0,67	0,74	0,79	0,67	0,67	0,67	0,67	0,75	0,67	0,67	0,67	0,67	0,67	0,71	0,79	0,67	0,67	0,67	0,67	0,77
$p_{7,8}$	0,81	0,83	0,78	0,85	0,89	0,8	0,77	0,79	0,75	0,81	0,85	0,76	0,89	0,91	0,85	0,93	0,97	0,88	0,72	0,7	0,73	0,77	0,79	0,73
# controlled	204	204	203	202	192	206	203	201	200	198	186	203	214	214	212	212	201	215	203	197	201	197	188	205
value of the object. funct.	212	211	212	208	197	216	211	209	210	206	192	212	220	218	219	216	205	223	214	209	211	206	196	213

Legend: #: number
A: Ahmed-method

Table 4: Comparison of the results of the ε-dependent LP-example of chapter 4 with the results of the Ahmed-method

Micro-Economic Aspects of Magnetic Resonance Tomography

Hildegard Feucht and Ernst Ostheimer

1 Magnetic resonance tomography, a modern large-scale system for medicine

Magnetic resonance (MR) tomography is a new diagnostic technique used in medicine. It belongs to the so-called imaging techniques, such as for instance the computerized X-ray tomography, scintigraphy, sonography or thermography. MR-tomography (MR-imaging) allows cross-sectional slice images of the human body. Within these cross-sectional slice images it is possible to differentiate between normal and pathological tissue conditions due to morphological changes. They are a helpful tool for the diagnosis of diseases.

Operational principles (see 26, 39, 40):
Such nuclei as for instance ^{1}H, ^{13}C, ^{23}Na, ^{31}P have a magnetic moment. If these nuclei are exposed to a static magnetic field, their magnetic moments are preferably aligned with this magnetic field. By irradiation of radio frequency pulses (= stimulating pulses) the nuclear magnets can be deflected from their preferred direction. By emission of radio frequency (RF) radiation, the nuclear magnets then return to their original position. This process is called relaxation. The half-value time herefore is the relaxation time. It is differentiated between spin-lattice relaxation time T1 and spin-spin-relaxation time T2. The emitted radiation during relaxation is received and evaluated by the MR-tomograph and allows the production of the known cross-sectional slice images of the human body. For finding the physical principle of the nuclear magnetic resonance in 1946 (see 2, 38), Felix Bloch and Edward M. Purcell were awarded the Nobel Prize for Physics in 1952. It took then about 20 years before in 1973, for the first time, the principle was applied by Paul C. Lauterbur for the reconstruction of cross-sectional slice images of the human body using his so-called technique of zeugmatography (see 31, 32). He was thereby successful, by means of additional gradient fields, in locating the origin of the electromagnetic RF radiation emitted du-

ring relaxation. Then, several research groups worked systematically on the development of MR-imaging systems (see 9, 16, 23, 30, 33). But it was only at the beginning of the 1980's, when suitable equipment for clinical application came onto the market (see 11, 36, 45). They are almost exclusively used to evaluate the ^{1}H-resonance signals for cross-sectional slice MR-imaging. The appropriate clinical systems presently used operate with the magnetic fields shown on the next page.

The sequences which are most commonly used to stimulate the relaxation radiation as well as to code the emission point of the induced relaxation radiation, are:

saturation recovery (SR)
inversion recovery (IR)
spin-echo-sequence (SE)

In addition to this there are many sequence combinations (e.g. multislice, multiecho sequences) and recently also fast-imaging procedures, such as for instance RARE (see 22), FLASH (see 20), FISP (see 37). All techniques have in common that they induce signals (i.e. RF-relaxation radiation) via RF-excitation pulses.

The main components of an MR-imaging system are:

- magnet (resistive magnet of up to 0.3 Tesla (T) or permanent magnet of up to 0.3 T or superconducting magnet), gradient coils, RF-coils, patient couch

- shielding (for RF-fields; if necessary, for the static magnetic field)

- energy supply, cooling

- computing system (computer)

- control console

- required space program (60-200 m^2 up to 0.5 T; 150-350 m^2 up to 1.5 T).

The MR-tomograph is a large-scale, high-tech medical equipment in the sense of the regulation of the federal committee of physicians and insurance companies in the Federal Republic of Germany (see 4, 34). MR-

- static magnetic field (for the alignment of nuclear magnets)	applied field strength range	0.02 - 2.0 Tesla (1 Tesla = 10.000 Gauss, earth magnetic field ~ 4.10^{-5} Tesla)
- irradiated electromagnetic RF-fields (pulses to deflect nuclear magnetization)	frequency of the RF-waves:	1 - 100 MHz
	specific energy absorption:	$\leq$ 1 W/Kg whole body 5 W/Kg partial body
- time-varying magnetic fields (gradient fields to locate the origin of the induced signals)	time variation:	< 3 T/sec whole and partial body (see 7)
	physical current density:	< 3 μA/m² } for switching times of 10 ms and longer (see 5)
	field strength:	< 2 mV/cm } for switching times of 10 ms and longer (see 5)
	physical current density:	$< \frac{30\ \mu A/cm^2}{\tau}$ } for switching times shorter then 10 ms (τ in ms) (see 5)
	field strength:	$< \frac{20\ mV/cm}{\tau}$ } for switching times shorter then 10 ms (τ in ms) (see 5)
	frequency range:	1 - 100 Hz
- emitted electromagnetic RF-fields (induced signals during relaxation)	frequency range corresponds to the irradiated electromagnetic RF-fields (see above).	

tomographs are classified in groups according to the type of magnet used (resistive magnet, permanent magnet, superconducting magnet)or according to the field strength of the static magnetic field. Most of the systems, presently used, have a field strength of 0.15 to 0.5 Tesla. A Finnish company offers a system with a field strength of 0.02 Tesla. The MR-tomographs still being developed indicate field strengths of 2.0 Tesla and more.

Already at the beginning of the 1980's, efforts were made by physicians and the industry to introduce, as quickly as possible, the MR-tomography for routine use in the medical diagnosis. It was thereby expected to make advances in the recognition of many diseases. Indeed, MR-tomography shows considerable advantages (see 10):

- MR-images show usually higher contrast differences in normal and pathological tissue than X-ray computerized tomography images.

- The MR-tomography offers a three-dimensional imaging possibility.

- The cross-sectional slice images of high spatial resolution no longer contain the artifacts which are known and feared in X-ray computerized tomography.

- Tumors as adenomas of the pituitary gland or acusticus-neurinomas can easily be reproduced by MR-tomography.

- By MR-tomography it is possible for the first time to make the spinal cord directly visible.

- Statements on biochemics, metabolic changes and the flow of fluids can, in general, be made.

- Health damage caused by RF and the currently applied static field strengths have not been proved. The risks seem to be very low and manageable.

- MR-tomography operates with contrast agents not containing iodine.

- For MR-tomography no ionizing radiation is necessary.

There are, however, some disadvantages involved with the application of MR-tomography:

- Blood flow, air and calcification produce no MR-signals and a differentiation is thus not possible.

- There are risks for patients with pacemakers and magnetic clips.

- Quantitative analyses (T1, T2, flow, diffusion) are presently feasible only to a limited extent.

- There are high space and manpower requirements to be met.

- The investment costs are very high (e.g. procurement prices between 1 an 5 Mio DM).

- The proceeds achieved depend on administrative prices (rates for medical treatment and care).

- The technology is advancing rapidly.

For each medical service centre (hospital or doctor's office) the procurement of an MR-tomograph bears a high risk, especially due to the high cost.

To reduce this risk a potential user of this equipment might be interested in the answer of the following questions:

a) What is the output of MR-tomography with respect to the present and future number of patients to be treated?

   - What configuration of equipment would thereby be most favourable and should be used in combination with what other diagnostical modalities?

   - What changes in the number of patients and the kinds of diseases to be treated can be expected after the procurement of such equipment?

b) What costs will arise from the use of such equipment?

c) Is there a chance to cover the costs and under what conditions?

Good and reliable analyses of the patients to be treated and the costs and proceeds will thus help to reduce the risk for the investment of an

MR-tomograph.

The following is a summary of micro-economic aspects concerning the operating conditions of the MR-tomography, the costs and proceeds to be expected as well as break-even evaluations. The calculations are based on simplifying model assumptions as outlined in section 2.

2 The basis for micro-economic cost and proceeds analysis (model assumptions)

The MR-tomograph should be installed in a health centre which works in the field of medical treatment and which makes routine use of this imaging technique. The specific tasks concerning clinical research as well as the training of physicians and technical personnel are not considered in this analysis.

The health centre is considered as a production unit, which tries to achieve its service targets by use of the MR-tomographic system. There can be different kinds of targets, such as for instance:

- improving and enlarging the examination and medical treatment spectrum

- keeping up with the progress in medicine

- maintaining and achieving the preferred position in the offered regional medical care

- covering the population's demand for medical care

- increasing proceeds, profit or efficiency.

Independent of the aims which the health centre tries to achieve by the use of an MR-tomographic system, it is assumed that it at least tries to cover the costs which are caused by the use of the system.

Input factors for the health centre to operate the MR-tomograph are manpower, material and organization. It is assumed that the costs of the operation of the MR-tomographical system can be clearly separated from the costs of other activities.

The production costs are derived from the values of the input factors. It must thereby be differentiated between the fixed costs and the variable costs dependent on the number of medical examinations (see 13,14). The following cost determinants are considered in the cost calculation:

investment costs
utilization period
depreciation
capital costs
maintenance costs
costs for documentation and archival registration
manpower costs
room costs.

The output of the health centre is the number of MR-tomographic examinations performed, including the medical finding. A further breakdown of the output into subquantities has not been made, as all cost intensive operational means of MR-tomography are used for each MR-tomographic examination.

Due to the existing demand it is assumed that the capacity of the MR-tomographic system will be fully utilized.

Such questions as the selection of the site for the health centre and thus, the definition of the regional distribution of MR-tomographs are not considered. It is assumed that these questions have already been clarified. (Distribution plans and characteristic figures in terms of equipment density can herefore serve as decision aids. In the Federal Rebulic of Germany, for example, a figure of 1.5 Mio inhabitants per 1 MR-tomograph is considered as standard figure for the regional equipment density (see 4, 34).)

The proceeds of performed examinations are in compliance with the rules provided by the health service policy in the Federal Republic of Germany, that means, in the outpatient sector all examinations are liquidated on the basis of fixed fee rates, in the inpatient sector either on the basis of the general hospital rate, a sector specific hospital rate or on the basis of specially agreed fees.

The health centre model is statically formulated by taking into account a period of one year. The calculation uses the average values of the time required for a tomographic examination. It is thereby assumed that variations in the time per examination and fluctuations in the demand can be balanced by a good organization (e.g. ordering system), so that a uniform capacity utilization will be possible. On the basis of this, the economic output of the medical service is derived as difference between costs and proceeds. Break-even point calculations are carried out to make evident by what conditions the costs are exceeded by the proceeds.

3 Operational conditions of MR-tomography

3.1 Indications

Due to the advantages of MR-tomography (described in section 1) a wide range of clinical applications for this new diagnostic technique can be expected. However, due to its high complexity and measurement variability, higher research efforts and a longer period of time than initially assumed were necessary for its implementation into routine medical care (see 14). At present, clinical research is also interested in

- still further defining the diseases for which the MR-tomography is indicated

- determining the optimal procedure for doing the examination (measurement sequences, resolution, measurement time, contrast material, optimal field strength range)

- integrating the MR-tomography in diagnostical and strategical procedures (e.g. additive, substitutive application)

- realizing further developement possibilities (quantitative tomography, chemical shift, high resolution MR-spectroscopy of nuclei of a higher ordinal number).

In the Federal Republic of Germany the health policy authorities try to reduce the costs of the health care system. The reason why MR-tomography is critically considered, can be seen in the high costs involved with this technique. Therefore, a routine use of the MR-tomography is only supported where, according to clinical studies, important reasons are evident. Such reasons are given (see 24):

- if MR-tomography is the only method which enables the diagnosis of a suspected disease

- if MR-tomography provides reliable additional information to the diagnosis with therapeutical consequence (e.g. localization, malignancy)

- if other associated methods are contraindicated (e.g. radiation risks, contrast material allergy).

As provided by the current regulations in the Federal Republic of Germany by the end of 1986, there are only four indications concretely determined which can be charged by a physician (see 6, 18):

- tumors of the brain
- temporal lobe epilepsy
- tumors of the spinal cord including syringomyely
- multiple sclerosis.

This catalogue will have to be extended in the future. The following indications for MR-tomography can now already be stated (see 10):

1) suspected tumor in case of negative or uncertain X-ray computerized tomography findings

2) suspected voluminous expansions of posterior fossa

3) differential diagnosis
multiple sclerosis or other morphological alteration in the brain or spinal channel (esp. for therapeutical consequence or therapeutical control)

4) suspected syringomyely

5) suspected intraspinal voluminous expansions

6) searching for intracardial tumors and thrombs as well as cardiomyopathy, if suspected and negative or uncertain echocardiogram

7) mediastinal tumors, if necessary for therapy planning

8) pediatric oncological follow-up examinations

9) indications from the sector of pediatric neuroradiology

10) diseases of male and female renal organs (internal genitals, bladder rectum) and, especially, for malignant processes in connection with the primary and staging diagnosis.

For allergies against contrast material containing iodine and by the exclusion of the X-ray computerized tomographical examination, only the MR-tomograph can be used. The direct imaging of the spinal cord is possible with this new technique.

Although a comprehensive indications catalogue for MR-tomography has not yet been prepared, every potential user of an MR-tomographic system shoul investigate whether his present number of patients and the patients to be expected would meet these indications and if he would thus efficiently utilize such an MR-tomography system. He must additionally take into account that not all indications can be appropriately and successfully examined by every MR-tomographic system. In principle, it applies that with increasing magnetic field strength the spatial resolution capacity of the MR cross-sectional slice images increases. It is therefore possible by the use of MR-tomographs with higher magnetic field strength to image smaller organs and lesions as it would be possible by the use of MR-systems with lower field strength. There are, however, also indications and technique-related limits for the magnetic field strength. The following examinations depend on a low and high field strength, respectively (see 10):

up to 0.5 Tesla

- natal examinations
- T2-weighted fast imaging techniques
- CPMB-sequences (Carr-Purcell-Meiboom-Gill-seq.)
- multislice-, multiecho-techniques

1.0 to 2.0 Tesla

- for the examination of lesions of small volume (e.g. disease of the orbita) equipment with high field strength (0.5 Tesla and more) has an advantage due to its higher spatial resolution.
- for magnetic field strengths of 1.5 Tesla and more the combination of the MR-tomography and the MR-spectroscopy (of nuclei of higher ordinal figure) is possible. Due to the present state of the art, however, such equipment is not available for the clinical routine operation.

- T1-weighted fast-imaging techniques
- high-resolution techniques (e.g. examination of the temporal bone).

It must also be considered that with increasing field strength the procurement and installation costs of an MR-tomograph will increase considerably.

3.2 Operational conditions of MR-tomography

The operational conditions are an important factor for the calculation of the operational costs and the effectiveness of the system. In general, the operational conditions depend on the following parameters:

a) site requirements
b) expendable goods requirements
c) manpower requirements
d) examination time and patients throughput.

3.2.1 Site requirements

The site requirements include the space and room requirements as well as special infrastructure requirements. The total room requirements for an MRI-system (in terms of combination and area) depend on the one hand on the field strength of the static magnetic field. On the other hand, however, they depend on whether the MRI-system is run as an independent diagnostical service or whether the system is integrated into the diagnostic department of a hospital or into a health centre. The specific purpose of use determines the requirements for auxiliary rooms.

The rooms needed for the installation of the facility consist of the actual examination room for the magnet and the patient couch, the control room for the operational control facilities of the system, the computer room for the data-processing hardware (control computer, imaging computer, disk storage, magnetic tape storage, printer, HF-, control- and gradient field boards) as well as the space for the power supply (cooling aggregate circuit distributor, shim-coil supply, magnet current supply).

For the systems which are operated by the comparably very low field strength of 0.02 Tesla, the control room can be integrated into the examination room.

As auxiliary rooms are considered:

- day- and workrooms for the staff (physician, physicist/technician, secretary)
- waiting rooms for patients
- dressing cabins for patients
- wash rooms and toilets for patients and the staff
- emergency treatment rooms and waiting rooms for stretchered patients unable to walk
- archival registration room
- dark room.

The space requirement is summarized in detail in table 1. In general, MR-imaging systems with high magnetic field strength will have a higher space requirement than systems with low field strength.

Table 1: Space requirement for MR-tomography (see 25, 29)

Rooms	Space requirement *)in m^2 at field strengths o		
	0.02 Tesla	to 0.5 Tesla	to 1.5 Tesla
examination room	25 - 35	40 - 80	80
control room		9 - 18	9 - 18
computer room	5 - 10	12 - 18	18 - 22
operational material room		7,5 - 18	18 - 22
waiting room	15 - 30	15 - 30	15 - 50
auxiliary rooms	15 - 45	15 - 50	15 - 150
total area	60 - 120	100 - 200	150 - 350**)

*) (The ceiling height of the examination room with resistive magnets should be at least 2.60 m, for superconducting magnets at least 3.70 m.)

**) (The total space requirement depends on whether the MR-systems is run as independent diagnostical department or not.)

During the operation of an MR-tomograph interferences and interactions with the environment can occur. There can be

- interactions of the static magnetic field and other system components with the environment

- interferences of the electromagnetic radio frequency fields (RF-radiation of the MR-tomograph as well as RF-radiation emitted from the environment)

- other types of interactions with the environment (e.g. heat dissemination, gas exhaustion).

The most intensive interaction of the MRI-system with the environment is in the area of the strong static magnetic field. The spatial expansion of the magnetic field and the still existing field strength must thereby especially be taken into account. The static magnetic field is - as a function of the field strength - divided in spatial zones (see 29). Within these zones distinctive types of behaviour due to the influences of the magnetic field on ferromagnetic substances (iron, cobalt, nickel) and vice versa, must be taken into account. This applies, in particular, to the use and handling of ferromagnetic objects (instruments, cabinets on wheels, chairs, etc.), as the now used magnets with field strengths of up to 2.0 Tesla are able to attract metallic parts at high speed.

In zone 1 there are field strengths stronger than 10 Gauss (= 1 Millitesla, mT). Access to this zone should only be allowed to the staff and the patients. For safety reasons, it is necessary that the access to this area is controlled. This measure is necessary with respect to potential danger for persons carrying pacemakers, the frequency of which could be changed already in cases of magnetic field strengths of over 5 Gauss. Potential danger also exists for persons with paramagnetic implants.

In zone 1 information on storage media, such as magnetic tapes, magnetic records and credit cards can be deleted. Interferences with the function of electronical and mechanical equipment (e.g. video systems, watches, etc.) can also occur.

In zone 2 are field strengths of 10 to 5 Gauss. In this zone traffic areas often exist, the entire control of which is not possible. In respect of the potential relay-interference of pacemaker implants every person should be made aware of this danger by suitable warning signals before entering this area.

In zone 3 with field strengths of 5 to 1 Gauss functional disturbances of nuclear medical and radiological equipment can occur. For electronic microscopes this can already occur in cases of field strengths of 1 Gauss and below.

There can also be environmental influences on the static magnetic field of the MR-tomograph leading to functional disturbances. Such disturbance can be caused by iron-reinforcements in ceilings, floors and walls, by moved heavy ferromagnetic objects (elevators, automobiles, street cars, trucks, etc.) or by already existing magnetic fields.

The interferences due to local sources can usually be eleminated by favourable positioning of the magnet (e.g. arrangement in alignment with the symmetrical axis of iron reinforcements) and by shimming the magnet on site. Interferences caused by moved iron masses can often be eliminated only by appropriate spacing or by stopping the movement. It can be stated that the shielding measures are the more expensive the higher the field strength of the magnet is.

Interferences of the RF-electromagnetic fields of the MR-tomograph with the environment could be avoided, if shielding measures within the magnet are already provided by the manufacturer or if a shielding cabin covering the magnet and the patient couch would be made. Furthermore, it should be ensured that the following infrastructure requirements are met:

- maintaining the load capacity of the floor at the installation site of the magnet (magnets can have a weight of several tons)

- maintaining the necessary height and width of the rooms, doors and windows

- securing the vibration freedom at the installation site

- using non-magnetic material to equip the examination room (wood, plastics, copper, brass, aluminium)

- securing a free accessibility to the magnet and the patient couch from all sides

- ensuring the patient's optical and acoustic contact to the operating personnel (if necessary, by radiophone or optical mirror)

- securing the air conditioning of the computer room according to the instructions of the manufacturer

- securing the circulation of cooling agents (water, oil) for resistive magnets by a separate power supply

- taking precautionary measures for the storage of pressure-cans for fluid helium and fluid nitrogen as safety stock in the case of an MR-tomograph with superconducting magnet; securing the free evaporation of the cooling agents to the outside (also during quenching)

- ensuring the magnetic field compatibility spacing for other electronical equipment in the environment of the MR-tomograph.

To meet the above infrastructural requirements, suitable construction measures should be taken. Furthermore, it must often be taken into account that no special building tract with the appropriate rooms is provided for the operation of an MR-tomograph. The installation and operation of an MRI-system will rather be executed within a more or less well suitable building structure. This can cause considerable costs for structural alterations. These additional costs must be considered in the production cost calculation.

3.2.2 Demand for expendable goods

The demand for expendable goods is mainly determined by the energy consumption for the operation of an MR-tomograph (equipment, air conditioning), by the consumption of cooling agents (water, helium, nitrogen) as well as by the archival registration (floppy, multiformat camera). While the consumption of energy and cooling material depends on the full or stand-by operation times of the MR-tomography system, the documentation and archival registration costs depend only on the number of the examined patients and thus on the patients troughput. The costs for energy and cooling material for the stand-by operation are thus considered as fixed costs, however the costs for energy and cooling material for full operation as well as the costs for documentation and archival registration as variable costs.

In table 2, the consumption values are listed as they can presently be assumed for MR-tomographs with a resistive, permanent or superconducting magnet. Deviations from the stated values may occur for individual cases. Such deviations, however, must then be considered by every MRI-system owner in his individual cost calculation. Changes in the values for the helium consumption for superconducting magnets must also be taken into account for the future, in view of the new magnetic cooling systems being developed. According to the statements of a manufacturer, a consumption rate of 0.15 l helium per hour can be expected (see 43).

As the costs for offices supplies, laundry, disinfecting material etc., compared to the above expendable material, are low in value they are here not separately specified. In the cost calculation (section 4) these costs are added to the other variable costs.

3.2.3 Manpower requirements

Highly qualified staff is required for the operation of an MR-tomograph. The figures in terms of the required manpower capacity, however, vary. The manpower requirement depends on various factors, such as for instance the daily operation hours of the MR-tomograph, the patients throughput and the measurement variability of the MR-tomograph used. It also depends an the type of tasks of the health centre using the MR-tomography. It should, for instance, be considered whether also tasks in the fields of clinical research or training of physicians and technical personnel are covered. According to the assumptions made in section 2, these tasks however are not considered here.

In general, the presence of a physician is required during the MR-tomographic examination. For each specific examination he must give instructions for the positioning of the patient, select the slices to be imaged as well as the measurement sequences and vary the parameters during the examination depending on the momentary examination result. The rest of the physician's working hours is used for the finding, case discussions, conferences, training measures, leave and sickness.

For a normal daily operation time of 8 hours and full utilization of the equipment capacity two qualified radiotechnologists are needed.They take over such tasks as patients' care, patients' positioning, handling of equipment, documentation and filing. - It still has to be clarified,

Table 2: Demand for expendable goods for the operation of a MR-tomograph

Expendable goods	Consumption values as a function of the type of the MR-tomograph				
	resistive magnet 0.02 T	resistive magnet 0.28 T	permanent magnet 0.3 T	superconducting magnet 0.5 T	superconducting magnet 1.0 T
electrical power			75 KWh		
- stand by	3 KWh	2 KWh		2.2 KWh	2.2 KWh
- in operation	7 KWh	100 KWh		30.8 KWh	30.8 KWh
electrical power, air conditioning, water cooling	---		23 KWh		
- stand by		4 KWh		3.1 KWh	3.1 KWh
- in operation		12 KWh		12 KWh	12 KWh
nitrogen	---	---	---		
- stand by				1.0 l/h	1.0 l/h
- in operation				1.4 l/h	1.4 l/h
helium *)	---	---	---		
- stand by				0.3 l/h	0.3 l/h
- in operation				0.6 l/h	0.6 l/h
water	0.3 cbm/h	3.6 cbm/h	---	---	---
documentation per examined body region	6 X-ray films 24/30 cm	6 X-ray films 24/30 cm	6 X-ray films 24/30 cm	6 X-ray films 24/30 cm	6 X-ray films 24/30 cm
archival registration per examined body region	2 floppy discs or 1/7 magnetic tape	2 floppy discs or 1/7 magnetic tape	2 floppy discs or 1/7 magnetic tape	2 floppy discs or 1/7 magnetic tape	2 floppy discs or 1/7 magnetic tape

*) (There are no recovery possibilities considered in the helium consumption values)

whether an additional typist is necessary for a smooth operation in the case of the use an MR-tomograph with higher field strength, due to its possible higher capacity.

Often, a physicist is employed for the technical operation of the system, the control of the proper functional conditions and the operational security. Sometimes, the physicist is replaced by a technician. For the operation of an MR-tomograph allowing spectroscopic examinations, a physicist or physical chemist should be employed.

For the determination of the manpower requirement, the personnel absence (leave, sickness) as well as a possible increase of the daily operational hours of the MR-tomograph must be considered. To guarantee a high performance standard and a wide use of the MR-tomographic system a sufficient number of personnel (staffing flexibility) should be ensured.

As the manpower costs are low in comparison to the capital costs the MR-tomographic systems should mainly be used in shift operation.

In table 3, the manpower requirement for MRI operation of 8 and 12 hours per day is shown. The manpower requirement indicates the variation as derived from the data of different sources. Thereby, a full utilization of the MR-tomograph and a routine use are assumed. Tasks like clinical research and training of physicians and technical assistants are not separately indicated. If such tasks are considered, the patients troughput will become lower at equal manpower.

Table 3: Manpower for MR-tomography during routine operation at varying operational hours (evaluation of the data from ref. 1, 3, 8, 12, 17, 21, 25, 27, 28, 41, 42; without replacements for leave)

Manpower	8-hour operation	12-hour operation
specialist *)	1	1 (0.5)
assistant	-	0.5 (1)
physicist/physical chemist	to be clarified	to be clarified
technician	0 - 0.5	0 - 1
radiotechnologist	1.5 - 2	2 - 3
typist	0 - 1	0 - 1.5
total	to be clarified	to be clarified

*) (Sometimes the consultory participation of additional specialists (as for example neuroradiologist) may be required.)

3.2.4 Examination time and patient throughput

The time required for the MR-examination of patients includes the time for the positioning of the patient, the preparation of the measurement, the measurement and adjustment of images as well as the image control and the filing. Due to the high complexity and measurement variability of the technique good organization and a high degree of experience are needed to get smooth operation with favourable examination times. It must also be considered that additional time is required for the application of specific techniques (e.g. triggering or gating during imaging).

Empirical data on the time requirement per examination are available, however not sufficient in quality. The average time required per examination ranges, according to different sources, between about 50 and 90 minutes (see 1, 3, 8, 12, 17, 21, 25, 27, 28, 41, 42).

It can, however, definitely be said that the examination times depend on the localization of the disease to be examined (head, spinal channel, heart, abdomen, etc.). Delays during imaging can sometimes occur due to insufficient rest positioning of the patient. It may also be possible that due to metallic implants, a claustrophoby or due to patients not keeping the agreed examination date, the examination cannot be performed as scheduled. This altogether influences the average examination time per patient and the total number of examinations to be carried out per day, week or year.

The maximum number of examinations performed per year is called the "capacity" of an equipment. The capacity depends on the average operation time of the equipment (e.g. 8 hours, 12 hours per day), on dead times during maintenance, repairs etc., but also on the effectiveness of the system itself and here, in particular, on the field strength of the static magnetic field as well as the available software. Systems with a high magnetic field strength allow, due to their favourable signal to noise ratio, in general, shorter measurement times with better spatial resolution than systems with a lower magnetic field strength. For a decreasing field strength the spatial resolution can, however, become so poor that lesions with minor voluminous dimension (e.g. in orbita, internal ear) can no longer be imaged. Furthermore, there have been, for some time, specific fast-imaging sequences (see section 1) that allow the production of images within a few seconds. Here again, magnets with a high field strength are superior to the systems with low field strength.

Only the future development and practical experience will, however, show to what extent fast-imaging sequences can be applied.

Hence, great uncertainty exists at present in respect of the required average examination time and the number of the annual performable examinations. It is not yet excluded that the capacity of MR-tomographs can meet the capacity of X-ray computer tomographs (see 10). But this would require a reduction of the current achievable measurement and evaluation time at routine use of MR-tomography.

In table 4, the estimated values for the capacity of MR-tomographs are summarized. Every potential user of an MR-tomographic system should check to what extent he could utilize his considered system due to the number of patients to be expected.

Table 4: Estimation of the capacity of MR-tomographs

Parameters	Field strength and operational time			
	0.02 Tesla		ca. 0.3 to 1.0 Tesla	
	8 hours	12 hours	8 hours	12 hours
working days per week	5	5	5	5
total hours per year	2.000	3.000	2.000	3.000
deduction for interruptions and dead times	8 %	8 %	8 %	8 %
examination hours per year	1.840	2.760	1.840	2.760
average examination time (estimated values)	90 min.	90 min.	60 min.	60 min.
examinations per year (capacity)	1.227	1.840	1.840	2.760

If the capacity of an MR-tomograph is exceeded, a reduction of the examination quality must be taken into account. This would be of great disadvantage, because MR-tomography represents, in general, the last stage of medical diagnosis and thus accumulates critical cases.

4 Costs and proceeds

4.1 Basic data of the cost calculation

For the cost analysis in section 4.2 below only MR-tomographs with field strengths of up to 1 Tesla were considered, as at present no MR-tomographs with field strengths of more than 1 Tesla are exclusively used in routine operation. Therefore, the cost arising from a routine operation of systems with field strengths of more than 1 Tesla can at present not be estimated for practical reasons.

Table 5 shows the technical and economical data, on which the cost analysis (in section 4.2) is based. For resistive MR-tomographs, systems with 0.02 Tesla and 0.28 Tesla, for superconducting MR-tomographs, systems with field strengths of 0.5 Tesla and 1.0 Tesla are considered. In addition a permanent magnet system with a field strength of 0.3 Tesla is taken into account.

The consumption values indicated in table 5 are based on the data received from different manufacturers (see 30, 38, 41, 42) and from a system user (see 32). They have already been explained in section 3.2.2. The data in terms of space and manpower requirements as well as patients throughput are also based on the conditions outlined in section 3.2.

In respect of the whole economic utilization period of an MR-tomograph, differing data are stated in the literature and by the manufacturers. These data vary between 4 and 7 years (see 30, 32, 38, 41, 42). This cost calculation has been based on an economic utilization period of 7 years. The definite economic utilization period is at present not known.

The depreciation amount is often subject to reasons of tax or financing policy. In the cost calculation, however, the depreciation has to consider the definitely expected value reductions, if the cost causing principle is to be taken into account. Under the assumption of a linear value reduction for the MR-tomographic facility and for the necessary installation and reinstallation measures, there is an annual calculatory depreciation of 14.29 % for an MR-tomograph with an utilization period of 7 years. For the required construction measures the calculated depreciation is 10 % in respect of a utilization period of 10 years.

In general, the annual interest payments for the investment capital depend on the type of financing. The higher the loan capital share of the total capital is, the higher the costs of the interest are. In the cost calculation, however, the interest for the total capital used for the procurement of an MR-tomograph must be accounted, independent of whether it is own or loan capital. Otherwise, it would be more feasible to use

Table 5: Basic data for the cost calculation

	Price/Unit	Resistive magnet		Permanent magnet	Superconducting magnet	
		0.02 T	0.28 T	0.3 T	0.5 T	1.0 T
Consumption Values						
Electricity	0.30 DM/KWh					
- stand by		3 KWh	6 KWh	98 KWh	5.3 KWh	5.3 KWh
- operation		7 KWh	112 KWh		42.8 KWh	42.8 KWh
Water	3 DM/m^3	0.3 m^3/h	3.6 m^3/h	---	---	---
Nitrogen	1.45 DM/l					
- stand by		---	---	---	1.0 l/h	1.0 l/h
- operation		---	---	---	1.4 l/h	1.4 l/h
- losses (refilling etc.)		---	---	---	5 %	5 %
Helium	20 DM/l					
- stand by		---	---	---	0.3 l/h	0.3 l/h
- operation		---	---	---	0.6 l/h	0.6 l/h
- losses (refilling etc.)		---	---	---	20 %	20 %
Documentation per examination	3.60 DM	6 X-ray films 24/30 cm				
Archival registration per examination	6.70 DM	2 discs				
Area requirement	25 DM/m^3 (incl. additional costs)	60 - 120 m^2	100 - 150 m^2	100 - 150 m^2	100 - 200 m^2	150 - 350 m^2
Operational hours per year						
Alternative A (8 h/day)	1.840					
Alternative B (12 h/day)	2.760					
Patients throughput/year						
Alternative A		1.200	1.800			
Alternative B		1.800	2.700			

Table 5 : Basic data for the cost calculation

(cont'd)

	Price/unit	Resistive magnet		Permanent magnet	Superconducting magnet	
		0.02 T	0.28 T	0.3 T	0.5 T	1.0 T
Manpower requirement	DM/year					
Alternative A						
physician	110.000	1	1	1	1	1
physicist	90.000	-	-	-	-	0.5
technician	60.000	-	-	-	0.5	-
radiotechnologist	50.000	1.5	2	2	2	2
typist	35.000	0.5	0.75	0.75	0.75	0.75
cleaning personnel	25.000	0.2	0.4	0.4	0.5	0.7
Alternative B						
physician	110.000	1.5	1.5	1.5	1.5	1.5
physicist	90.000	-	-	-	-	0.5
technician	60.000	-	-	-	0.5	-
radiotechnologist	50.000	2	3	3	3	3
typist	35.000	0.75	1	1	1	1
cleaning personnel	25.000	0.4	0.6	0.6	0.75	1
Additional manpower needed for leave and vacation replacement	15 %					
Utilization period						
- MR-tomographic system	7 years					
- installations and reinstallations	10 years					
Calculatory interest rate	9 %					

the capital for other interest-bearing types of purposes. For the calculatory interest as seen in table 5, an interst rate of 9 % is assumed. The calculatory interest has been calculated on the basis of 50 % of the investment costs, since - for linear depreciation - these are normally bound during the total utilization period.

The data on which the cost calculation is based are used as an example. Deviations can occur for every user; they must then be considered in the individual cost calculations.

The construction and equipment requirements vary from one MR-tomographic system to the other and, within the same system classes, from one manufacturer to the other. This leads to considerable differences in the financial burden both in the procurement costs and the necessary scope of construction measures.

Table 6 shows a summary of the financial resources required for the procurement and the operation of different MR-tomographic systems. The procurement price usually includes in addition to the cost for the real magnetic facility, the following service items:

- control and evaluation desk
- computer facility together with control and evaluation software
- disk storage
- multiformatting camera
- patients' monitoring system.

The delivery of the MRI-system is usually free home, that means without transportation and installation costs. But, if extremely high installation costs incur due to special local circumstances, they are in most cases not borne by the manufacturer. Such costs were not included in the procurement costs as outlined in table 6.

In general, the economic utilization period of an equipment can be extended due to regular modification and improvement measures. The amount of the average financial resources required per utilization year usually depends on the duration of the total utilization period. This cost calculation uses a total utilization period of 7 years. Under this assumption an average amount of approx. 100.000 DM per year must be considered for modification and improvement of the MRI-system. This amount includes the modification and improvement costs for hard- and software.

Furthermore, it was assumed that after an utilization period of 7 years the scrap-value of the old facility equals the disassembling costs, i.e. an amount of zero is entered in the cost calculation for the scrap-value minus the disassembling costs.

Table 6: Procurement price *) of different MR-tomographic systems

	Resistive magnet		Permanent magnet	Superconducting magnet	
	0.02 T	0.28 T	0.3 T	0.5 T	1.0 T
Procurement price (incl. shielding measures) in DM	1.117.200	2.300.000	3.650.000	4.000.000	4.400.000
Construction measures (DM)	20.000	500.000	200.000	600.000	700.000
Total (DM)	1.137.200	2.800.000	3.850.000	4.600.000	5.100.000
Annual modification and improvement measures for hard- and software, beginning with the 2. year (DM)	100.000	100.000	100.000	100.000	100.000

*) (All prices include 14 % value-added tax)

Source: Verbal statements of the manufactures and data from manufacturer's advertising material

4.2 Cost calculation

Tables 7 and 8 show the total operating costs per year for different MR-tomography systems and for differing operating times (1.840 and 2.760 operation hours per year). The values listed in these tables are based on the operation data provided in table 5 and the procurement costs presented in table 6.

The annual insurance premium was based on an insurance rate of 0.8 % of the procurement costs of an MR-tomography system. Included in this amount is the 5 % insurance tax to be paid by the policy holder. The amount of the insurance premium is decisive in the calculation of the

Table 7: Annual costs of operation of different MR-tomography systems; Alternative A: 1.840 hours of operation per year

Costs	Resistive magnet 0.02 T	Resistive magnet 0.28 T	Permanent magnet 0.3 T	Superconducting magnet 0.5 T	Superconducting magnet 1.0 T
I. Fixed costs					
Rent (incl. supplementary charges)	18.000 DM to 36.000 DM	30.000 DM to 45.000 DM	30.000 DM to 45.000 DM	30.000 DM to 60.000 DM	45.000 DM to 105.000 DM
Insurances	9.385 DM	19.320 DM	33.660 DM	33.600 DM	36.960 DM
Maintainance/repair	70.000 DM	105.000 DM	140.000 DM	205.000 DM	205.000 DM
Expendable goods					
helium	---	---	---	63.072 DM	63.072 DM
nitrogen	---	---	---	13.337 DM	13.337 DM
electricity	7.884 DM	15.768 DM	---	13.928 DM	13.928 DM
water	7.884 DM	---	---	---	---
Interim total	113.153 DM to 131.153 DM	170.088 DM to 185.088 DM	200.660 DM to 215.660 DM	358.937 DM to 388.937 DM	377.297 DM to 437.297 DM
Calculated depreciation					
- MR-tomograph (incl. shielding measures)	159.600 DM	328.571 DM	521.429 DM	571.429 DM	628.571 DM
- construction measures	2.000 DM	50.000 DM	20.000 DM	60.000 DM	70.000 DM
Modification and improvement measures	100.000 DM	100.000 DM	100.000 DM	100.000 DM	100.000 DM
Calculated interest rate					
- MR-tomograph (incl. shielding measures)	50.274 DM	103.500 DM	164.250 DM	180.000 DM	198.000 DM
- construction measures	1.170 DM	29.250 DM	11.700 DM	35.100 DM	40.000 DM
Total of the fixed costs	426.197 DM to 444.197 DM	781.409 DM to 796.409 DM	1.018.039 DM to 1.033.039 DM	1.305.466 DM to 1.335.466 DM	1.414.818 DM to 1.474.818 DM
II. Variable costs					
Personnel					
physician	110.000 DM	110.000 DM	110.000 DM	110.000 DM	110.000 DM
physicist	---	---	---	---	45.000 DM
technician	---	---	---	30.000 DM	---
radiotechnologist	75.000 DM	100.000 DM	100.000 DM	100.000 DM	100.000 DM
typist	17.500 DM	26.250 DM	26.250 DM	26.250 DM	26.250 DM
cleaning personnel	5.000 DM	10.000 DM	10.000 DM	12.500 DM	17.500 DM
replacement for leave	31.125 DM	36.938 DM	36.938 DM	41.813 DM	44.813 DM
Expendable goods					
helium	---	---	---	13.240 DM	13.240 DM
nitrogen	---	---	---	1.121 DM	1.121 DM
electricity	2.208 DM	58.512 DM	14.400 DM	20.700 DM	20.700 DM
water	---	19.872 DM	---	---	---
Archival registration	16.080 DM	24.120 DM	24.120 DM	24.120 DM	24.120 DM
Documentation	25.920 DM	38.880 DM	38.880 DM	38.880 DM	38.880 DM
Other variable costs	18.000 DM	27.000 DM	27.000 DM	27.000 DM	27.000 DM
Total costs per year	727.030 DM to 745.030 DM	1.232.981 DM to 1.247.981 DM	1.405.627 DM to 1.420.627 DM	1.751.090 DM to 1.781.090 DM	1.883.442 DM to 1.943.442 DM
Costs per year (without investment costs)	413.986 DM to 431.986 DM	621.660 DM to 636.660 DM	588.248 DM to 603.248 DM	804.561 DM to 834.561 DM	845.921 DM to 905.921 DM

Table 8: Annual costs of operation of different MR-tomography systems; Alternative B: 2.760 hours of operation per year

Costs	Resistive magnet 0.02 T	Resistive magnet 0.28 T	Permanent magnet 0.3 T	Superconducting magnet 0.5 T	Superconducting magnet 1.0 T
I. **Fixed costs**					
Rent (incl. supplementary charges)	18.000 DM to 36.000 DM	30.000 DM to 45.000 DM	30.000 DM to 45.000 DM	30.000 DM to 60.000 DM	45.000 DM to 105.000 DM
Insurances	9.385 DM	19.320 DM	30.660 DM	33.600 DM	36.960 DM
Maintainance/repair	70.000 DM	105.000 DM	140.000 DM	205.000 DM	205.000 DM
Expendable goods					
helium	---	---	---	63.072 DM	63.072 DM
nitrogen	---	---	---	13.337 DM	13.337 DM
electricity	7.884 DM	15 768 DM		13.928 DM	13.928 DM
water	7.884 DM	---	---	---	---
Interim total	113.153 DM to 131.153 DM	170.088 DM to 185.088 DM	200.660 DM to 215.660 DM	358.937 DM to 388.937 DM	377.297 DM to 437.297 DM
Calculated depreciation					
- MR-tomograph (incl. shielding measures)	159.600 DM	328.751 DM	521.429 DM	571.429 DM	628.571 DM
- construction measures	2.000 DM	50.000 DM	20.000 DM	60.000 DM	70.000 DM
Modification and improvement measures	100.000 DM	100.000 DM	100.000 DM	100.000 DM	100.000 DM
Calculated interest rate					
- MR-tomograph (incl. shielding measures)	50.274 DM	103.500 DM	164.250 DM	180.000 DM	198.000 DM
- construction measures	1.170 DM	29.250 DM	11.700 DM	35.100 DM	40.950 DM
Total of the fixed costs	426.197 DM to 444.197 DM	781.409 DM to 796.409 DM	1.018.039 DM to 1.033.039 DM	1.305.466 DM to 1.335.466 DM	1.414.818 DM to 1.474.818 DM
II. **Variable costs**					
Personnel					
physician	165.000 DM	165.000 DM	165.000 DM	165.000 DM	165.000 DM
physicist	---	---	---	---	45.000 DM
technician	---	---	---	30.000 DM	---
radiotechnologist	100.000 DM	150.000 DM	150.000 DM	150.000 DM	150.000 DM
typist	26.250 DM	35.000 DM	35.000 DM	35.000 DM	35.000 DM
cleaning personnel	10.000 DM	15.000 DM	15.000 DM	18.750 DM	25.000 DM
replacement for leave	45.188 DM	54.750 DM	54.750 DM	59.813 DM	63.000 DM
Expendable goods					
helium	---	---	---	19.880 DM	19.880 DM
nitrogen	---	---	---	1.681 DM	1.681 DM
electricity	3.312 DM	87.768 DM	21.600 DM	31.050 DM	31.050 DM
water	---	29.808 DM	---	---	---
Archival registration	24.120 DM	36.180 DM	36.180 DM	36.180 DM	36.180 DM
Documentation	38.880 DM	58.320 DM	58.320 DM	58.320 DM	58.320 DM
Other variable costs	27.000 DM	40.500 DM	40.500 DM	40.500 DM	40.500 DM
Total costs per year	865.947 DM to 883.947 DM	1.453.735 DM to 1.468.735 DM	1.594.389 DM to 1.609.389 DM	1.951.640 DM to 1.981.640 DM	2.085.429 DM to 2.145.429 DM
Costs per year (without investment costs)	552.903 DM to 570.903	842.414 DM to 857.414 DM	777.010 DM to 792.010 DM	1.005.111 DM to 1.035.111 DM	1.047.908 DM to 1.107.908 DM

insurance tax. Costs for telephone, office materials, patients' records, laundry, hygiene and transaction fees are included in the other variable costs. A sum of 15 DM per examination was set for these costs.

The fixed costs listed in tables 7 and 8 were subdivided into two groups. The first group comprises the fixed costs incurred by the operation of the system. The second group contains the fixed costs incurred in acquisition and financing of the MR-tomography system and their distribution over the individual years of operation. This procedure was necessary due to special circumstances regarding hospitals in the Federal Republic of Germany. In this country the investment costs connected with the purchasing of an MR-tomography system are not borne by the hospital itself (see section 4.3) and thus the hospital only finances the running operation costs. This situation, as it is shown in section 5, has considerable influence on the average costs per examination.

4.3 The proceeds achieved by MR-tomography

The proceeds to be expected by the use of MR-tomographic systems result from the number of examinations to be performed and the amount of fee received per examination. The rate of fee has to be in compliance with the legal directives applied to health services in the Federal Republic of Germany.

For outpatient MR-tomographic examinations which are directly paid by the patient himself (private patient), the directive for physicians' fee (Gebührenordnung für Ärzte, GOÄ, see 18) applies as the basis for determining the doctor's invoice. The physician can, at free choice, bill 100 % to 250 % of the standard fee rate. In general, however, he is only allowed to invoice 100 % to 180 %.

For inpatient or partially inpatient private medical examinations in a hospital the physician has to deduct his invoiced amount of fees by 15 % (§ 6 GOÄ). In addition, the hospital can request the physician to pay a proportional amount of its material costs caused by the examinations. In contrast thereto the hospital must consider a deduction of 5 % of its general rate asked for private patient care (see 44).

For outpatient MR-tomographic examinations which are paid by the compulsory health insurance companies (RVO insurance companies, alternative insurance companies), the physicians' fee has to comply with the so-called uniform assessment measure (Einheitlicher Bewertungsmaßstab, EBM, see 6).

In complicance with EBM the MR-tomographic examinations are to be billed according to EBM-position number 6,100. This position has been valued in 1986 by a number of 4,700 points. The GOÄ has no own position for MR-tomographic examinations. MR-tomography is therefore invoiced by using an equivalent GOÄ-position. MR-tomographic examinations are seen equivalent to GOÄ-position number 5,650. This position has been valued in 1986 by a number of 6,810 points.

The standard fee rate is then computed according to the following formula:

standard fee rate = (number of points) x (scoring value)

The scoring value is 0.10 DM for examinations carried out for private patients and members of the RVO insurance companies. The alternative insurance companies accept a scoring value of 0.114 DM on average. For private medical examinations the additional charges and deductions mentioned above are to be considered for determining the physicians' fee.

Hence, in the Federal Republic of Germany for MR-tomographic examinations a registered physician can achieve the following fees (applicable for 1986):

- fee per private patient examination: DM 1.225,80 (maximum general value)
- fee paid by compulsory insurance companies per examination:

  RVO insurance companies: DM 470,--
  alternative insurance companies: DM 536,-- (average value)

There are, however, only four indications as already mentioned in section 3.1, for which MR-tomographic examinations can accordingly be charged:

- tumors of the brain
- temporal lobe epilepsy
- tumors in the spinal channel (incl. syringomyely)
- multiple sclerosis.

For MR-tomographic examinations performed in a hospital very differing rules of billing (see 6, 18, 19, 44) apply in the Federal Republic of Germany. In these rules it is distinguished between outpatient, partially inpatient and inpatient services. Standard services are defined against optional services. Furthermore, it is distinguished whether the physician or the hospital charges the services or whether the method of billing each examination or invoicing a global hospital rate or even a mixed procedure is used. For all these forms of performing and liquidating medical examinations, appropriate rules are to be applied for determining the amount of fees. This, however, shall not be considered in greater detail here.

A hospital which intends to procure an MR-tomograph should clarify what form of billing would be used how often and what proceeds could be expected. It can then use these proceeds as a basis for a comparison with its costs. In respect of the costs for the use of an MR-tomographic system in the hospital sector, in the Federal Republic of Germany the investment costs are usually borne by a third party. Therefore, the costs for procurement, modification and construction measures as well as the costs of financing are not included in the utilization costs.

In the cost calculation of section 4.2 (tables 7 and 8) the utilization costs without the investment costs components are therefore stated in addition to the total costs.

5 Efficiency considerations

The output data for the following efficiency considerations are summarized in section 4. Table 6 (section 4.1) shows the costs of the procurement of an MR-tomography system, the necessary construction measures on its installation and the expected costs for the modification and improvement in the course of the utilization period. In tables 7 and 8 the annual costs to be expected, subdivided into fixed and variable costs, are given. In table 7, a daily operation time of 8 hours is assumed for the MR-tomography unit and in table 8, 12 hours a day are considered. Even if the costs listed in these tables are only to be taken as calculation examples, some conclusions can be drawn from them:

a) The procurement costs of an MR-tomography unit are high for all systems. However, there are considerable cost differences of more than 500 %. In particular, the procurement costs and the neccessary construction measures for the setting up rise considerably with increasing field strength of the static magnetic field.

b) The operating costs of an MR-tomography system are predominantly determined by the investment costs (procurement, financing, modification and improvement) divided over the utilization period (working life) of the system. Their proportion of the total costs can be easily obtained from the data in tables 7 and 8. It lies between 46 % and 59 % of the total costs. Contrasted with these figures the proportion of the personnel costs is between 17 % and 36 %.

Regarding the high investment cost differences, the potential user of an MRI-system must at first investigate which field strength area the system to be operated by him should have. Of primary interest is which diseases he can use the system for and which diagnoses with what degree of accuracy he can achieve. Unfortunately there is not yet a recognized catalogue of indications for the MR-tomography which reflects the magnetic field strength of the unit used. Reference is made to the basic comments in sections 3.1 and 3.2. Low field systems at about 0.02 Tesla clearly have a worse spatial resolution than medium and high field systems. Moreover, the capacity of the low field systems is smaller. High and even medium field systems permit the diagnostic evaluation of the effect of chemical shift. High field systems from 1.5 Tesla upwards permit the possibility of MR-spectroscopy on nuclei of higher ordinal number. Every potential user must therefore clarify in which areas he intends to use his MR-tomography unit. In this respect, future technological improvements should be taken into account.

Due to the high proportion of the investment costs in the total costs, it makes economic sense to use the MRI-system intensively (as many examinations as possible, as long a utilization period as possible). In the example calculations, presented in tables 7 and 8, fully used systems with patients troughputs close to the systems capacities are assumed. As MR-tomographs with high magnetic field strength are more widely applicable than low field systems, high field systems may easier be used at a high throughput level. However, considerations should be paid to the fact that, at present in the Federal Republic of Germany, only 4 indications have been established for which outpatients MR-tomography examinations of compulsory health insurance members can be charged. (For possible future additions to the indications catalogue see section 3.1.) A similar limitation of indications does not exist for private medical treatment.

There is no limit of indications for inpatient treatment in hospitals, as far as the treatment is covered by the genral hospital fee rate or carried out for a private patient.

It is important for a health centre to know, under which conditions it can cover the costs incurred by using the MR-tomography. As already stated in section 4.3, a difference is to be made between hospitals and registered physician's surgeries. In the case of hospitals, it is usually a third party which bears the investment costs.

To clarify the question whether it is possible that the proceeds exeed the costs of MR-tomography or not, the costs per examination are presented in table 9 for the two alternatives considered earlier; alternative A includes 8 hours of operation per day, alternative B includes 12 hours of operation per day. Thereby a patients throughput close to the systems capacities is assumed.

Table 9: Costs per MR-tomography examination

	Resistive magnet		Permanent magnet	Superconducting magnet	
	0.02 T	0.28 T	0.3 T	0.5 T	1.0 T
Alternative A (8 hours/day)	1.200 E/a	1.800 E/a	1.800 E/a	1.800 E/a	1.800 E/a
whole cost calculation	606 DM to 621 DM	685 DM to 694 DM	781 DM to 790 DM	973 DM to 990 DM	1.047 DM to 1.080 DM
partial cost calculation	345 DM to 360 DM	346 DM to 354 DM	327 DM to 336 DM	447 DM to 464 DM	470 DM to 503 DM
Alternative B (12 hours/day)	1.800 E/a	2.700 E/a	2.700 E/a	2.700 E/a	2.700 E/a
whole cost calculation	481 DM to 491 DM	539 DM to 544 DM	591 DM to 596 DM	723 DM to 734 DM	773 DM to 795 DM
partial cost calculation	308 DM to 318 DM	312 DM to 318 DM	288 DM to 294 DM	373 DM to 384 DM	389 DM to 411 DM

Legend: E/a = Examinations per year DM = DM per Examination

The partial cost calculation includes no cost for procurement, construction, modification/improvement and financing.

The figures presented in table 9 show

- that in the case of the whole cost calculation the costs per examination rise with increasing field strength
- that in the case of the whole cost calculation the costs per examination (even given full utilization of the systems) are partially above the fee levels, in accordance with which outpatient MR-tomography examinations are paid (see section 4.3)
- that in the case of the partial cost calculation which is usually valid for the hospitals, about 40 % to 60 % lower costs per examination incur than in the case of the whole cost calculation.

At present, the number of patients and their health insurance status (private patient or member of a compulsory health insurance scheme) define the possibility of reaching the break-even point for a registered physician.

A further model calculation shows for the outpatient treatment in a registered physician's surgery, by which average fee rate and by which annual examinations number the proceeds exeed the costs. An analogue calculation could be carried out for the hospitals.

The results of the calculations are presented in diagram form in figure 1. The proceeds and the costs are shown on the ordinate, the annual number of examinations on the abscissa. The cost straight lines are the result, taking the fixed and variable cost components into consideration. The proceeds are presented as a family of lines which emanate from the origin of the coordinate system. In addition the estimated capacity limits of the MRI-systems up from 0.28 Tesla and the 0.02 Tesla system are given as vertical straight lines.

It can be concluded that the costs of the 0.02 Tesla low field system are covered by the fee rates laid down in the Federal Republic of Germany even at low throughput levels. For medium and high field systems they do not break even under certain circumstances. This applies, for example, if the capacity of the MR-tomograph does not permit the necessary patients throughput to cover the costs.

If, however, there are MRI-systems with field strengths over 0.3 Tesla in operation in doctor's surgeries, this may be due to the fact that the owners of such systems expect either a high alternative benefit or that they expect an increase in the fee rate. Perhaps they are aiming at a better economic result by a mixed calculation including other medical procedures and equipment.

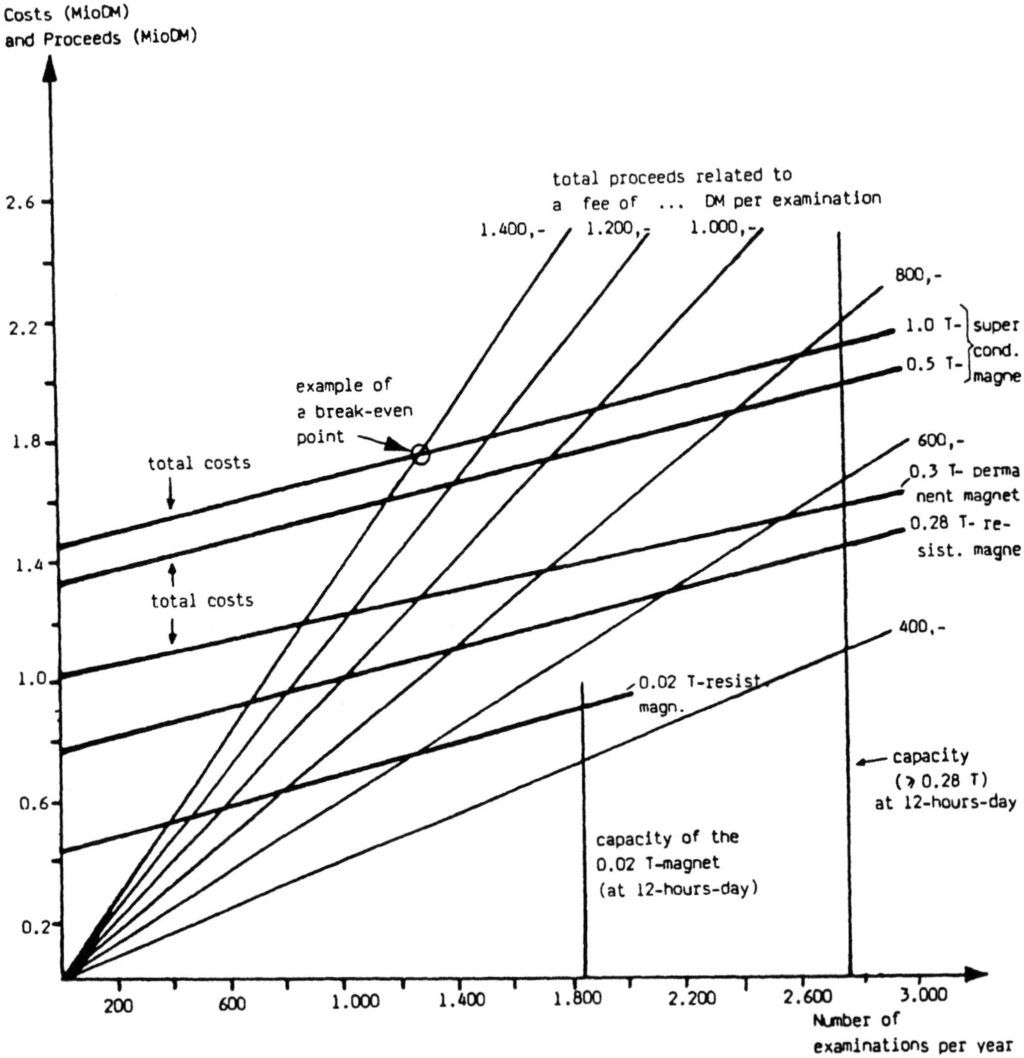

Figure 1: Annual costs and proceeds of MR-tomography related to the number of performed examinations and **to** the height of fee (break-even point calculations)

Literature:

1 Baum, H., Kühnert, A., Sundermeyer, R., et al. (eds.): Kernspintomographie 1985: Untersuchungen, Betriebszeit, Untersuchungszeit, Dietzenbach 1985.

2 Bloch, F.: Nuclear Inductions, in: Physical Review 70, 1946, pp. 460.

3 Bruker Medizintechnik GmbH (ed.): Zusammenstellung der jährlichen Betriebskosten für einen Bruker Kernspintomographen TOMIKON BMT 1100 mit resistivem Magneten (0,28 T), Rheinstetten without year.

4 Bundesausschuß der Ärzte und Krankenkassen: Richtlinien für den wirtschaftlichen Einsatz von medizinisch-technischen Großgeräten, in: Deutsches Ärzteblatt, no. 3, edition B, 1985, pp. 90.

5 Bundesgesundheitsamt: Empfehlungen zur Vermeidung gesundheitlicher Risiken verursacht durch magnetische und hochfrequente elektromagnetische Felder bei der NMR-Tomographie und In-vivo-NMR-Spektroskopie, in: Bundesgesundheitsblatt 27, no. 3, 1984, pp. 92.

6 Bundesmantelvertrag Ärzte, Anlage 5 (Stand 1. April 1986), Einheitlicher Bewertungsmaßstab (EBM) nach § 368g Abs. 4 RVO, Bonn-Bad Godesberg.

7 Bureau of Radiological Health (United States of America): Guidelines for Evaluating Electromagnetic Risk for Trials of Clinical NMR Systems, Department of Health and Human Services, Public Health Service, Food and Drug Administration, Rockville 1982.

8 Cherryman, G.R.: Cost of operating a nuclear magnetic resonance imaging system, in: British Medical Journal 291, 1985, pp. 1437.

9 Damadian, R., Minkoff, L., Goldsmith, M., et al.: Field Focussing Nuclear Magnetic Resonance (FONAR): Visualization of a Tumor in a Live Animal, in: Science 194, 1976, pp. 1430.

10 Diekmann, F., and Riefenstahl, R.: Medizinisch-technische Großgeräte - Symposium, Berlin 1987.

11 Edelstein, W.A., Hutchinson, J.M.S., et al.: Spin-warp NMR-imaging and Applications to Human whole-body Imaging, in: Physics in Medicine and Biology 25, 1980, pp. 751.

12 Evans, R.G., Jost, R.G., and Evans, R.G. jun.: Economic and Utilization Analysis of Magnetic Resonance Imaging Units in the United States in 1985, in: American Journal of Radiology 145, 1985, pp. 31

13 Fandel, G., and Prasiswa, A.: Zur Planung und Organisation wirtschaftlicher Betriebseinheiten im ambulanten medizinischen Versorgungsbereich, in: Operations Research Spektrum 4, 1982, pp. 15.

14 Feucht, H., König, D., and Ostheimer, E.: Kernspintomographie - Analyse der Einsatzmöglichkeiten, Köln 1984.

15 Fonar (ed.): New 3000 Gauss Permanent Magnet in the Fonar QED ß3000 NMR Scanner, Melville/New York without year.

16 Garroway, A.N., Grannel, P.K., and Mansfield, P.: Image Formation in NMR by a Selective Irradiative Process, in: Journal of Physics C: Solid State Physics 7, 1974, pp. 457.

17 Gautschi, H., and Schmutz, G.: Entwicklungsstand, Bedarf und Betrieb von MRI- und MRS-Anlagen in der Schweiz, Aarau 1984.

18 Gebührenordnung für Ärzte (GOÄ) vom 12. Nov. 1982, in: BGBl I, p. 1522, (Nach Änderungen Stand vom 1. April 1986).

19 Gesetz zur wirtschaftlichen Sicherung der Krankenhäuser und zur Regelung der Krankenhauspflegesätze (Krankenhausfinanzierungsgesetz - KHG) vom 29. Juni 1972 (BGBl I, p. 1009); lastly altered by Krankenhaus-Neuordnungsgesetz vom 20. Dezember 1984 BGBl I, p. 1716.

20 Haase, A., Frahm, J., Matthaei, D., et al.: Rapid Images and NMR Movies, Fourth Annual Meeting of the Society of Magnetic Resonance in Medicine, Book of Abstracts 2, pp. 980.

21 Halbsguth, A., and Lochner, B.: Wirtschaftlichkeitsanalyse, NMR-Symposium an der Deutschen Klinik für Diagnostik, Wiesbaden 1984.

22 Henning, J., Nauerth, A., Friedburg, H., et al.: Ein neues Schnellbildverfahren für die Kernspintomographie, in: Radiologie 24, 1984, pp. 579.

23 Hinshaw, W.S.: Spin Mapping: The Application of Moving Gradients to NMR, in: Physical Letters, 48A, 1974, pp. 87.

24 Huk, W.: Indikationen der NMR-Tomographie bei Untersuchungen im Bereich des zentralen Nervensystems, NMR-Symposium an der Deutschen Klinik für Diagnostik, Wiesbaden 1984.

25 Instrumentarium Corp. (ed.): Acutsan, the cost-effective approach, Helsinki without year.

26 Kaufmann, L., Crooks, L.E., and Margulis, A.R.: Nuclear Magnetic Resonance in Medicine, IGAKU-SHOIN, New York/Tokyo 1981.

27 Knief, P., and Laufenberg, M.: Zur Wirtschaftlichkeit von Kernspintomographen, in: Arzt und Wirtschaft 11, 1984, pp. 15.

28 Knüttel, B., and Müller, W.: Magnetsysteme für die NMR-Tomographie - Technische Eigenschaften und Betriebskosten, in: Deutsches Ärzteblatt, no. 14, edition B, 1985, pp. 1002.

29 König, D.: Rahmenbedingungen für die Aufstellung und den Betrieb von Kernspintomographie-Anlagen, in: Kernspintomographie, 2. Bericht 1984 Bundesministerium für Forschung und Technologie, Bonn 1984.

30 Kumar, A., Welti, D., and Ernst, R.B.: NMR-Fourier-Zeugmatography, in: Journal of Magnetic Resonance 18, 1975, pp. 69.

31 Lauterbur, P.C.: Image Formation by Induced Local Interactions: Examples Employing Nuclear Magnetic Resonance, in: Nature 242, 1973, pp. 190.

32 Lauterbur, P.C.: Magnetic Resonance Zeugmatography, in: Pure and Applied Chemistry 49, 1974, pp. 149.

33 Mansfield, P., Maudsley, A.A., and Baines, T.: Fast Scan Proton Density Imaging by NMR, in: Journal of Physics E: Scientific Instruments 9, 1976, pp. 271.

34 Ministerium für Arbeit, Gesundheit, Familie und Sozialordnung Baden-Württemberg: Bekanntmachung über Anschaffung, Nutzung und Mitbenutzung medizinisch-technischer Großgeräte, in: Staatsanzeiger Baden-Württemberg Nr. 19, 1985, pp. 5.

35 Morneburg, M.: Gesichtspunkte bei der Standortsuche und Planung für ein Magnetom, in: Electromedica 51, 1983, pp. 65.

36 NMR-Tomographie, Informationsschrift der Fa. Bruker, Rheinstetten 1982

37 Oppelt, A., Graumann, R., Barfuss, H., et al.: FISP: eine neue schnell Pulssequenz für die Kernspintomographie, in: Electromedica 1, 1986, pp. 15.

38 Purcell, E.M., Torrey, H.C., and Pound, R.V.: Resonance Absorption by Nuclear Magnetic Moments in a Solid, in: Physical Review 69, 1946, p. 37.

39 Rinck, P.A.: Magnetresonanz in der Medizin, Stuttgart/New York 1985.

40 Roth, K.: NMR-Tomographie und -Spektroskopie in der Medizin, Berlin/Heidelberg/New York/Tokyo 1984.

41 Rühl, H.L.: Kernspintomographie, Bundesverband Deutscher Radiologen und Nuklearmediziner - Interessengemeinschaft für Computertomographie, Dietzenbach 1984.

42 Rühl, H.L., (ed.): Kernspintomographie: Standort, Untersuchungszeit, Jahresbetriebskosten, Kosten/Zeiteinheit, Roedermark 1985.

43 Siemens AG: Magnetom Daten, Erlangen without year.

44 Verordnung zur Regelung der Krankenhauspflegesätze (Bundespflegesatzverordnung - BPflV) 1973, in: BGBl. I. p. 333, lastly altered by Vierte Verordnung zur Änderung der Bundespflegesatzverordnung vom 20. Dezember 1984, BGBl. I, p. 1680.

45 Zeitler, E., and Ganssen, A.: Erste klinische Erfahrung mit der Kernspintomographie (KST), in: Fortschritte auf dem Gebiet der Röntgenstrahlen und Nuklearmedizin 135, no. 5, 1981, pp. 517.

Regional Location and Capacity Planning for ESW Lithotripters and CT Scanners

Lüder Bach

1 The current planning situation concerning AMT installations

Extracorporal shock wave kidney lithotripters (ESW lithotripters) and computerized tomographic scanners (CT scanners) are part of the group of so-called machines for advanced medical technology (AMT machines). For both types as well as for other AMT types there exists a planning need in order to guarantee their medical utilization as well as their locational distribution at a desirable service level. In this context it is the planner's objective to avoid either over-provision or under-provision of AMT services.

The different types of AMT machines on the market require different planning needs. Using ESW lithotripters as an example to represent all AMT types it will be shown how and why a planning need can materialize.

In mid-1985 an ESW lithotripter was installed in Erlangen, Bavaria, to be used in non-operative shock wave kidney stone treatment.[1] This was the third installation of its kind in Bavaria, following previous installations in Munich and Würzburg. According to the Bavarian location and capacity plan in effect at the time the installations at these three locations provided a sufficient service capacity for the annual demand for extracorporal shock wave kidney lithotripsy (ESWL) for all of Bavaria. Thus it was assumed that the long term ESWL demand to be expected for a population of approximately 11 million would be met by these three installations.[2] However, only two years later, in mid-1987, a fourth unit was installed in the Nuremberg City Clinic, one of the largest municipal hospitals in the Federal Republic of Germany. The further installation of units in other locations can be safely assumed.

A similar development took place in the state of Baden-Württemberg: Here too, by the end of 1985 three ESW lithotripters were in operation, located in Stuttgart, Ulm, and Heidelberg. In this case also, total capacity and individual locations were considered to service the needs of this state and its population of approximately 9 million sufficiently. And yet, the actual situation in mid-1986 demanded new planning considerations leading to the decision in early 1987 to install three additional ESWL units in Freiburg, Karlsruhe, and Ulm, and possibly a fourth one in Mannheim.

Such developments in Bavaria and Baden-Württemberg are representative of parallel developments in all other federal states of West Germany, and they suggest that the total planning situation in the Federal Republic of Germany, which originally estimated the need for a total of 21 ESWL units, has become obsolete.[3]

This need for a rapid updating of the original plans for ESWL installations was decidedly influenced by two factors. One of these was the fact that in the first planning phase several of the larger urological clinics were not considered as ESWL locations. The fear of exclusion from medical-technological progress and the feeling of being disadvantaged resulted in the coalition of several hospitals and local politicians exercising considerable political pressure to have additional locations for ESW lithotripters authorized. The administration in charge of health care and planning in the individual states was able for some time to resist this pressure, referring to high investment and operation costs and thus to high treatment costs, and claiming that the existing ESWL capacity provided for sufficient services statewide. This position no longer could be claimed when in 1986 the second factor gained influence: two new models of ESW lithotripters were marketed, one by Siemens, the other by Wolf.[4] Both models were offered at a considerably lower price than the only model on the market until then, the model offered by Dornier.[5]

The combination of these two influential factors resulted in a decidedly new situation, for planners and decision-makers alike. In 1986, the Dept. of Social Affairs in the state of Baden-Württemberg, which is responsible for the public health care sector, took up the issue and developed planning-based decisions concerning the effectiveness of regional decentralization by way of increasing ESWL installations in hospitals on the following conditions: a calculated choice among the ESWL models on the market, acceptance of the needs and demands of hospitals and politicians in the different regions of the state as well as acceptance of the general guidelines, such as those issued by the state hospital plan concerning specified service levels.[6]

Against this background of the development and distribution of ESWL installations [7] in the Federal Republic and their consequences as specified in new planning and decision-making needs, the factors relating to AMT machines in general and ESW lithotripters and CT scanners in particular lead to the following considerations:

- general planning tasks concerning AMT installations,
- specific planning tasks for regional location and capacity planning concerning AMT systems,
- the basic structure of a model of the overall utilization and transportation costs, to be applied to AMT systems in regional location and capacity planning,
- regional location and capacity planning for ESWL systems, with Baden-Württemberg as an example,
- regional location and capacity planning for CT systems, with the northeastern region of Baden-Württemberg as an example.

The analyses presented base their considerations and suggestions on the general guidelines specified by the public health system of the Federal Republic of Germany.

2 General planning tasks

The increasing demand for AMT installations generates specific requirements for various interest groups to plan, to make decisions and to execute such decisions.[8] These groups include the different associations formed by certified physicians, health insurance agencies, hospitals and hospital doctors, the Depts. of Health in the several states, and others. The requirements are a direct result of the following developments, actual situations and conjectures about AMT technology and services:

- they open up new diagnostic and therapeutic possibilities which are generally identified with medical progress;

- they usually incur high investments generating debates about cost increases or decreases;

- they tend to support an uneven sectoral dissemination in the out-patient and in-patient areas;

- they tend to support an uneven regional distribution with a concentration in metropolitan areas and urban agglomerations;

- they support an uneven structural dissemination tending to concentrate either in larger hospitals or in physicians' offices;

- they generate fear among individual doctors, hospitals, cities, or counties that in refusing to install AMT technology they will cut themselves off from medical progress and be forced to accept less qualified medical services for their population.

The requirements for planning, decision-making, and action-taking relate to the following areas and aspects:

- medical services [9]:
  - fields of indication,
  - medical necessity,
  - diagnostic and therapeutic advantages and disadvantages,
  - substitutive and cumulative range of utilization,
  - effectiveness of the installation;

- economy [10]:
  - substitutive and cumulative effects of expenditures,
  - effects of expenditures on treatment costs,
  - the unit's durability,
  - the unit's efficiency;

- management/administration/operation [11]:
  - location of unit
    (e.g. physician's office or hospital),
  - locational conditions and demands on medical apparatus
    (e.g. need for other medical technology),
  - locational conditions and demands on manpower
    (e.g. need for additional qualified personnel),
  - locational conditions and demands on functioning
    (e.g. need for specialized departments/clinics),

- locational conditions and demands on organization (e.g. joint-use regulations);

- public health policy [12]:
  - need for regulation and control (e.g. in decisions about investment and location),
  - distribution of competences (e.g. for planning, investment, governing boards),
  - procedural rules and regulations (e.g. for planning, coordination, management, administration);

- regional development policy:
  - regional conditions,
  - spatial service levels,
  - medical service levels,
  - regional effects.

Certain individual aspects are, without doubt, more significant for some AMT types than for others, more important for some interest groups than for others, and more prominent in certain planning and decision-making situations than in others.[13] It should also be noted that it is not necessary to evaluate and decide upon all aspects evenly at one time; instead, sequential decisions reflect a more typical procedure, where in a first step general decisions concerning primarily medical and economic aspects are made which then, for example, are followed by more concrete administrative and operative decisions, where locational conditions and demands enter in as secondary factors.[14]

The locational decision for an AMT installation, which implicitly is connected to a decision about an investment, is governed by two basically different sets of circumstances: The decision can either be an "exclusive" one, calculated only in terms of a single unit's profitability, with no explicit consideration of its implications, neither for other units already installed or still in the planning stages, nor for the region's service level or its indication rate. Such a procedure in financial and locational decision-making, which could be justified only from the position of the individual operator of an AMT installation, does, as a rule, not meet the standards and objectives of current health policies or regional development policies. Instead, a more "inclusive" constellation of decision-making has developed as part of the objective to make investment and location decisions which are economically and spatially efficient and effective. That is to say, the decision for a new AMT installation can only be made when all other identical units in the region, already installed or still in the planning stages, are taken into account; this region can be a metropolitan area, an urban agglomeration, part of a federal state, or a state as such.

In this context of a demand for efficient end effective investment and location decisions it is important to note the following findings of regional anlyses since they may serve as examples for successful decision-making procedures: [15] It is possible to prove that under specified conditions an increasing number of CT scanners leads to decreasing costs and, at the same time, to a higher indication rate and a higher degree of accessibility, i.e. improved medical as well as spatial service levels for the region's population. In the case of ESW lithotripters, new model-developments currently allow for drastic financial reductions, which in turn open up a greater range of freedom to decide for more installations in additional locations within a given total budget of an entire region. This, of course, results in an improved spatial service level.

3 Specific planning tasks

Specific planning tasks relate to the location decision within a regional context. Locationally defined planning tasks for AMT installations usually gain importance only after previous decisions have been made in the medical and economic areas, i.e. after the range of medical applications and the medical/economic cost-benefit relations have in turn been clarified. These more fundamental decisions about an AMT service then lead to a decision about the number of AMT units needed by one region to meet its demands. This question is answered superficially only, and thus insufficiently, when the total demand in one region is taken to be equal the total capacity of all the units in that region. Here the locational, i.e. regional distribution of the units plays an important role for the following reasons:

- An AMT unit may have a certain maximum service range, i.e. the greater the distance between the AMT location and the user location the greater the tendency not to use AMT services.

- A substitutive relation may possibly exist between patient tranportation costs and AMT utilization costs since a larger number of installations will result in reduced transportation costs; such savings may exceed the investments for additional units.

- The effects of this substitutive relation between transportation costs and AMT utilization costs is possibly influenced considerably when the purchasing price of an AMT unit changes, e.g. when prices decline due to new technologies.

- The capacity of utilization, possibly also the excess of maximum capacity levels, depends on the size of the district which is to be served by the unit.

An approach which incorporates all actual expenses in an investment and location decision, even when such expenses are to be shared by different fund suppliers, enforces greater precision, and the question concerning the number of units therefore should read: How many AMT units of a specific type - such as ESW lithotripters or CT scanners - must be present in a specific region, and at which locations should these units be installed?[16]

The two relevant variables in a decision about an investment and location therefore are:

- the number of AMT units,
- the locations of the AMT units.

The relevant goal parameters are:

- the total costs for a region,
- the costs per treatment,
- the capacity utilization of an AMT unit,
- the medical service level
  (e.g. as measured by the indication rate) [17],
- the spatial service level
  (e.g. as measured by transportation distances) [18].

The distinct form of these parameters depends primarily on the two decision variables. Each individual parameter contains the information necessary for investment and location decisions.

4 A model of utilization and transportation costs

For the purpose of evaluating the goal parameters in their dependence on the decision variables, a "model of overall utilization and transportation costs for AMT systems" has been developed into which the two decision variables are incorporated as input variables. This model determines total costs consisting of:

- transportation costs for the transportation of patients to an AMT installation and back;

- utilization costs, i.e. a combination of three related cost categories:
  - fixed costs per AMT unit (expenses for equipment, operation, and personnel),
  - fixed threshold costs per AMT unit (expenses incurred by exceeding the maximum workload of operating personnel),
  - variable costs per treatment (expenses for supplies and materials).

In such a model the following input parameters may have to be accounted for:

- different modes of transportation for patients (e.g. private car or taxi, ambulance, critical care vehicle, subway, bus, train, etc.),
- different groups of patients (e.g. out-patients, in-patients),
- different indication rates (e.g. dependent or not dependent on distance),
- number of AMT units per location,
- different AMT models and different unit prices (e.g. choice among models on the market),
- different suppliers of services (e.g. hospital, physician's office),
- maximum unit capacity,
- minimum unit capacity,
- maximum workload capacity of operating personnel.

The basic structure of this model resembles that of the location-allocation-model with central points [19]: In such a mathematical model the total costs, consisting of utilization and transportation costs, are minimized. A specific description of the model and its application to ESW lithotripters and CT scanners is provided in the following sections.

Table 1: Breakdown of costs for different models of ESW lithotripters (in DM as in 1986)

CATEGORIES	ESWL MODELS DORNIER	SIEMENS	WOLF
FIXED COSTS:			
- equipment	1,019,325	709,417	397,575
- operation	332,940	198,900	82,550
- personnel	325,000	325,000	190,000
TOTAL	1,677,265	1,233,317	670,125
FIXED THRESHOLD COSTS:			
- personnel	80,000	80,000	-
TOTAL	80,000	80,000	-
VARIABLE COSTS:			
- supplies and materials	900	50	50
TOTAL	900	50	50

Note: (a) FIXED COSTS and FIXED THRESHOLD COSTS are costs per ESW lithotripter and per year.
(b) VARIABLE COSTS are costs per ESWL treatment.

5 Regional planning for ESW lithotripters

Regional location and capacity planning for ESW lithotripters has already been carried out for the region comprising the state of Baden-Württemberg.[20] The population of approximately 9 million, and the population inhabiting the areas bordering on Baden-Württemberg, together require a total of 4,259 ESWL treatments per year. This estimate was based on an indication rate of 425 ESWL treatments per 1 million inhabitants and year. Such planning consists of an analysis of given locational alternatives which differ with respect to the number of locations and the regional distribution of locations. All locational alternatives are analysed in terms of their financial, capacitary and spatial consequences, all of which are measured using the goal parameters. A further analysis is made of the sequence in which a gradual expansion from currently 3 ESWL locations to a future total of 7 could be achieved. Finally, the question is addressed whether hospitals of the so-called "level of intermediate services"-group can also be selected for locations, in addition to the existing 7 ESWL units

Table 2: Locational alternatives for regional systems of ESW lithotripters, as used in analysis

NO. OF ALTER-NATIVE	ESWL LOCATIONS	S	U	H	F	K	T	M
		ALTERNATIVE INCLUDES:						
1	3	X	X	X				
2	3 + 1	X	X	X	X			
3	3 + 1	X	X	X		X		
6	3 + 2	X	X	X	X	X		
7	3 + 2	X	X	X	X		X	
9	3 + 2	X	X	X		X	X	
12	3 + 3	X	X	X	X	X	X	
13	3 + 3	X	X	X	X	X		X
14	3 + 3	X	X	X	X		X	X
15	3 + 3	X	X	X		X	X	X
16	3 + 4	X	X	X	X	X	X	X

LEGEND: S = Stuttgart, U = Ulm, H = Heidelberg, F = Freiburg, K = Karlsruhe, T = Tübingen, M = Mannheim

X = ESWL location

all of which are located in hospitals of the "maximum level of services"-group. In order to clarify the procedure and the essential contextual claims of the analysis concerning ESWL locations in Baden-Württemberg, the following sections will address these issues:

- the input variables and parameters on which the study is based,
- the adaptation and application of the model of utilization and transportation costs to those questions which are relevant for this study,
- the essential findings of location and capacity planning in Baden-Württemberg.

5.1 Input variables and parameters

The state of Baden-Württemberg has three locations for ESWL installations, one unit each in Stuttgart, Ulm, and Heidelberg. Possible new locations are maximum service level hospitals in the following cities: Freiburg or Karlsruhe (first stage), plus Tübingen (second stage),

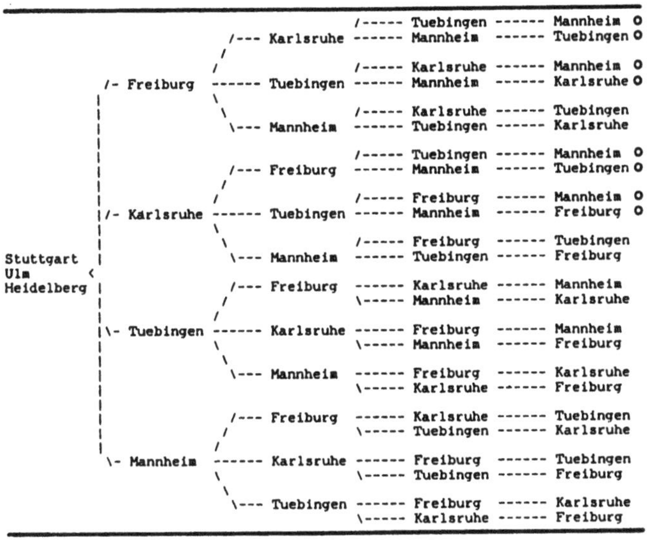

Figure 1: Tree diagram of all potential expansion-sequences with 3 current ESWL locations and 7 ESWL locations in the 4th stage (sequences analysed are marked "o")

plus Mannheim (third stage). In the fourth stage a location for an ESWL unit will be selected in one of the cities not selected in stages 1 through 3. Since such expansion can only be achieved in graded steps, the sum total of all conceivable expansion sequences results in 8 sequences with a total of 11 locational alternatives (see fig. 1 in connection with table 2). For the input parameters the following assumptions are made:

- Only one group of patients is defined, i.e. those patients exclusively who have been accepted into hospitals as in-patients and who undergo ESWL treatment.

- All patients use private automobiles in reaching their treatment locations, so that the transportation costs can be calculated on the basis of rates per kilometer and the distances travelled, with both trips to and from the hospital counted separately.

- The demand for ESWL treatment is not made dependent on distance, which allows for the use of a constant indication rate independent of the size of the service districts and thus of the distances each patient must travel.

- Each ESWL location has only one lithotripter.

- All ESWL treatment is supplied in hospitals only.

- Each locational alternative is analysed in terms of its suitability for each of the specific ESWL models on the market, i.e. for each locational alternative identical calculations are made four times, the only difference being that the first calculation is made for the Dornier model, the second for the Siemens model, the third for the Wolf model, and the fourth for the so-called "Special Payment Agreement KfH/Dornier" [21]. The individual models vary in all three categories, fixed costs, fixed threshold costs and variable costs (see table 1).

- The maximum ESWL capacity is set at 1,600 treatments per year and unit and must be adhered to. In case this limit is exceeded patients are then assigned to other ESWL locations.

- The minimum ESWL capacity is set at 1,000 treatments per year and unit and must be adhered to. In case of a shortfall of this limit the location is no longer considered.

- A maximum workload capacity of 1,000 treatments per unit, year and treatment team must be adhered to. In order to avoid fixed threshold costs for additional personnel, excess treatments should be assigned to other locations wherever possible.

5.2 Procedure and application of the mathematical model

The approach followed in this study is similar to that of a locational analysis, i.e. different given locational alternatives are analysed and compared with regard to the same set of goal parameters. For this reason the application of the model of utilization and transportation costs is simplified in that an optimization of the locations themselves is no longer necessary since these can be assumed as given in the locational alternatives themselves. This reduces the need for optimization to the service districts by allocating the population distributed in the state of Baden-Württemberg to the ESWL locations. Once the service districts have been determined all cost-factors of the utilization and transportation costs (and thus also of the total costs) are included in the calculation. Most of the goal parameters can then be determined from the service districts and the sum total of costs (see fig. 2 in connection with table 3).

The total costs as well as the goal parameters of each locational alternative are then taken as information to be included in the decision-making process about the selection and sequence of locational

Table 3: Sequence of main steps for calculating utilization and transportation costs for a regional ESWL system

CALCULATION-SEQUENCE	INFORMATION GAINED
1. Delimitation of service district for each ESW lithotripter	- Service districts - Demand for ESWL treatments per district - Maximum distance per district - Average distance per district - Average distance in planning region
2. Calculation of total fixed threshold costs	- Fixed threshold costs - Level of utilization per ESW lithotripter - Correction of locational alternative if necessary
3. Calculation of total variable costs	- Variable costs
4. Calculation of total fixed costs	- Fixed costs
5. Calculation of total utilization costs	- Utilization costs
6. Calculation of total transportation costs	- Transportation costs
7. Calculation of overall utilization and transportation costs	- Overall utilization and transportation costs - Average costs per ESWL treatment

alternatives, thus enabling decision-makers to compare the locational alternatives and the sequences of development and expansion in terms of their financial, capacitary and spatial implications.

The following three sections outline and illustrate the mathematical model for ESWL systems, the symbols used in the model, and finally the input variables for its application as well as their specification.

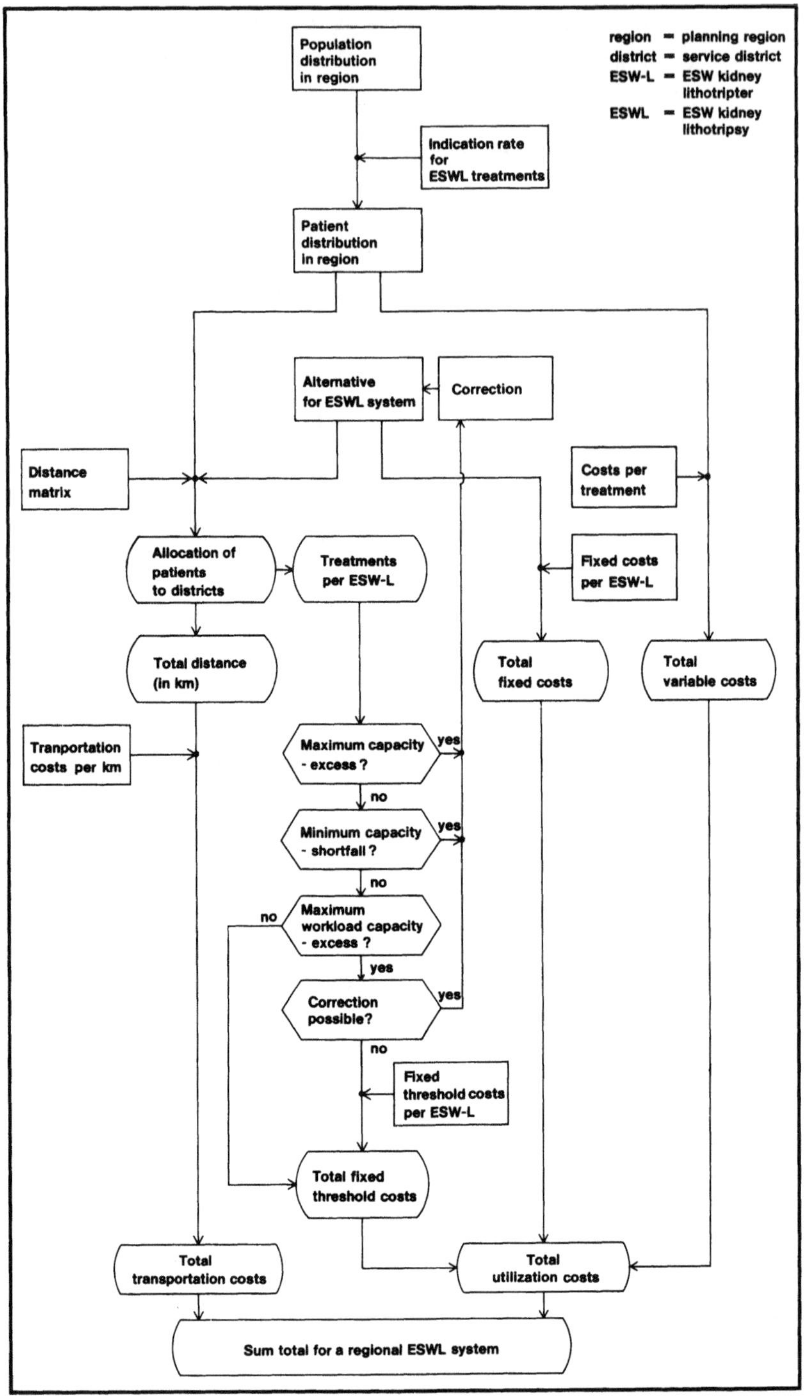

Figure 2: Flow chart for calculating overall utilization and transportation costs for a regional ESWL system

5.2.1 Mathematical model for regional ESWL systems

The equation for the overall utilization and transportation costs, i.e. for the total costs K per year of a regional ESWL system is:

$$K = T + U \qquad (1.0)$$

The equation for transportation costs T in equation (1.0) is:

$$T = 2 \cdot \left(\sum_{j=1}^{n} \sum_{i=1}^{m} X_{ji} \cdot T^{*} \cdot d_{ji} \right) \qquad (2.0)$$

where

$$X_{ji} = E_{i \varepsilon Q j} \cdot I^{*} \qquad (2.1)$$

The equation for overall utilization costs U in equation (1.0) is:

$$U = F + V + S \qquad (3.0)$$

In equation (3.0), the three terms F, V, and S are defined as follows. The equation for fixed costs F is:

$$F = F^{*} \cdot Z^{*} \qquad (4.0)$$

The equation for variable costs V is:

$$V = E_{i} \cdot I^{*} \cdot V^{*} \qquad (5.0)$$

The equation for fixed threshold costs S is:

$$S = S^{*} \cdot \sum_{j=1}^{n} y_{j} \qquad (6.0)$$

where

$$y_{j} = 1 \quad \text{if} \quad \left(\sum_{i=1}^{m} X_{ji} / c^{*} \right) > 1$$

$$\text{for all } j, j=1,\ldots,n \qquad (6.1)$$

in all other cases:

$$y_{j} = 0 \qquad (6.2)$$

with X_{ji} defined as in equation (2.1).

In equation (2.1), the service districts Q_j are defined as follows:

$$Q_j = \{ P_i : d_{ji} \le d_{ki} \text{ for } i=1,\dots,m \text{ and } k = 1,\dots,n \text{ with } k = j \text{ as well as } c' \le \sum_{i=1}^{m} X_{ji} \le c'' \} \text{ for all } j,\ j=1,\dots,n \quad (7.0)$$

5.2.2 List of symbols

K	total costs (per year)
T	transportation costs (per year)
U	utilization costs (per year)
F	fixed costs (per year)
V	variable costs (per year)
S	fixed threshold costs (per year)
i	index for demand locations, i=1,...,m
j	index for supply locations, j=1,...,k,...,n
P_i	i-th demand location
E_i	population at P_i
M_j, M_k	j-th, respectively k-th, supply location
Q_j	service district of M_j
X_{ji}	number of ESWL treatments from P_i at M_j
I^*	indication rate
T^*	transportation costs per kilometer
F^*	fixed costs per ESW lithotripter
V^*	variable costs per ESWL treatment
S^*	fixed threshold costs per ESW lithotripter
Z^*	number of ESW lithotripters
d_{ji}, d_{ki}	distance between P_i and M_j, P_i and M_k respectively
c^*	maximum workload capacity of an ESWL operating team
c'	minimum capacity of an ESW lithotripter
c''	maximum capacity of an ESW lithotripter
y_j	0-1-variable

5.2.3 List and specification of input variables and parameters

For the purpose of analysing eleven alternative locational systems for ESW lithotripters the following input variables and parameters were used:

- the locations for ESW lithotripters according to each of the eleven alternative locational systems (see table 2),

- the distances d_{ji} and d_{ki} between demand locations P_i and supply locations M_j or M_k respectively, as measured in kilometers in the road network,
- the population at E_i,
- the indication rate I*=425 ESWL treatments/1 million inhabitants,
- the factor of transportation costs T*=0.50 DM/km,
- the fixed costs F*, the variable costs V*, and the fixed threshold costs S* (see table 1),
- the capacity limits per ESW lithotripter: c*=1,000 treatments, c'=300 treatments, and c"=1,600 treatments.

5.3 Results

For each of the locational alternatives for ESWL systems in Baden-Württemberg included in the study the financial, capacitary, and spatial consequences were determined (see figs. 3 to 6). From these individual results the following essential conclusions can be drawn:

(a) From a purely computational perspective the three ESWL units existing in Baden-Württemberg in 1986 are sufficient to meet the demand in this state of 4,259 ESWL treatments per year, assuming that the Stuttgart and Heidelberg locations are utilized at full capacity while the Ulm installation has an extra 541 ESWL treatments in reserve (see fig. 5).

(b) Each additional ESWL unit and thus each additional location leads to an increment of the total costs incurred, thus increasing also the average cost for an individual ESWL treatment. Only in case of the "Special Payment Agreement KfH/Dornier" can costs retain a near-constant level (see fig. 3).

(c) Increasing the number of ESWL locations in most cases leads to a reduction of the average distance of patient travel (see fig. 4). Generally, this means an improvement in regional accessibility of ESWL services.

(d) Costs for individual ESWL treatments change when one or more of these variables change: the number of ESWL installations, the spatial distribution of units, and/or the unit model. This allows to draw the conclusions that:

- 7 ESWL locations using the Wolf model incur total costs per treatment considerably below those incurred by 3 ESWL locations using

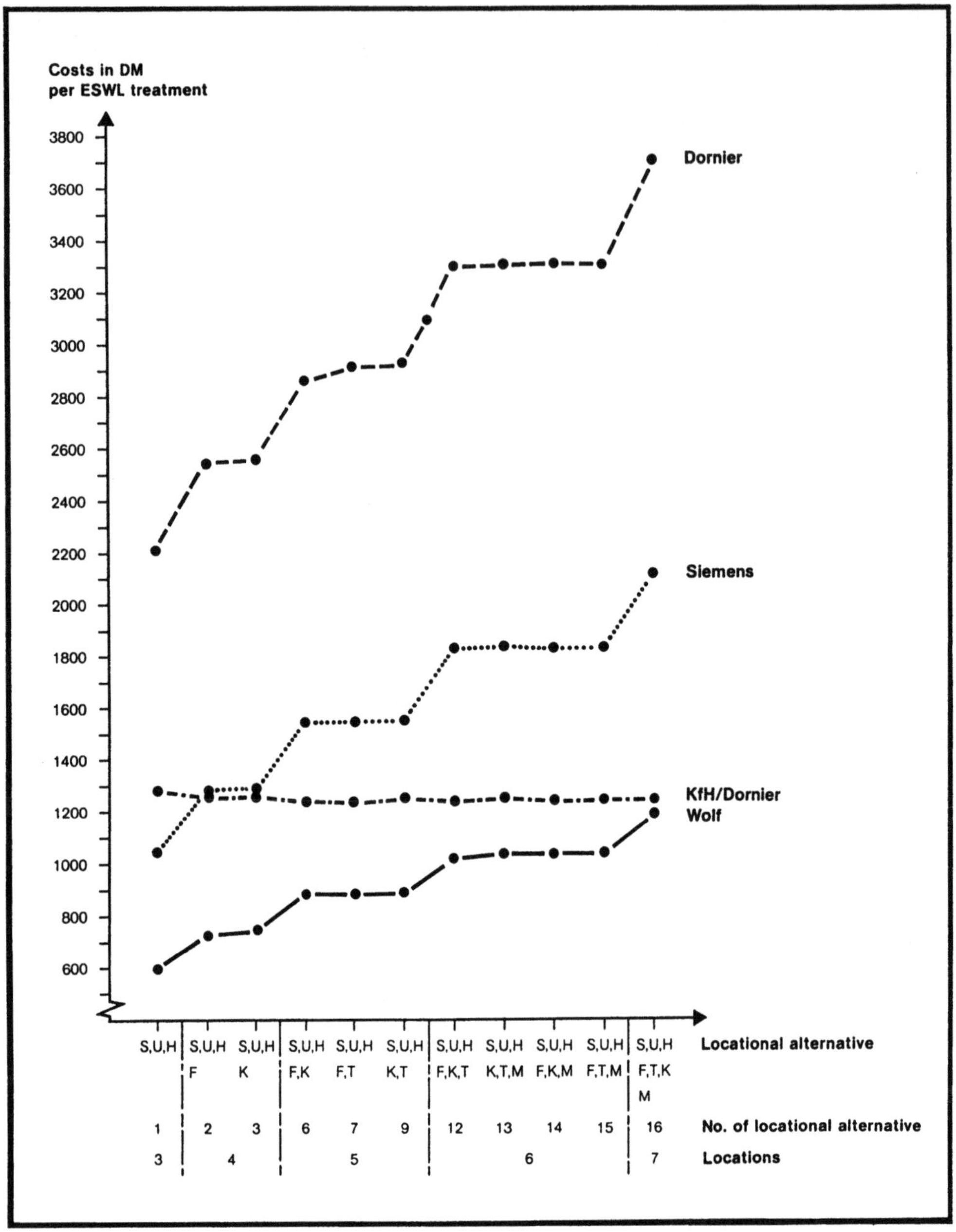

Figure 3: Cost development per ESWL treatment based on eleven alternative ESWL systems for Baden-Württemberg

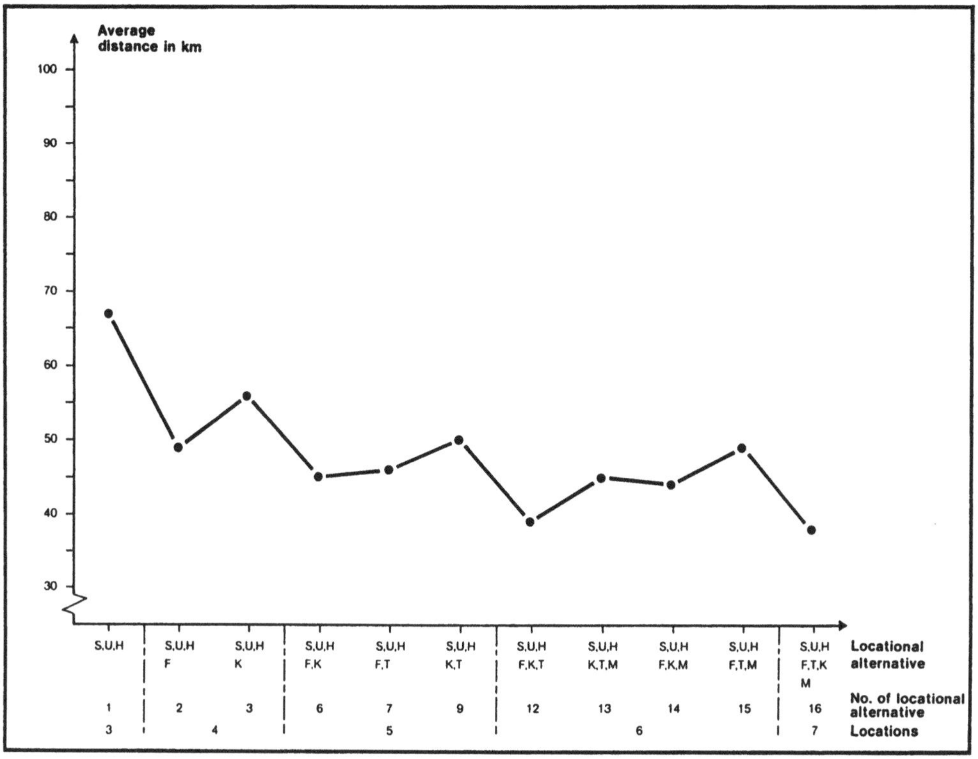

Figure 4: Average distances (in km) to nearest ESWL location, calculated for eleven alternative ESWL systems in Baden-Württemberg

Dornier models, and slightly above those incurred by 3 ESWL locations using Siemens models.

- 7 ESWL locations using the Siemens model incur total costs per treatment slightly below those incurred by 3 ESWL locations using the Dornier model.

(e) Due to its fringe location Mannheim, if it is chosen for an ESWL location, will never be allocated more than 293 patients (see fig. 6). Since this means a shortfall of the minimum capacity limit the decision for this location can only be retained if Mannheim and Heidelberg agree to joint treatment services or if patients from the bordering areas of Rhineland-Palatinate are allocated to Mannheim.

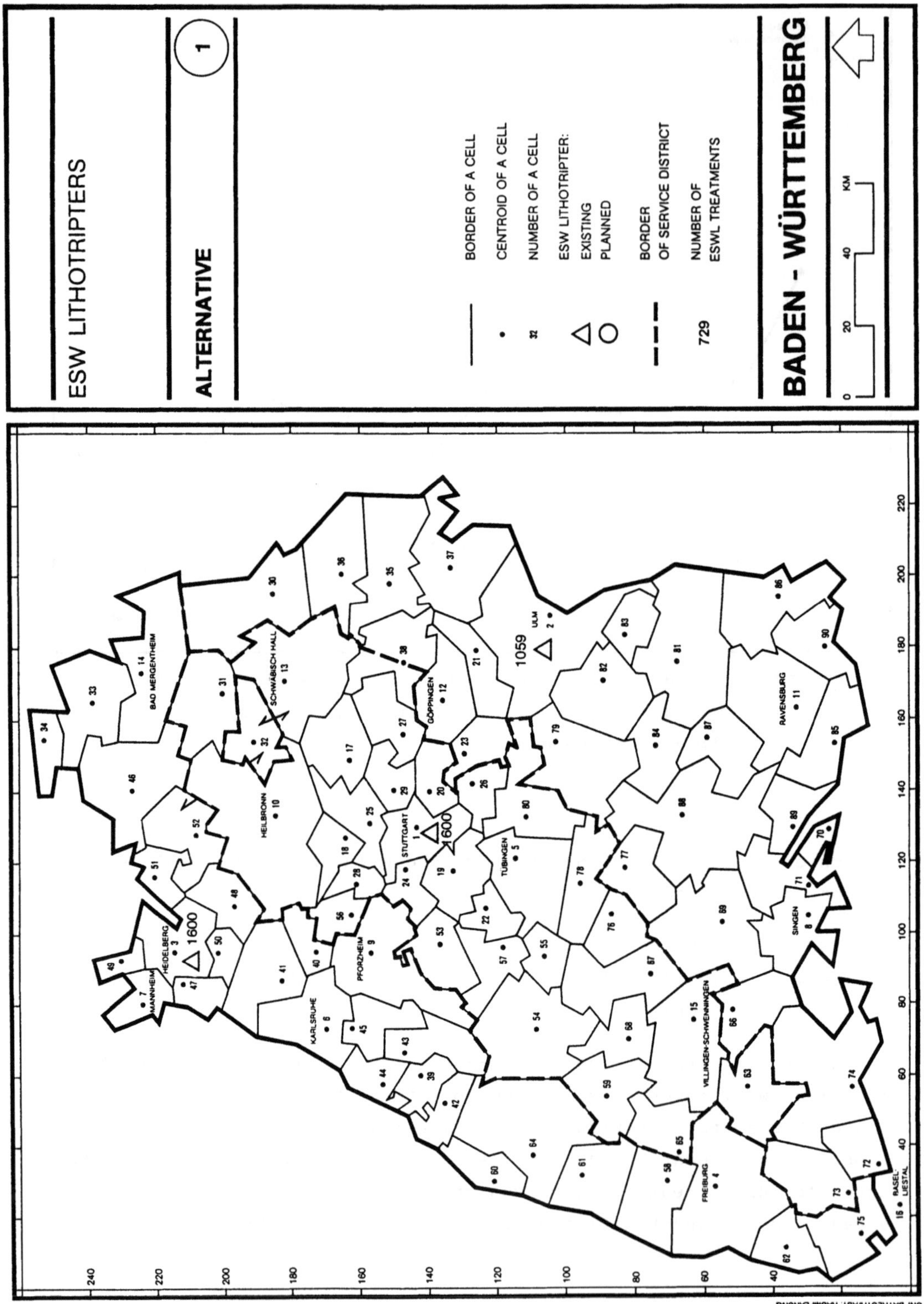

Figure 5: Alternative 1 for an ESWL system with 3 ESWL locations in Baden-Württemberg

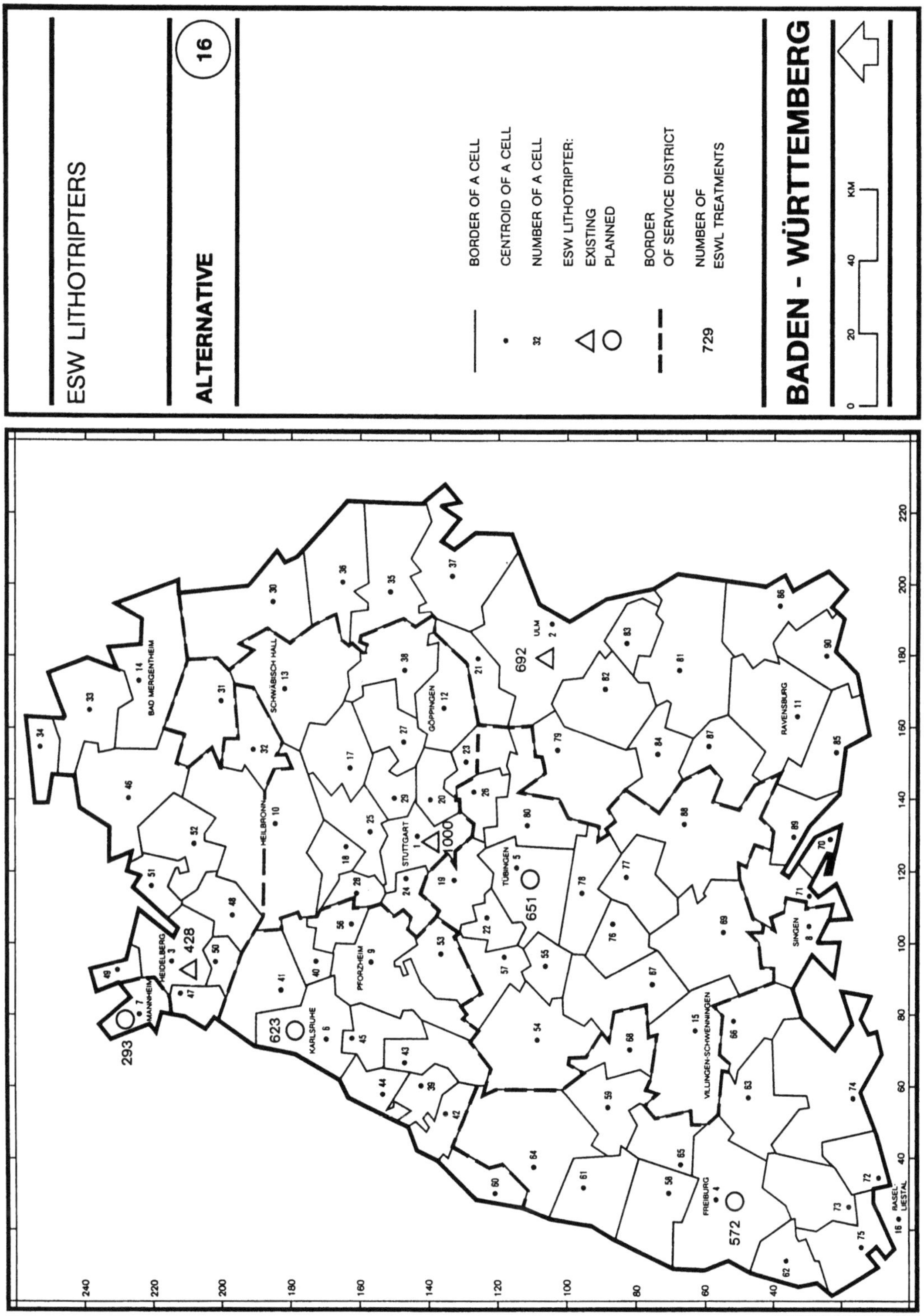

Figure 6: Alternative 16 for an ESWL system with 7 ESWL locations in Baden-Württemberg

(f) The optimal expansion sequence for a statewide ESWL locational system from currently 3 locations (Stuttgart, Ulm, and Heidelberg) to a total of 7 locations is: Freiburg first, Karlsruhe second, Tübingen third, and Mannheim fourth. All other expansion sequences are suboptimal sequences.

(g) A further increase of the number of ESWL locations beyond these seven locations, all of which are hospital locations at the so-called "maximum service level", would mean expansion to selected hospital locations of the "intermediate service level" - as for example in Bad Mergentheim, Ravensburg, Singen, Villingen-Schwenningen, Heilbronn, Göppingen, Pforzheim, or Schwäbisch-Hall. To choose one of these locations is not feasible since services at any of them as well as the Heidelberg and Mannheim locations would fall below the the minimum capacity level.

6 Regional planning for CT scanners

Regional location and capacity planning has been carried out for CT scanners in much the same way as it was done for ESW lithotripters. The planning area here was limited to the northeastern region of the state of Baden-Württemberg, one of the most sparsely populated areas in the state. The average population density in the planning region is 171 inhabitants/square km, and the total population is 2.6 million. In comparison, the average population density for Baden-Württemberg as a whole is 260 inhabitants/square km. Densely populated areas are found along the western and southern border of the planning region, around the cities of Heilbronn (population 278,500), Ludwigsburg (242,100), Stuttgart (703,300), Göppingen (174,400), and Ulm (210,800). In all of these cities CT scanners already are in service, whereas there are none in the core of the region excepting the city of Bad Mergentheim (25,200). In order to secure appropriate CT services in this planning region for the future, additional possible CT locations are in hospitals of Schwäbisch-Hall (40,000), Aalen (73,000), and Heidenheim (53,100). The existing locations and the possible future locations for CT units have been combined for analytical purposes into a base solution 0 plus 7 locational alternatives, all of which are part of the analysis and comparison in terms of their financial, capacitary, and spatial consequences.[22]

Table 4: Breakdown of costs for different suppliers of CT services (in DM as in 1984)

CATEGORIES	SUPPLIER HOSPITAL	SUPPLIER PHYSICIAN'S OFFICE
FIXED COSTS:		
- equipment	358,700	495,000
- operation	204,000	209,000
- personnel	163,000	230,000
- overheads	40,000	20,000
TOTAL	765,700	954,000
FIXED THRESHOLD COSTS:		
- personnel	66,000	46,000
TOTAL	66,000	46,000
VARIABLE COSTS:		
- supplies and materials	42	42
TOTAL	42	42

Note: (a) FIXED COSTS and FIXED THRESHOLD COSTS are costs per CT scanner and per year.
(b) VARIABLE COSTS are costs per CT scan.

6.1 Input variables and parameters

Eight alternative locational systems for CT services are analysed all of which differ in the number of CT units as well as the CT locations (see table 5). For the input parameters the following assumptions are made:

- There are three groups of patients, defined as out-patients, in-patients (transferred), and in-patients (resident). The German health care system defines the group of out-patients as those patients who are treated by physicians working in the so-called "ambulatory" sector, as opposed to those working in the "stationary" hospital sector. An out-patient thus is transferred by a physician for CT diagnosis to a CT location, which can either be a hospital or a radiologist's office. A transferred in-patient is stationed in a hospital without a CT unit and who is transferred for CT diagnosis to a different hospital or radiologist where CT services are available. A resident in-patient is stationed in a hospital offering CT services.

Table 5: Locational alternatives for regional systems of CT scanners, as used in analysis

NO. OF ALTER-NATIVE	CT LOCATIONS	CT SCANNERS	ALTERNATIVE INCLUDES: S	L	H	G	U	BM	AL	SH	HE
0	5	11	3/2	1/-	1/1	1/-	2/-	-/-	-/-	-/-	-/-
1	5 + 2	12	3/2	1/-	1/-	1/-	2/-	1/-	1/-	-/-	-/-
2	5 + 2	12	3/2	1/-	1/-	1/-	2/-	1/-	-/-	1/-	-/-
3	5 + 2	12	3/2	1/-	1/-	1/-	2/-	1/-	-/-	-/-	1/-
4	5 + 3	13	3/2	1/-	1/-	1/-	2/-	1/-	1/-	1/-	-/-
5	5 + 3	13	3/2	1/-	1/-	1/-	2/-	1/-	1/-	-/-	1/-
6	5 + 3	13	3/2	1/-	1/-	1/-	2/-	1/-	-/-	1/-	1/-
7	5 + 4	14	3/2	1/-	1/-	1/-	2/-	1/-	1/-	1/-	1/-

LEGEND:

S = Stuttgart
L = Ludwigsburg
H = Heilbronn
G = Göppingen
U = Ulm
BM = Bad Mergentheim
AL = Aalen
SH = Schwäbisch Hall
HE = Heidenheim

3/2 = 3 CT scanners in hospitals and 2 CT scanners in physicians' offices

- To access a CT scanner patients use one of three transportation modes: private automobile/taxi, ambulance, or critical care vehicle. Each transportation case is calculated on the basis of a flat rate per case plus a rate per km (see tables 6 and 7). Transportation to and from the location are counted separately.

- The demand for CT scans is made dependent on distance, which allows for the use of different indication rates depending on 3 distance ranges (see table 8).

- Each CT location may have more than one unit (see table 5).

- A CT unit can be installed either in a hospital or in a physician's office (see table 5). This generates different costs in the three categories of fixed costs, fixed threshold costs, and variable costs (see table 4).

- Each patient is allocated to the nearest CT location. In those cases where several units are available in a single location, requests for scans at this location are distributed proportionally according to a predetermined "weight" allotted to each CT unit.

- CT unit capacity is not restricted to maximum or minimum limits.

Table 6: Modal split (in %) of patients among three modes of transportation for regional CT systems

GROUP OF PATIENTS	MODE OF TRANSPORTATION		
	CAR/TAXI	AMBULANCE	CRITICAL CARE VEHICLE
Out-Patients	80	20	0
Referred in-patients	50	45	5
Resident in-patients		not relevant	

Table 7: Costs for three modes of transportation for regional CT systems (in DM as in 1984)

TRANSPORTATION COSTS	MODE OF TRANSPORTATION		
	CAR/TAXI	AMBULANCE	CRITICAL CARE VEHICLE
Flat rate	5.00	170.00	340.00
Rate per kilometer	1.10	3.20	6.50

Table 8: Indication rates for regional CT systems, i.e. number of CT scans per year for three groups of patients with respect to three ranges of distances

GROUP OF PATIENTS	GROUP OF REFERENCE	3 RANGES OF DISTANCES IN KILOMETERS		
		0≤10	>10≤20	>20
Out-patients	1000 inhabitants	7.2	6.0	4.2
In-patients (referred)	1000 inhabitants	6.0	6.0	6.0
In-patients (resident)	1000 in-patients of hospitals with CT scanner	45.0	Not relevant	Not relevant

Table 9: Sequence of main steps for calculating utilization and transportation costs for a regional CT system

CALCULATION-SEQUENCE	INFORMATION GAINED
1. Delimitation of service district for each CT scanner	- Service districts - Latent demand for CT scans per district - Maximum distance per district - Average distance per district - Average distance in planning region
2. Calculation of actual demand for CT scans per district	- Demand of out-patients, referred in-patients, and resident in-patients
3. Distribution of demand among modes of transportation	- Transport cases and kilometers by car, ambulance, and critical care verhicle
4. Calculation of total transportation costs	- Transportation costs
5. Calculation of total utilization costs	- Utilization costs
6. Calculation of overall utilization and transportation costs	- Overall utilization and transportation costs - Average costs per CT scan

- More than 3,500 scans per year at one CT unit will result in fixed threshold costs for additional personnel.

6.2 Procedure and application of the mathematical model

Similar to the planning task defined for ESWL systems, regional location and capacity planning for CT systems, in this case in the northeastern area of Baden-Württemberg, requires that all cost-factors of the utilization and transportation costs are included in the calculation, so that in a next step the goal parameters can then be determined (see fig. 7 in connection with table 9).

The following sections outline and illustrate the mathematical model for CT systems, the symbols used in the model, as well as the input variables and their specification.

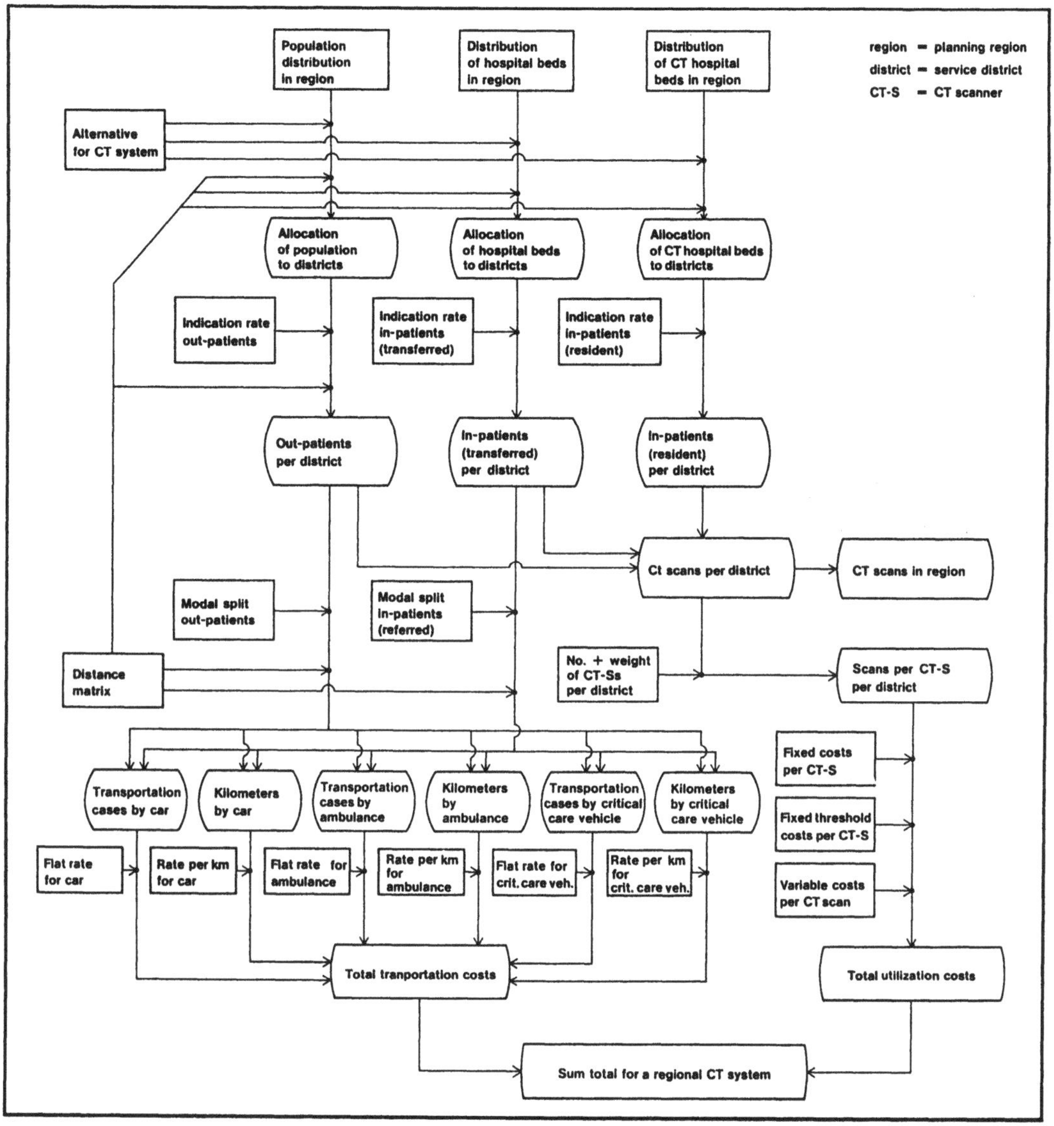

Figure 7: Flow chart for calculating overall utilization and transportation costs for a regional CT system

6.2.1 Mathematical model for regional CT systems

The equation for the overall utilization and transportation costs, i.e. for total costs K per year of a regional CT system is:

$$K = T + U \qquad (8.0)$$

The equation for the transportation costs T in equation (8.0) is:

$$T = T^a + T^s \qquad (9.0)$$

The two terms T^a and T^s are defined as follows. The equation for transportation costs T^a of the group of out-patients is:

$$T^a = \sum_{v=1}^{w} \sum_{j=1}^{n} \sum_{i=1}^{m} X^a{}_{ji} \cdot T^a{}_v \cdot 2 \cdot (TP_v + (TE_v \cdot d_{ji})) \qquad (10.0)$$

where

$$X^a{}_{ji} = E_{i \varepsilon Q j} \cdot I^a (d) \qquad (10.1)$$

$$\begin{aligned} I^a (d) &= I_1 \quad \text{for} \quad 0 < d_{ji} \leq d_1 \\ &= I_2 \quad \text{for} \quad d_1 < d_{ji} \leq d_2 \\ &= I_3 \quad \text{for} \quad d_2 < d_{ji} \end{aligned} \qquad (10.2)$$

The equation for transportation costs T^s of the group of transferred in-patients is:

$$T^s = \sum_{v=1}^{w} \sum_{j=1}^{n} \sum_{i=1}^{m} X^s{}_{ji} \cdot T^s{}_v \cdot 2 \cdot (TP_v + (TE_v \cdot d_{ji})) \qquad (11.0)$$

where

$$X^s{}_{ji} = \sum_{i=1}^{m} E_i \cdot I^s \cdot (B_{i \varepsilon Q j} / \sum_{i=1}^{m} B_i) \qquad (11.1)$$

The equation for the overall utilization costs U in equation (8.0) is:

$$U = F + V + S \qquad (12.0)$$

In equation (12.0), the three terms F, V, and S are defined as follows. The equation for fixed costs F is:

$$F = \sum_{t=1}^{p} \sum_{j=1}^{n} (Z_{tj} \cdot F_t) \qquad (13.0)$$

The equation for variable costs V is:

$$V = \sum_{t=1}^{p} \sum_{j=1}^{n} \sum_{e=1}^{f} (V_t \cdot X_{tje}) \qquad (14.0)$$

where

$$X_{tje} = X_j \cdot ((Z_{tje} \cdot g_{tje}) / (\sum_{t=1}^{p} \sum_{e=1}^{f} Z_{tje} \cdot g_{tje})) \qquad (14.1)$$

$$X_j = \sum_{i=1}^{m} (X^a_{ji} + X^s_{ji}) + X^b_j \qquad (14.2)$$

$$X^b_j = L_j \cdot I^b \qquad (14.3)$$

The equation for fixed threshold costs S is:

$$S = \sum_{t=1}^{p} \sum_{j=1}^{n} \sum_{e=1}^{f} (Z_{tje} \cdot (S_t \cdot y_{tje})) \qquad (15.0)$$

where

$$y_{tje} = 1 \quad \text{if} \quad (X_{tje} / Z_{tje}) > c^*$$

$$\text{for all } e, e=1,...,f$$
$$\text{for all } j, j=1,...,n$$
$$\text{for all } t, t=1,...,p \qquad (15.1)$$

in all other cases:

$$y_{tje} = 0 \qquad (15.2)$$

with X_{tje} defined as in equation (14.1).

In equations (10.1) and (11.1), the service districts Q_j are defined as follows:

$$Q_j = \{ P_i : d_{ji} \leq d_{ki} \text{ for } i=1,...,m \text{ and } k=1,...,n$$
$$\text{with } k = j \}$$
$$\text{for all } j, j=1,...,n \qquad (16.0)$$

6.2.2 List of symbols

K total costs (per year)

T transportation costs (per year)

U utilization costs (per year)

F fixed costs (per year)

V variable costs (per year)

S fixed threshold costs (per year)

a	index for group of out-patients
s	index for group of transferred in-patients
b	index for group of resident in-patients
i	index for demand locations, i=1,...,m
j	index for supply locations, j=1,...,k,...,n
v	index for transportation mode, v=1,...,w v_1 = private automobile, taxi v_2 = ambulance v_3 = critical care vehicle
t	index for type of CT scanner, t=1,...,p t_1 = CT scanner in a physician's office t_2 = CT scanner in a hospital
e	index for CT scanner of one supply location, e=1,...,f
P_i	i-th demand location
E_i	population at P_i
B_i	number of hospital beds at P_i
M_j, M_k	j-th, respectively k-th, supply location
L_j	number of hospital patients per year in those hospitals at M_j that have a CT scanner
Q_j	service district of M_j
X^a_{ji}	number of CT scans for out-patients from P_i at M_j
X^s_{ji}	number of CT scans for transferred in-patients from P_i at M_j
X^b_j	number of CT scans for resident in-patients from M_j at M_j
X_j	number of all CT scans at M_j
X_{tje}	number of all CT scans at M_j performed with the e-th CT scanner of the t-th type
$I^a(d)$	indication rate for out-patients
d_1, d_2	threshold of distance for $I^a(d)$
I^s	indication rate for transferred in-patients
I^b	indication rate for resident in-patients
T^a_v	rate of out-patients using the v-th transportation mode
T^s_v	rate of transferred in-patients using the v-th transportation mode
TP_v	basic fee per transport case for the v-th transportation mode
TE_v	transportation costs per kilometer for the v-th transportation mode
d_{ji}, d_{ki}	distance between P_i and M_j, P_i and M_k respectively

F_t	fixed costs for the t-th type of CT scanner
V_t	variabel costs for the t-th type of CT scanner
S_t	fixed threshold costs for the t-th type of CT scanner
Z_{tje}	number of e-th CT scanner of the t-th type at M_j
g_{tje}	weight factor of e-th CT scanner of the t-th type at M_j
c^*	maximum workload capacity of a CT operating team
y_{tje}	0-1-variable

6.2.3 List and specification of input variables and parameters

For the purpose of analysing eight alternative locational systems for CT scanners the following input variables and parameters were used:

- the locations for CT scanners according to each of the alternative locational systems (see table 5),
- the distances d_{ji} and d_{ki} between demand locations P_j and supply locations M_j or M_k respectively, as measured in kilometers in the road network,
- the number of inhabitants E_i as well as the number of hospital beds B_i at demand location P_i,
- the number of patients L_j in hospitals at supply location M_j owning a CT scanner,
- the number Z_{tje} and the weight factor g_{tje} for each CT scanner at supply location M_j,
- the distance thresholds d_1 and d_2 as well as the indication rates $I^a(d)$, I^s, and I^b (see table 8),
- the rates of modal split $T^a{}_v$ and $T^s{}_v$ as well as the factors of transportation costs TP_v and TE_v (see tables 6 and 7),
- the fixed costs F_t, the variable costs V_t, and the fixed threshold costs S_t (see table 4),
- the maximum workload capacity of a CT operating team c^*=1,600 scans/CT scanner.

6.3 Results

For each of the eight locational alternatives for CT systems the financial, capacitary, and spatial consequences were determined (see figs. 8 and 9 in connection with tables 10 and 11). Based on these individual results the essential conclusions are:

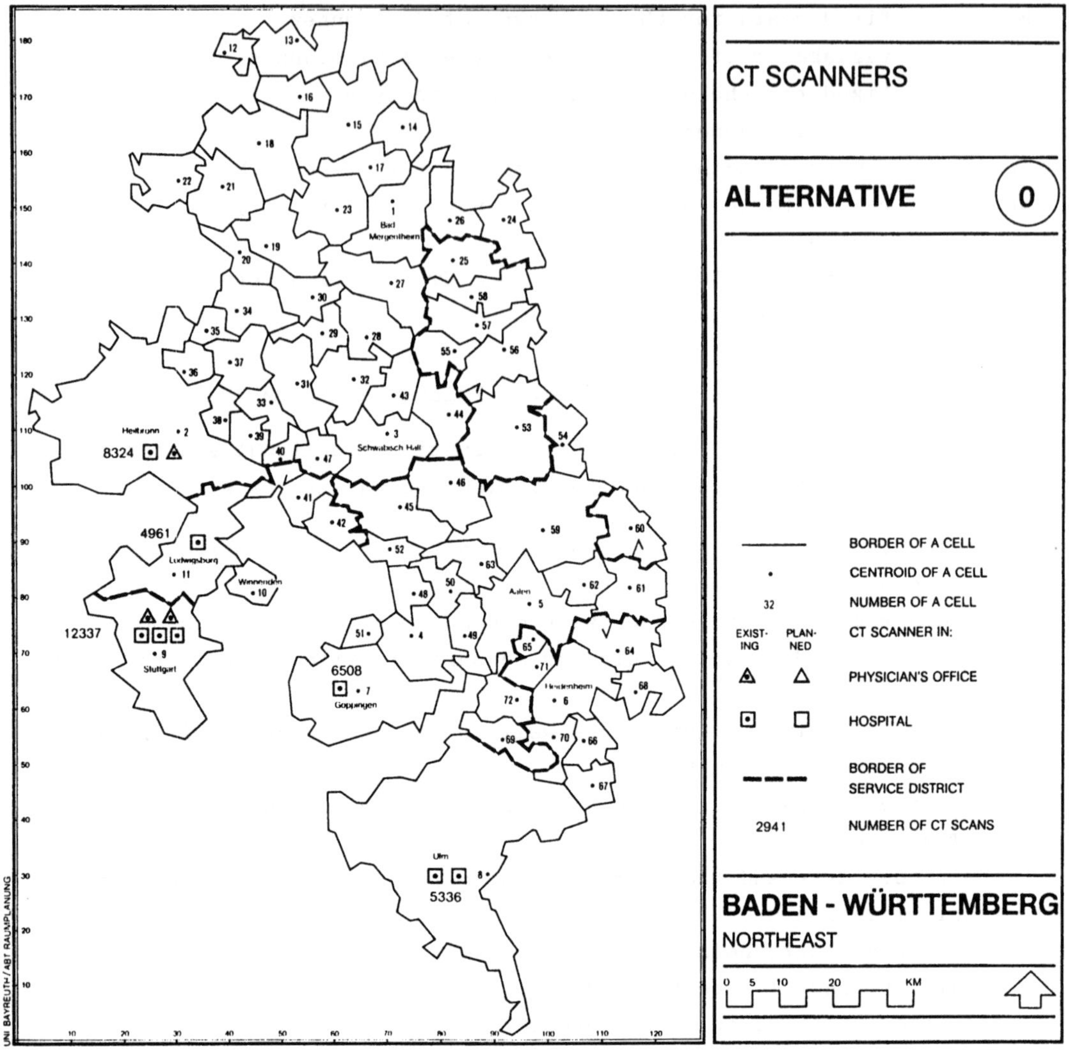

Figure 8: Alternative 0 for a CT system with 6 CT locations and 11 CT scanners in the northeastern region of Baden-Württemberg

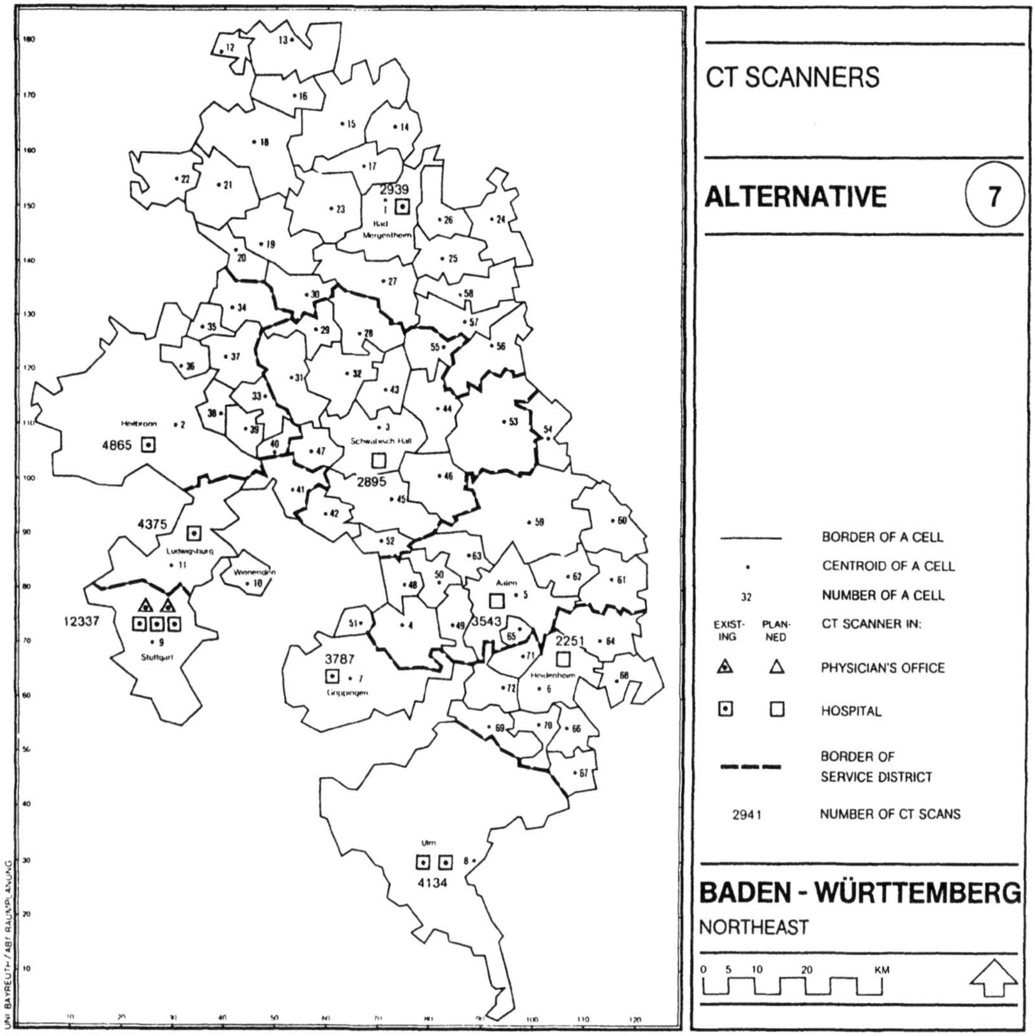

<u>Figure 9:</u> Alternative 7 for a CT system with 9 CT locations and 14 CT scanners in the northeastern region of Baden-Württemberg

Table 10: Results for base solution (alternative 0) and alternatives 1 to 7, with respect to decision criteria for a regional CT system in the northeastern region of Baden-Württemberg (DM as in 1984)

DECISION CRITERIA	ALTERNATIVES							
	0	1	2	3	4	5	6	7
(1)	(2)	(3)	(4)	(5)	(6)	(7)	(8)	(9)
CT scanners	11	12	12	12	13	13	13	14
CT scans	37467	39230	39049	39228	40101	40253	40099	41124
Average indication rate	14.6	15.3	15.2	15.3	15.7	15.7	15.7	16.1
Total costs (in mill. DM)	17.3	17.1	17.5	17.2	17.7	17.9	17.8	18.4
% of these for:								
- utilization	62.1	67.6	65.2	67.3	69.6	69.2	69.4	71.1
- transportation	37.9	32.4	34.8	32.7	30.4	30.8	30.6	28.9
Costs per CT scan (in DM)	461	436	448	437	440	443	444	448
Average distance to nearest CT scanner (in km)	22.6	12.8	14.7	13.6	11.2	12.0	11.6	10.4
Maximum distance to nearest CT scanner (in km)	128.0	66.0	74.0	66.0	66.0	66.0	66.0	66.0

(a) Increasing the number of CT scanners does not necessarily lead to an increase of the total costs incurred by a regional CT system. In comparison, alternatives 1 and 3 each incur lower total costs than alternative 0, despite the fact that both locations use one CT unit more than alternative 0.

(b) For 5 of the 7 alternatives an increase in CT units results in an increase of the total costs incurred by the regional CT system. Total costs increase from a minimum range of DM 0.2 million (alternative 2, using 12 scanners at 7 locations) to a maximum range of DM 1.1 million (alternative 7 using 14 scanners at 9 locations).

(c) All other parameters indicate that their values in alternatives 1 to 7 are better than in alternative 0. This especially counts for a higher indication rate, lower costs for an individual CT scan, and

Table 11: Potential expansion-sequence of CT installations in the northeastern region of Baden-Württemberg, and annual utilization and transportation costs for each alternative regional CT system (DM as in 1984)

CURRENT SITUATION	STEP 1	STEP 2	STEP 3
	Alternative 1: B. Mergentheim Aalen (DM 17.1 mill.)	Alternative 4: B. Mergentheim Aalen Schwäb. Hall (DM 17.7 mill.)	
Alternative 0: (Base solution) (DM 17.3 mill.)	Alternative 2: B. Mergentheim Schwäb. Hall (DM 17.5 mill.)	Alternative 5: B. Mergentheim Aalen Heidenheim (DM 17.9 mill.)	Alternative 7: B. Mergentheim Aalen Heidenheim Schwäb. Hall (DM 18.4 mill.)
	Alternative 3: B. Mergentheim Heidenheim (DM 17.2 mill.)	Alternative 6: B. Mergentheim Schwäb. Hall Heidenheim (DM 17.8 mill.)	

lower average as well as maximum transportation distances to individual CT locations (see table 10).

(d) For a gradual expansion of CT services all alternative locations are combined to form expansion sequences. The optimal sequence then is the one with the optimal value-rates rendered by either one or several parameters. Following this decisionary guideline the optimal expansion sequence for alternatives reads: 0 - 1 - 4 - 7 (see table 11). This sequence stipulates that with each additional CT location optimal rates are effected for each of the following: total costs, costs for each individual CT scan, average transportation distance, and maximum transportation distance. According to this expansion sequence additional CT units should be installed at these locations: Aalen first, Schwäbisch-Hall second, and Heidenheim third.

7 Conclusions

The planning considerations concerning location and capacity planning for ESW lithotripters are based on a decision context prevalent in the state of Baden-Württemberg in early 1987; for CT scanners they are based on a decision context prevalent in 1984. Although they have been occasioned by actual demands they are not limited to time and place. Instead, they are exemplary cases from which the following generalizations about regional location and capacity planning concerning AMT systems can be concluded. The decision to install an AMT unit demands a locational decision which should only be made within the context of a regional locational system. Calculations leading to an individual decision about the efficiency of an individual AMT unit, total treatment costs caused by a regional system of AMT units, medical or spatial service levels in individual regions etc., are effective only from an urban, regional or statewide planning perspective. In this respect, the model of utilization and transportation costs presented here can serve as a structural model which can be applied to other AMT technologies as well. This concerns not only AMT technologies marketed already but also includes new technological developments such as MRI (magnetic resonance imaging) units or extracorporal shock wave lithotripters for gall stone treatment. The explicit designation of input variables and parameters as components for the application of the mathematical model allows for a systematic inclusion of the planning options into the decision-making process. At the same time the model can be used as an instrument to display systematically the consequences of different planning options, corresponding for instance to the demands of various interest groups, and thus to serve as an information base for evaluation processes.

References:

[1] cf. Forßmann et al. 1977, Kehr 1984, Schmiedt/Chaussy 1985, on medical technologies developed for non-operative extracorporal shock wave kidney lithotripsy (ESWL).

[2] cf. Ortskrankenkasse 1985a.

[3] cf. Ortskrankenkasse 1985b.

[4] Diekmann et al. 1986, pp. 425-426, contains a brief description of ESW lithotripters of the so-called second generation. For a more detailed description of the Siemens model cf. Ziegler 1987, of the Wolf model cf. Krauss et al. 1987.

[5] cf. Diekmann et al. 1986, pp. 436-441, for calculations concerning costs for three different ESWL models (Dornier, Siemens, Wolf).

[6] cf. calculations for optimal capacity and location distribution of ESWL units in Baden-Württemberg as prepared by Bach et al. 1987.

[7] The following figures indicate the rapid increase of ESWL installations in the Federal Republic of Germany: 1980: 1, 1983: 4,

1985: 16, 1986: 20 installations; cf. Kehr 1984, Bruckenberger 1985a, Diekmann et al. 1986.

[8] Besides ESW lithotripters and CT scanners, AMT technology also provides the following : machines for diagnosis (e.g. left heart catheter workstations, magnetic resonance imaging (MRI) machines, etc.) and machines for therapy (e.g. cyclotrons, tele-cobalt therapy machines etc.). The problem of AMT definition is addressed in: Hinderer/Siebig 1984, p. 190; Bopp 1986, pp. 24-26; Hoberg 1986a, pp. 2-3, and 1986b, p. 73. AMT catalogues are offered by: Großgeräte-Richtlinien-Ärzte 1986; Sozialministerium 1985. For the most recent update of AMT discussion cf. Sozialministerium 1986.

[9] For medical evaluations of ESWL technology cf.: Aeikens et al. 1985; Chaussy 1984, pp. 62-63; Diekmann et al. 1986, pp. 426-429; Rassweiler et al. 1985, pp. 80-83; Ortskrankenkasse 1986, p.430. For medical evaluations of CT technology cf.: Abshoff 1979; Bekier 1977; Brenner et al. 1986, pp. 278-284.

[10] Economic factors of ESWL utilization are dealt with in: Aeikens 1986; Rassweiler et al. 1985, pp. 81-83; Diekmann et al. 1986, pp. 436-444; Ortskrankenkasse 1986, p. 430. For a cost-benefit-analysis concerning kidney stone lithotripsy by ESWL cf. Schäfer 1982. For economic factors in CT utilization cf.: Brenner et al. 1986, pp. 298-306; Deckner 1980; Fischer 1980; Schicke 1984; Schölmerich 1983, pp. 42-45.

[11] Conditions for ESWL locations are dealt with in: Kehr 1984, p. 299; Diekmann et al. 1986, pp. 432-434 and p. 446; Rassweiler et al. 1985, p. 83. Conditions for CT locations are dealt with in: Brenner et al. 1986, pp. 289-294; Müller 1982.

[12] The rapid expansion of AMT services - as documented by Bruckenberger 1985a, table 2, or Hoberg 1986b, survey 1 - have led to intensive deliberations about planning and coordination procedures for AMT installations, particularly among administrators in the health departments of the individual states, health insurance agencies and doctors' associations. As a result the Federal Republic of Germany today works with operational guidelines regulating investment and planning for AMT installations, both in the in-patient and out-patient sectors. For a survey of the sometimes extremely controversial discussion and the regulations currently

agreed upon cf.: Ärzteblatt 1984; Bopp 1984 and 1986, pp. 28-30; Brenner 1984; Bruckenberger 1983, 1985a, 1985b, and 1985c; Clade 1984; Großgeräte-Richtlinien-Ärzte 1986; Hinderer/Siebig 1984; Hoberg 1986a and 1986b; Kassenärztliche Bundesvereinigung 1984; Lubecki 1986; Ortskrankenkasse 1984; Pohl 1982; Schölmerich 1983. For AMT planning for Baden-Württemberg cf. Sozialministerium 1985, for Rhineland-Palatinate cf. Wabnitz 1985. For critical remarks on the effectiveness of regulating guidelines cf. Münnich 1984, pp. 37-41.

[13] cf. the proposal for a multi-dimensional cost-benefit analysis in Tsubo, 1984. Pohlenz, 1980, presents the concept of a cost-benefit-analysis for AMT services.

[14] cf. Hoberg's (1986a, p. 4, and 1986b, pp. 73-74) argument that health policies supporting cost-reduction need to pursue three objectives in dealing with AMT utilization: objectives of standard, of structure, and of dynamics of utilization.

[15] This reference anticipates results detailed below in sections 5.3 and 6.3.

[16] Wagner, 1984, pp. 378, poses the same type of question within the context of macro-economic evaluation for AMT installations.

[17] The level of medical services is counted as a goal parameter only when AMT utilization is dependent on the distance patients are forced to travel to an AMT location. Only in such a case an actual indication rate is distance-dependent, i.e. dependent on the locations of AMT units.

[18] Criteria for measurement can be the regional average traveling distance for all patients as well as the maximum traveling distance within the region.

[19] cf. Bach 1978, pp. 122-124.

[20] For details cf. Bach et al. 1987.

[21] Based on a trustee agreement with the West German Federations of Statutory Health Insurance Organizations (Bundesverbände der gesetzlichen Krankenversicherung) the Management Board for Home Dialysis (Kuratorium für Heimdialyse - KfH) was commissioned in 1982 to install 21 ESWL units in hospitals in return of a flat-

rate special payment for each ESWL treatment. For details cf. Ortskrankenkasse 1986.

[22] For details of this planning project cf. Bach/Hoberg 1984; also Bach/Hoberg 1985a and 1985b.

Literature:

Abshoff, J.: Die Versorgung mit Computer-Tomographen im stationären Bereich am Beispiel Nordrhein-Westfalen, in: Das Krankenhaus 71, 1979, pp.369-375.

Aeikens, B.: Aspekte der Kosten-Nutzen-Analyse des Nierenlithotripters an der Medizinischen Hochschule Hannover, in: Krankenhaus-Umschau 55, 1986, pp. 171-173.

Aeikens, B., Fritz, K., Drimalla, H., and Kolle, P.: Behandlungskonzept der Nierenlithotripsie an der MHH, in: Niedersächsisches Ärzteblatt 58, 1985, pp. 32-34.

Anon.: Großgeräte für die Kassenpraxis - Empfehlung der Kassenärztlichen Bundesvereinigung zum Einsatz und zur Standortbestimmung medizinisch-technischer Großgeräte in der ambulanten kassenärztlichen Versorgung, in: Deutsches Ärzteblatt, series B, 81, 1984, p. 192. (cited as: Ärzteblatt 1984).

Anon.: Medizinisch-technische Großgeräte - Gesetzentwurf durch Bundesrat eingebracht, in: Die Ortskrankenkasse 66, 1984, pp. 384-385. (cited as: Ortskrankenkasse 1984).

Anon.: Bayern - Dritter Nierensteinzertrümmerer im Betrieb, in: Die Ortskrankenkasse 67, 1985, p. 383. (cited as: Ortskrankenkasse 1985a).

Anon.: Medizinisch-technische Großgeräte - Wirtschaftlicher Einsatz - Regelungen der Selbstverwaltung für die ambulante Versorgung, in: Die Ortskrankenkasse 67, 1985, pp. 506-507. (cited as: Ortskrankenkasse 1985b).

Anon.: Richtlinien des Bundesausschusses der Ärzte und Krankenkassen für den bedarfsgerechten und wirtschaftlichen Einsatz von medizinisch-technischen Großgeräten (Großgeräte-Richtlinien-Ärzte), in: Die Ortskrankenkasse 68, 1986, pp. 239-241. (cited as: Großgeräte-Richtlinien-Ärzte 1986).

Anon.: Erfolg der Nierenlithotripter - Bisher 30000 Nierensteinzertrümmerungen in der Bundesrepublik, in: Die Ortskrankenkasse 68, 1986, pp. 430-431. (cited as: Ortskrankenkasse 1986).

Bach, L.: Methoden zur Bestimmung von Standorten und Einzugsbereichen zentraler Einrichtungen, Interdisciplinary Systems Research Vol. 55 , Basel/Stuttgart 1978.

Bach, L., Ehm, H., and Friedl, W.: Modellrechnungen zur Optimierung der Kapazität und Standortverteilung von ESWL-Geräten in Baden-Württemberg, Bayreuth 1987. (Publication in preparation).

Bach, L., and Hoberg, R.: Regionale Standortplanung für medizinische Großgeräte am Beispiel von Computertomographie-Geräten im Nordosten Baden-Württembergs, Forschungsmaterialien No. 10 , Bayreuth 1984.

Bach, L., and Hoberg, R.: A Planning Model for Regional Systems of CT Scanners, in: Socio-Economic Planning Sciences 19, 1985a, pp. 189-199.

Bach, L., and Hoberg, R.: Planungsmodell für regionale Systeme medizinischer Großgeräte, in: Raumforschung und Raumordnung 43, 1985b, pp. 233-247.

Baden-Württemberg, Land, Ministerium für Arbeit, Gesundheit, Familie und Sozialordnung: Grundsätze für die Abstimmung der Anschaffung, Nutzung oder Mitbenutzung medizinisch-technischer Großgeräte gemäß §10 KHG und für das Verfahren nach §368n Abs.8 RVO, in: Staatsanzeiger für Baden-Württemberg vom 6. März 1985, pp. 5f. (cited as: Sozialministerium 1985).

Baden-Württemberg, Land, Ministerium für Arbeit, Gesundheit, Familie und Sozialordnung (ed.): Symposium Medizinisch-technische Großgeräte - Indikationen, Substitutionen, Leistungen, Kapazitäten, Standorte, Wirtschaftlichkeit, Report of a Symposium on June 23-24, 1986 in Stuttgart, prepared by F. Diekmann and R. Riefenstahl , Stuttgart 1986. (cited as: Sozialministerium 1986).

Bekier, A.: Die Computertomographie - einmal anders betrachtet, in: Therapiewoche 27, 1977, pp. 8825-8828.

Bopp, U.: Gesetzesinitiative zum wirtschaftlichen Einsatz medizinisch-technischer Großgeräte, in: Management und Krankenhaus, No.9, 1984, pp. 181-187.

Bopp, U.: Methoden, Verfahren und Verbindlichkeit der Großgeräteplanung, in: Ministerium für Arbeit, Gesundheit, Familie und Sozialordnung des Landes Baden-Württemberg (ed.): Symposium Medizinisch-technische Großgeräte, Report of a Symposium on June 23-24, 1986 in Stuttgart, prepared by F. Diekmann and R. Riefenstahl , Stuttgart 1986, pp.19-32.

Brenner, G.: Großgeräte - Planungsbürokratie völlig überflüssig, in: Deutsches Ärzteblatt, series C, 81, 1984, pp. 765-766.

Brenner, G., Diekmann, F., Hacker, H., et al.: Computer-Tomographen, in: Ministerium für Arbeit, Gesundheit, Familie und Sozialordnung (ed.): Symposium Medizinisch-technische Großgeräte, Report of a Symposium on June 23-24, 1986 in Stuttgart, prepared by F. Diekmann and R. Riefenstahl , Stuttgart 1986, pp. 271-330.

Bruckenberger, E.: Zur Problematik der abgestimmten Nutzung medizinisch-technischer Großgeräte, in: Vogel, H.R. (ed.): Bedarf und Bedarfsplanung im Gesundheitswesen, Stuttgart 1983, pp. 49-57.

Bruckenberger, E.: Aktive Kooperation zur Steuerung medizinisch-technischer Großgeräte, in: Krankenhaus-Umschau 54, 1985a, pp. 431-435.

Bruckenberger, E.: "Diagnostischer Overkill" - und das niedersächsische Kooperationsmodell, in: Deutsches Ärzteblatt, series B, 82, 1985b, pp. 2175-2178.

Bruckenberger, E.: Medizinisch-technische Großgeräte - Aktive Kooperation zur Steuerung, in: Die Ortskrankenkasse 67, 1985c, pp. 751-755.

Chaussy, Ch.: Wie wirtschaftlich sind Nierentransplantationen und extrakorporale Stoßwellenlithotripsie von Nierensteinen?, in: Arzt und Krankenhaus 57, 1984, pp. 60-63.

Clade, H.: Damit die "Gerätemedizin" nicht aus dem Ruder läuft, in: Deutsches Ärzteblatt, series B, 81, 1984, pp. 190-194.

Deckner, R.: Wirtschaftlichkeit der Computertomographie, in: Röntgenpraxis 33, 1980, pp. 209-234.

Diekmann, F., Eisenberger, F., Riefenstahl, R., et al.: Nierenlithotripter, in: Ministerium für Arbeit, Gesundheit, Familie und Sozialordnung des Landes Baden-Württemberg (ed.): Symposium Medizinisch-technische Großgeräte, Report of a Symposium on June 23-24,

1986 in Stuttgart, prepared by F. Diekmann and R. Riefenstahl , Stuttgart 1986, pp. 419-454.

Fischer, N.: Grundsätze für die Beschaffung und den Einsatz von Computer-Tomographen, in: Die Ersatzkasse 60, 1980, pp. 310-312.

Forßmann, B., Hepp, W., Chaussy, Ch., et al.: Eine Methode zur berührungsfreien Zertrümmerung von Nierensteinen durch Stoßwellen, in: Biomedizinische Technik 22, 1977, pp. 164-168.

Greenwald, H.P., Woodward, J.M., and Berg, D.H.: Transportation or CT Scanners - A Theory and Method of Health Resources Allocation, in: Health Services Research 14, 1979, pp. 207-219.

Hinderer, E.,and Siebig, J.: Staatliche Bedarfsplanung medizinischer Großgeräte, in: Das Krankenhaus 76, 1984, pp. 189-193.

Hoberg, R.: Standortentscheidung für medizinisch-technische Großgeräte, in: Zeitschrift für öffentliche und gemeinwirtschaftliche Unternehmen 9, 1986a, pp. 1-13.

Hoberg, R.: Standortplanung für medizinisch-technische Großgeräte, in: Medizin - Mensch - Gesellschaft 11, 1986b, pp. 72-81.

Kassenärztliche Bundesvereinigung: Großgeräte für die Kassenpraxis - Empfehlungen der Kassenärztlichen Bundesvereinigung zum Einsatz und zur Standortbestimmung medizinisch-technischer Großgeräte in der ambulanten kassenärztlichen Versorgung, in: Deutsches Ärzteblatt, series B, 81, 1984, p. 192.

Kehr, H.: Nierensteinentfernung ohne Operation - Sachstand der extrakorporalen Stoßwellenlithotripsie, in: Die Ortskrankenkasse 66, 1984, pp. 299-300.

Krauss, W., Vallon, P., and Wurster, H.: Der Piezolith - eine piezoelektrische Geräteeinheit zur extrakorporalen Zertrümmerung von Nierensteinen, in: Ziegler, M. (ed.): Die extrakorporale und laserinduzierte Stoßwellenlithotripsie bei Harn- und Gallensteinen - Grundlagen - Anwendung - Klinik, Berlin/Heidelberg/New York/London/Paris/Tokyo 1987, pp. 28-32.

Lubecki, P.: Wirtschaftlichkeit medizinisch-technischer Großgeräte - Richtlinien und Vergütungsregelungen für die kassenärztliche Versorgung, in: Die Ortskrankenkasse 68, 1986, pp. 218 .

Müller, H.W.: Voraussetzungen für die Beschaffung und den Betrieb von CT-Geräten, in: Arzt und Krankenhaus, No.9, 1982, p. 325.

Münnich, F.E.: Kosten- und Allokationswirkungen des technischen Fortschritts im Gesundheitswesen, in: Münnich, F.E., and Oettle, K. (eds.): Ökonomie des technischen Fortschritts in der Medizin, Beiträge zur Gesundheitsökonomie Vol.6 , Gerlingen 1984, pp. 13-45.

Pohl, D.: Planungspoker um medizinische Großgeräte, in: Der Deutsche Arzt 32, 1982, pp. 4-8.

Pohlenz, O.: Gedanken zur Computertomographie, in: Arzt und Krankenhaus 5, 1980, pp. 34-35.

Rassweiler, J., Miller, K., Fuchs, G., et al.: Kosten und Nutzen der berührungsfreien Nierensteinlithotripsie, in: Lebensversicherungsmedizin 35, 1985, pp. 80-84.

Schäfer, Th.: Nutzen-Kosten-Untersuchung zur berührungsfreien Nierensteinzerkleinerung, Dornier Studienergebnis No. 281 , Friedrichshafen 1982.

Schicke, R.K.: Computer-Tomographie - zur Effektivität technologischer Innovation, in: Münnich, F.E., and Oettle, K. (eds.): Ökonomie des technischen Fortschritts in der Medizin, Beiträge zur Gesundheitsökonomie Vol.6 , Gerlingen 1984, pp. 107-135.

Schmiedt, E., and Chaussy, Ch.: Die extrakorporale Stoßwellenlithotripsie von Nieren- und Harnleitersteinen, in: Deutsches Ärzteblatt, series B, 82, 1985, pp. 247-251.

Schölmerich, P.: Der Bedarf an Großgeräten in der Klinik aus ärztlicher Sicht, in: Vogel, H.R. (ed.): Bedarf und Bedarfsplanung im Gesundheitswesen, Stuttgart 1983, pp. 39-48.

Tsubo, R.-J.: Cost Benefit and Interest Group Analysis, in: van Eimeren, W., Engelbrecht, R., and Flagle, Ch.D. (eds.): System Science in Health Care, Berlin/Heidelberg/New York/Tokyo 1984, pp. 705-709.

Wabnitz, R.-J.: Medizinisch-technische Großgeräteplanung in Rheinland-Pfalz, in: Krankenhaus-Umschau 54, 1985, pp. 842-844.

Wagner, J.L.: Makroökonomische Evaluation der Computertomographie, in: Culyer, A.J., and Horisberger, B. (eds.): Technologie im Gesundheitswesen - Medizinische und wirtschaftliche Aspekte, Berlin/Heidelberg/New York/Tokyo 1984, pp. 376-391.

Ziegler, K.: Der Lithostar - ein elektromagnetisches System zur extrakorporalen Zertrümmerung von Nierensteinen, in: Ziegler, M. (ed.): Die extrakorporale und laserinduzierte Stoßwellenlithotripsie bei Harn- und Gallensteinen - Grundlagen - Anwendung - Klinik, Berlin/Heidelberg/New York/London/Paris/Tokyo 1987, pp. 20-23.

Planning and Organization of Economic Units in the Field of Out-Patient Medical Care

Günter Fandel and Antonius Prasiswa

1 Introductory remarks

The idea of applying economic concepts to decisions in the field of health in order to use resources efficiently is not new. Initially it was macroeconomic aspects, for example the advantage of investment in the health service per se (Billerbeck 1968), that were at the forefront of these considerations. More recently in the German speaking area - stimulated by Anglo-Saxon publications - questions relating to the area of hospital economics in a wider sense have increasingly taken up a central position in these reflections. Up to now interest has been shown in a very varied range of both general and specific problems. With regard to the system of in-patient hospital treatment a number of authors within the framework of hospital management have considered questions in general terms about the objectives and aim strategies of hospitals (Adam 1972, Axtner 1978) as well as questions about the structure and analysis of the hospital care service (Herder-Dorneich/Kötz 1972). The first attempt specifically orientated towards interpreting an hospital as a production unit and to laying down definite types of production functions with specification of both input and output goes back to Feldstein (1967). At approximately the same time other authors endeavoured to determine the best minimum number of beds for hospitals (Smith/Solomon 1966, Egle 1970, Kolesar 1970) whereby it was mostly assumed that hospitals can be seen as treatment and waiting systems for urgent and less urgent cases. With the help of the simulation or queueing theory the best admission policies, with regard to a socially acceptable refusal quota and waiting times for the different types of patients, were correspondingly deduced. Some perspectives of the question, which automatically leads on from there, as to the significance of operational research for hospital planning have been shown in a general article by Meyer and Rohde (1971). Subsequently a large number of publications concerning this area appeared, the most important results of which are to be found in the Proceedings in Operations Research 1976 - 1978 under the headwords health service or application in public administration. More recent attempts to solve medically orientated economic problems in hospital practice, with the help of methods of system research, are collated in the Meyer volume (1979).

In contrast to the works on the in-patient sector of the health service, which have been briefly mentioned above, the economic problems in the area of out-patient care, apart from isolated expositions on the analysis of the location of doctors' practices (Heinhold 1974) and on the advantages of group practices (Pfeffer-Küppers/Esch 1977) have been largely neglected. It is precisely aspects such as the optimal size and organization of a doctor's practice which, when a rational calculation of the professional risk a doctor takes when he decides to set up on his own is required, will gain increasingly in significance. For on the one hand the personnel expenses, excluding the owner of the practice, which in 1975 accounted for 45% of the total expenses of a doctor's practice, rise continually. On the other hand the cost fraction of the operating funds of about 31% can, on account of the progressively apparatus intensive patient care, hardly be reduced, in fact it is more likely to increase further. Thirdly this cost pressure will possibly also be intensified on the profits side because an increase in the number of doctors in private practice in the different specialist areas is to be reckoned with within the next few years. Against this factual background the managerial leadership of a doctor's practice - analogous to other service businesses - with its obligation to perform efficiently, besides the special responsibility held by the doctor, will in the future have to be accepted as an equally central task in out-patient care. In this context a decision to set up an autonomous business of a professional nature in the field of medical service goes hand in hand with the question as to how this service process, apart from specialisation, should be organized, whereby basically two forms of organization are open to the doctor: a one-doctor practice or a group practice with other doctors. This problem of the optimal size of the business and the form of organization as well as the equipping of a doctor's practice, in correspondence with the number of patients to be cared for, forms the object of the following exposition. The principle of profit maximization will serve as the basis of the methodological examination to be adopted. Thus it is at the same time possible to determine both the production procedure involved in the service process and the overall input-structure of a docter's practice in the best possible way. Apart from that the analysis facilitates the revelation of the possible economies of scale expected for group practices and of their extent. The methodological reflections will then be concretized using the example of a specialist practice for ophthalmology.

2 Formulation of a general model for doctor's practice

2.1 Premises and notation

In order to achieve a fairly adequate formulation of a general model for a doctor's practice, despite the multitude of exceptional features of out-patient care, which are mainly connected with the supply and demand side of medical services and the medical renumeration system (Prasiswa 1979), the remainder will be based on the following simplified assumptions:

1) The output of a doctor's practice corresponds to the quantity of the various services, which during a particular period of time are medically necessary for the treatment of patients which fall under the care of the practice. The demand for such services should, therefore, correspond with the production of the doctor's practice. In addition it will be assumed that the question as to the location of the doctor's practice has already been resolved. In the methodological treatment of this sub-problem, for which decision-orientated solution methods are largely lacking, it is possible, by way of a substitute, to apply the process of product positioning (e.g. Brockhoff/Rehder 1978), usually associated with economic marketing planning. As far as the practical localisation of the practice is concerned the requirement plans of the 'Kassenärztliche Vereinigungen' (panel doctor associations) for out-patient care provide a basis upon which a decision can be made. It is also assumed that, on account of the distribution of doctors in the catchment area along with the morbidity and demand structure, the demand for the individual services is assured by the number of patients to be treated. Whilst morbidity expresses the probability of becoming ill and needing a doctor within a particular period of time, the demand structure should be understood as the quantitative combination of the individual services required on average for each case of illness. The latter are dependent on technical progress and on changes in the illness structure. With regard to the scale of the

services required it is unproblematic to assume that the amount is not necessarily constant but rather continously changeable.

2) Within the framework of indirect payment of service, which dominates in the health service, the fees for the accountable services are laid down in the scale of charges. In these scales of charge the various services in a specialist area are described in detail and, in order to simplify payment, they are coded and evaluated in terms of points. The evaluation of the points in terms of money and the scales of charge are negotiated between the 'Kassenärztliche Vereinigungen' (panel doctor associations) and the holders of the 'Krankenkassen' (sick benefit funds).

3) On the input side of a doctor's practice the personnel, the capital goods, the tangible assets and the organi zation and disposition are to be regarded as production factors. The personnel consists of the medical personnel (owner of the practice, assistent doctors and a deputy doctor) and the non-medical personnel (medical technical assistant, nurse, doctor's receptionist), who support the doctors in their work. The capital goods of a practice are the practice rooms and their equipment, whereby in the case of a group practice the number of consulting rooms must at least correspond to the number of doctors who are working together. The tangible assets are essentially the materials required for the practice and the laboratory. On the whole these are, however, of relatively little individual value. As the input factor organization is not generally represented by one particular worker in a doctor's practice direct personnel costs are unlikely to arise, although material goods are necessary. The factor prices can be established from the tarif agreements, from price lists for medical instruments and for equipments and with the help of the usual rents for the area. It will be presupposed that the input types can only be acquired in integer quantities.

4) In the description and analysis of the production procedure in an out-patient doctor's practice a linear-limitational technology will be assumed. This can certainly be justified on a medium and/or long term basis in accordance with the law of large numbers of the services to be carried out, whereby the individual production coefficients are to be regarded as average values. As a number of services can, in view of the possible combinations of production factors, be carried out by various procedures the problem of choice of procedure has often to be solved at the same time as the optimal size of a doctor's practice

is being determined.

5) In order to facilitate an evenly balanced use of capacity and/or to avoid capacity bottlenecks, in which the patients' demand for medical attention can temporarily not be satisfied, it will furthermore be required that the practice is organized as an appointment practice.

6) The economic product of a doctor's practice can be regarded, at will, as either the income of the owner of the practice or the profit of a practice. The discrepancy between profit and income is attributable to the calculable costs - employer's wage, rent, depreciations, and interest. In this context the calculable employer's wage is accounted a particular significance because it has to be estimated according to the principle of opportunity costs for the work carried out by the doctor, as an entrepreneur, and possibly by members of his family. These calculable expenses must, therefore, be added to the total value of goods used in order to ascertain the profit of a doctor's practice. The criterion of profit maximization is thus quite acceptable for a doctor's practice in so far as it corresponds with the usual postulate of efficiency, given the demand and appropriate renumeration, to produce the medically necessary services with a minimum of costs. Whereas in a one-doctor practice the practice's profit matches that of the doctor this is notthe case in a group practice. If, therefore, in order to better compare the advantages of alternative forms of organization for a doctor's practice, the profit per doctor is to be included as a criterion, it is necessary to undertake an appropriate mathematical modification of the optimization approach for a group practice.

7) The model of the doctor's practice will be statically formulated, whereby the period of examination should be identical with that of the usual accounting period of a practice, namely a quarter.

On the basis of these assumptions let:

$x = (x_1,\ldots,x_n)'$ the vector of the amounts produced from the various types of output;

$\hat{x} = (x_1^1,\ldots,x_1^{v_1},\ldots,x_n^1,\ldots,x_n^{v_n})'$ the vector of the production quantities $x_j^{s_j}$, which are produced from the output j, $j=1,\ldots,n$, with the help of the production process s_j, $s_j=1,\ldots,v_j$;

$E = (e_{jw})$, $j=1,\dots,n$, $w=1,\dots,\sum_{j=1}^{n} v_j$, the matrix of the row vectors e_j, which at the points $\sum_{j'=0}^{j-1} v_{j'}+1$ to $\sum_{j'=0}^{j} v_{j'}$, $v_0=0$, posses ones and otherwise only exhibit zeros; with this matrix E the notation $x=E\hat{x}$ applies;

$y = (y_1,\dots,y_n)'$ the vector of the demand structure, the components of which show the services to be rendered on average per patient;

p the number of patients to be cared for by the practice;

$\bar{y} = (\bar{y}_1,\dots,\bar{y}_n)' = p\cdot y'$ the vector of the average demand quantities with p patients;

$h = (h_1,\dots,h_n)'$ the price vector of the outputs in demand;

$c = (c_1^1,\dots,c_1^{v_1},\dots,c_n^1,\dots,c_n^{v_n})'$ the vector of the variable unit costs of the production quantities produced;

$r = (r_1,\dots,r_m)'$ the vector of the integer order quantities of the various types of input i, $i=1,\dots,m$, with r_1 as the number of doctors working in the practice;

$\hat{r} = (\hat{r}_1,\dots,\hat{r}_m)'$ the vector of the input amounts which are employed in the production of the output x;

$k = (k_1,\dots,k_m)'$ the vector of the rates of cost which are not dependent on use for the various types of input;

$A = (a_{ij}^{s_j})$, $i=1,\dots,m$, $j=1,\dots,n$, $s_j=1,\dots,v_j$, the matrix of the production coefficients;

$F = h'\cdot\bar{y} = h'\cdot p\cdot y$ the proceeds of the doctor's practice for the care of p patients;

$\bar{F} = F/p$ the case value, which indicates the average profit referring to one patient;

$K^V = c'\cdot\hat{x}$ the variable production costs;

$K = k'\cdot r$ the costs irrespective of use or fixed costs;

$G = F-K-K^V$ the profit of the doctor's practice;

$\bar{G} = G/r_1$ the profit per doctor;

$\bar{p} = p/r_1$ the number of patients per doctor.

The profit function of a doctor's practice, which has p patients to treat per quarter, reads therefore as follows:

(1) $G=h'\cdot p\cdot y-k'r-c'\hat{x}=h'\cdot\bar{y}-k'r-c'E^{-1}x$,

whereby in the following the condition which has already been mentioned above, namely that the output should always correspond with demand, should still be fulfilled i.e. always

(2) $x-\bar{y}=0$

holds.

2.2 Structural model and optimal equipment of a doctor's practice

Before the output orientated problem, which has been selected as the investigatory aim to be pursued here, concerning the determining of the optimal organization form and equipment of a doctor's practice is formulated in terms of the two variants of profit maximization, the structural model of a doctor's practice based on the notation should first be briefly outlined with the aid of diagram 1. In the upper part of diagram 1 it can be seen how the supply quantities x_j are produced upon utilization of the available input quantities and the various production processes. The bottom part shows how the demand quantities stem from the demand structure and the number of patients. As it has been presupposed that care is to be guaranteed, the supply of medical services must correspond with the demand.

As already noted, two variants come into question as criterion for the decision problem: the maximization of the practice's profit (variant 1) or, by way of a comparison, the maximization of the profit per doctor in a group practice (variant 2). In the first variant the question, as to how the practice should be equipped in order to care for p patients and with which production processes the individual supply amounts can be produced in order to achieve maximum profit, can now be clothed

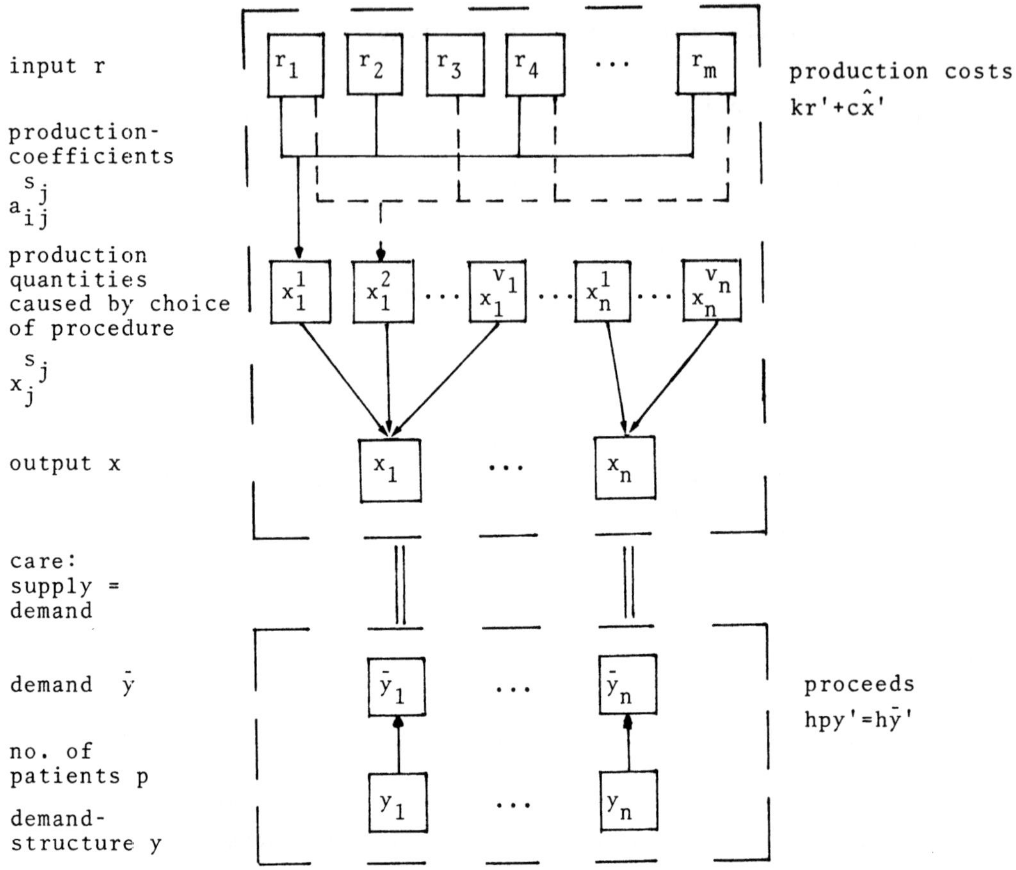

Diagram 1: Structural model of a doctor's practice

in the following mixed-integer linear programming formulation:

$$\max G = h'\cdot p\cdot y - k'r - c'x$$

subject to:

$$r - A\hat{x} = r - \hat{r} \geq 0,$$

$$E\hat{x} - py = x - \bar{y} = 0,$$

(3) $$\hat{x} \geq 0$$

$$r \geq 0 \text{ and integer,}$$

whereby the production programme $\hat{x}$ dependent on the choice of procedure and the supply quantities r represent the variables of the decision problem.

In the case of a group practice a disadvantage of this optimization approach might be seen in the fact that the profit per doctor $\bar{G}=G/r_1$ can, on the one hand, only be determined a posteriori; and, on the other hand, that it is not necessarily the optimal one. It is, however, precisely these amounts that should be of relevance for a doctor deciding to participate in the establishment of a group practice. The discrepancy between the optimal solutions, with regard to the profit of the practice and the profit per doctor, results from the substitution possibilities, within certain limits, of the input i.e. certain activities in the practice can be carried out by the medical personnel instead of by the doctors and vice versa. Under conditions which are otherwise the same the second optimization variant, in which the profit per doctor should be maximized, results in the fractional programme:

$$\max \bar{G} = \frac{1}{r_1} \; (h' \cdot p \cdot y - k' r - c' \hat{x})$$

subject to:

$$r - A\hat{x} = r - \hat{r} \geq 0,$$

$$E\hat{x} - py = x - \bar{y} = 0, \tag{4}$$

$$\hat{x} \geq 0,$$

$$r \geq 0 \text{ and integer.}$$

As such a fractional programme of the type (4) is difficult to deal with in certain circumstances the following two-step procedure is recommended for the solving of the thus modified decision problem. Firstly with the predetermination of the variable r_1, i.e. with the number of doctors working in the practice, the form of the practice is preset and at the same time the number of patients to be cared for is discretely varied. In a subsequent direct comparison of the feasible solutions the optimal decision alternatives for certain numbers of patients can then be established. This solution technique, which has been selected for reasons of simplification, is, with regard to the optimization rule which is to be observed for programme (4), acceptable in so far as, with a given number of doctors, the objective function and the constraints in problem (4) are linear and continuous. With the solution of the problems (3) and (4) one obtains the optimal equipment of a doctor's practice with regard to the various maximization variants resulting from the solution values for the input quantities.

3 An example of application in a specialist practice for ophthalmology

3.1 Collection and evaluation of the data

The data necessary for the application of the preceding methodical reflections to the example of a specialist practice for ophthalmology has been gathered from various sources (Prasiswa 1979):

- By means of an inquiry of 100 practizing ophthalmologists, undertaken with the help of a standard questionaire, general data about the practice (number of working days per year, number of consulting hours per week), were collected along with data about the equipment of the practice (personnel, rooms, apparatus) and about the service process (production technology) as well as about the variable unit costs which differ according to the production procedure.

- The purchase prices of the instruments required for a practice and the average commercial rent for practice rooms in a fairly good position in a large town were obtained from equipment manufacturers and from real-estate agents.

- The basis upon which the personnel costs are to be calculated was supplied by the 'Bundesangestelltentarif' (BAT) and the 'Gehalts- und Manteltarifvertrag' for medical assistants.

- Information about the fees for the various types of service which have been considered here, based on the evaluation procedure for medical services (BMÄ), was ascertained from a statutory sick benefit fund.

- On the basis of the information gathered from the sick benefit funds' reports about the demand structure, differentiated according to BMÄ numbers, it seemed sensible to concentrate on the eight kinds of service which altogether constituted 80% of the case value F of the specialist group for ophthalmology; the remaining types of service have been combined in a basket of available products called "other services".

- Finally plausibility assumptions have been introduced in order to determine, for example, the expected life and depreciation rate of the equipment and the interest rates.

The thus prepared data has been collated in tables 1-3. In the output table 1 the most important types of service of a practice for ophthalmology with their BMÄ numbers have been listed and designated. Their production variables have been differentiated according to the possible choice of procedure, and the demand structure, the fees and profit values have been indicated. Contrary to the fees it is only the variable production unit costs that are dependent on the choice of procedure. The possibility of producing specific types of output with differing production procedures means, for example, that with the single service type j=1 the output "consultation in surgery hours" can be carried out by the doctor on his own (variable x^1), by the doctor with the help of an orthoptist (variable x^2) or by the doctor with the help of an orthoptist and a medical assistant (variable x^3). The production coefficients which then also alter, are listed in table 3 in the form of a technology matrix, the columns of which characterize the individual procedure alternatives in terms of input.

The important production factors of an ophthalmology practice with their rate of cost are listed in table 2, whereby four types of personnel (variable numbers 17 - 20) and fourteen kinds of equipment (variable numbers 21 - 34) are dealt with. These input variables are measured in man-quarters (MQ) and apparatus-quarters (AQ), which, with an average of 12 working weeks per quarter and 40 working hours per week, having regard to an unavoidable percentage loss of 12% of work time which is not determined by demand, amounts to about 25.334 man-minutes and apparatus-minutes per quarter. Whilst the personnel costs can, by following the valid tarif agreements, be directly calculated for a quarter, in order to determine the rate of cost of the various instruments the depreciation and the interest per quarter in relation to the purchase price have to be estimated. To this end the instruments were attributed a useful life of 7 years; the interest rate was set at 6%. This leads altogether to depreciations and interest per quarter which constitute approximately 5% of the purchase price of the instruments. Over and above this the depreciation and interest for the personnel and for room costs for the personnel and for the instruments have to be considered because the premises of the practice and the non-specialized equipment of the practice (chairs, cupboards, office machines) have to be taken into account as further input variables which are not directly dependent on output. In accordance with the

Table 1: Types of service, demand structure, fees and variable production costs

Variable-number	Type of service	BMÄ-No.	Output variable $x_j^{s_j}$	Designation	Demand Structure y_j	Fee h_j	Profit value $h_j \cdot y_j$	Accumulative profit values $\sum_{z=1}^{j} h_z \cdot y_z$	Variable production costs[1)] $c_j^{s_j}$
1			x_1^1						0,10
2	1	1	x_1^2	Consultation in surgery hours	1,08	7,15	7.722	7.722	0,10
3			x_1^3						0,10
4			x_2^1						0,20
5	2	65	x_2^2	Thorough examination	0,47	10,60	4.982	12.704	0,15
6			x_3^1						0,05
7	3	1200	x_3^2	Subjective dioptometry/ spherical	0,59	5,90	3.481	16.185	0,05
8			x_4^1						0,10
9	4	1201	x_4^2	Subjective dioptometry/ spherical-cylindrical	0,45	8,90	4.005	20.190	0,10
10	5	1202	x_5^1	Objective diop-tometry	0,46	7,40	3.404	23.594	0,10
11			x_6^1						0,10
12	6	1216	x_6^2	Examination for heterophoria/ strabismus	0,27	9,10	2.457	26.051	0,10
13			x_6^3						0,15
14	7	1240	x_7^1	Slit miscropsia	0,65	7,40	4.810	30.861	0,10
15	8	1256	x_8^1	Tonometric examination with an applanation tonometer	0,32	10,00	3.200	34.061	0,10
16	9	-	x_9^1	"Other services"	1,00	7,765	7.765	$41.826=\bar{F}$	0,45

1) Mainly caused by the use of supplies like e.g. electricity and medicines as well as other medical aids.

Table 2: Input of an ophthalmology practice and costs

Variable number	Input variable r_i	Designation	Unit of measurement	Purchase price	Personnel costs	Depreciation and interest	Room costs [2]	Total costs k_i
17	r_1	Doctor	MQ	-	20000	1000[1]	1040	22040
18	r_2	Orthoptist	MQ	-	9000	75[1]	78	9153
19	r_3	Medical receptionist	MQ	-	6000	75[1]	78	6153
20	r_4	Trainee	MQ	-	2000	75[1]	78	2153
21	r_5	Phoroptor and projector/board	AQ	17120	-	856	65	921
22	r_6	Spectacle glass box	AQ	2980	-	149	65	214
23	r_7	Slit lamp	AQ	10160	-	508	65	573
24	r_8	Refractometer	AQ	7860	-	393	65	458
25	r_9	Skiascop	AQ	540	-	27	65	92
26	r_{10}	Applanationstonometer	AQ	1680	-	84	65	149
27	r_{11}	Synoptophone	AQ	8180	-	409	65	474
28	r_{12}	Other instruments for strabism diagnosis	AQ	2500	-	125	65	190
29	r_{13}	Impression tonometer	AQ	340	-	17	65	82
30	r_{14}	Other instruments for strabism and amblyopia therapy	AQ	1500	-	75	65	140
31	r_{15}	Perimeter/campimeter	AQ	13200	-	660	65	725
32	r_{16}	Infra-red lamp/hot air instrument	AQ	860	-	43	65	108
33	r_{17}	Short-/microwave irradiation apparatus	AQ	3460	-	173	65	238
34	r_{18}	Ophthalmometer	AQ	4120	-	206	65	271

[1] Caused by furnishings attributable to this input type

[2] Caused by average space requirement

Table 3: Matrix A of the production coefficients (in 10^{-5}MQ or AQ per output unit)

Outputvariable $x_j^{s_j}$ / Input-variable r_i	x_1^1	x_1^2	x_1^3	x_2^1	x_2^2	x_3^1	x_3^2	x_4^1	x_4^2	x_5^1	x_6^1	x_6^2	x_6^3	x_7^1	x_8^1	x_9^1
r_1	20	8	12	28	20	16	12	20	16	8	16	8	0	8	8	8
r_2	0	40	20	0	20	0	0	0	0	0	0	20	60	0	0	6
r_3	0	0	4	0	4	0	12	0	16	0	0	0	0	0	0	14
r_4	0	0	0	0	0	0	0	0	0	0	0	0	0	0	0	12
r_5	0	0	0	28	20	16	12	20	16	0	16	0	0	0	0	1
r_6	0	0	0	28	20	16	12	20	16	0	0	0	0	0	0	0
r_7	0	0	0	28	20	0	0	0	0	0	0	0	0	8	0	1
r_8	0	0	0	28	20	0	0	0	0	8	0	0	0	0	0	0
r_9	0	0	0	28	20	0	0	0	0	8	0	0	0	0	0	0
r_{10}	0	0	0	28	20	0	0	0	0	0	0	0	0	0	8	0
r_{11}	0	0	0	28	20	0	0	0	0	0	0	20	60	0	0	3
r_{12}	0	0	0	28	20	0	0	0	0	0	16	20	60	0	0	2
r_{13}	0	0	0	28	20	0	0	0	0	0	0	0	0	0	0	2
r_{14}	0	0	0	0	0	0	0	0	0	0	0	0	0	0	0	6
r_{15}	0	0	0	28	20	0	0	0	0	0	0	0	0	0	0	4
r_{16}	0	0	0	0	0	0	0	0	0	0	0	0	0	0	0	8
r_{17}	0	0	0	0	0	0	0	0	0	0	0	0	0	0	0	4
r_{18}	0	0	0	0	0	0	0	0	0	0	0	0	0	0	0	2

principle of cause the costs caused by these factors have been calculated for the individual types of personnel and instruments. In order to facilitate a clear evaluation of the results regarding the problem formulations (3) and (4) the input and output variables of tables 1 and 3 have also been coded with consecutive numbers. Amounts of money have all been indicated in the units of measurement DM or DM/item.

3.2 Results and discussion

The calculations on the basis of the two optimization variants (3) and (4) were carried out on an IBM 370/168 system with the programme packege IPMIXD. The numbers of patients p which have been fixed for the problem formulation (3) and the optimal sizes of a practice for ophthalmology resulting from these figures, expressed by the optimal production quantities for the individual types of service, which are dependent on the choice of procedure, and by the optimal input variables are collated in the synopsis of results presented in table 4. On the basis of these results the proceeds, costs, and profits as well as the income per doctor can be calculated for the various sizes of practice as shown in table 5. The income per doctor E - as already explained - is determined by adding the calculable employer's wage of 20.000 DM per quarter, which has been appropriated as personnel expenses for the input type 'doctor' in accordance with the opportunity cost principle, to the profit per doctor. This corresponds with the income of a 37 year old doctor, married with two children, who is employed in an hospital and who is paid according to the payment group BAT Ia (basis 1979) including additional wage costs for three months. The proceeds can be ascertained by simply multiplying the case value $\bar{F}$ = 41.826 DM from table 1 with the respective number of patients.

In this first optimization variant the practice form can only be found out a posteriori. On the basis of tables 4 and 5 the following statements can, however, be made:

- The transition from a one-doctor practice to a group practice with two doctors occurs when the number of patients is between 1800 and 2000.

- When the number of patients is between 600 and 1800 a one-doctor practice is most profitable. When the number of patients is between 2100 and 3600 or 3900 and 4800 or 5100 and 6000 a group practice with two or three or four doctors respectively is most profitable.

Table 4: Overview of the optimal production programme and of the optimal size of an ophthalmology practice with differing numbers of patients: Calculations according to approach (3)

Practice	(1)	(2)	(3)	(4)	(5)	(6)	(7)	(8)	(9)	(10)	(11)	(12)	(13)	(14)	(15)	(16)	(17)	(18)	(19)
No. of variable \ p	600	900	1.200	1.500	1.800	2.100	2.400	2.700	3.000	3.300	3.600	3.900	4.200	4.500	4.800	5.100	5.400	5.700	6.000
1	648	972	1.296	0	0	2.268	2.592	2.916	1.895	1.200	0	4.212	4.536	3.725	416	5.508	5.832	3.656	3.790
2	0	0	0	1.620	1.944	0	0	0	1.345	2.364	3.888	0	0	400	240	0	0	2.500	2.690
3	0	0	0	0	0	0	0	0	0	0	0	0	0	735	4.528	0	0	0	0
4	0	0	0	0	0	0	0	0	0	0	0	0	0	0	0	0	0	2.679	0
5	282	423	564	705	846	987	1.128	1.269	1.410	1.551	1.692	1.833	1.974	2.115	2.256	2.397	2.538	0	2.820
6	0	0	708	0	0	0	0	1.593	0	0	0	2.301	2.478	0	2.360	3.009	1.999	1.750	0
7	354	531	0	885	1.062	1.239	1.416	0	1.770	1.947	2.124	0	0	2.655	472	0	1.187	1.613	3.540
8	0	0	540	0	0	0	0	1.215	0	0	536	1.755	0	0	2.160	2.295	2.430	2.565	0
9	270	405	0	675	810	945	1.080	0	1.350	1.485	1.084	0	1.890	2.025	0	0	0	0	2.700
10	276	414	552	690	828	966	1.104	1.242	1.380	1.518	1.656	1.794	1.932	2.070	2.208	2.346	2.484	2.622	2.760
11	162	243	324	405	368	0	648	729	810	891	468	0	0	1.215	0	1.377	1.458	452	1.620
12	0	0	0	0	118	567	0	0	0	0	504	1.053	1.134	0	1.296	0	0	0	0
13	0	0	0	0	0	0	0	0	0	0	0	0	0	0	0	0	0	1.087	0
14	390	585	780	975	1.170	1.365	1.560	1.755	1.950	2.145	2.340	2.535	2.730	2.925	3.120	3.315	3.510	3.705	3.900
15	192	288	384	480	576	672	768	864	960	1.056	1.152	1.249	1.344	1.440	1.536	1.632	1.728	1.824	1.920
16	600	900	1.200	1.500	1.800	2.100	2.400	2.700	3.000	3.300	3.600	3.900	4.200	4.500	4.800	5.100	5.400	5.700	6.000
17	1	1	1	1	1	2	2	2	2	2	2	3	3	3	3	4	4	4	4
18	1	1	1	1	2	1	1	1	1	2	3	1	1	1	2	1	1	2	2
19	1	1	1	1	1	1	1	1	1	1	1	1	1	2	1	1	1	1	2
20	1	1	1	1	1	1	1	1	1	1	1	1	1	1	1	1	1	1	1
21	1	1	1	1	1	1	1	1	1	1	1	1	2	2	2	2	2	2	2
22	1	1	1	1	1	1	1	1	1	1	1	1	2	2	2	2	2	2	2
23	1	1	1	1	1	1	1	1	1	1	1	1	1	1	1	1	1	1	1
24	1	1	1	1	1	1	1	1	1	1	1	1	1	1	1	1	1	1	1
25	1	1	1	1	1	1	1	1	1	1	1	1	1	1	1	1	1	1	1
26	1	1	1	1	1	1	1	1	1	1	1	1	1	1	1	1	1	1	1
27	1	1	1	1	1	1	1	1	1	1	1	1	1	1	1	1	1	1	1
28	1	1	1	1	1	1	1	1	1	1	1	1	1	1	1	1	1	1	1
29	1	1	1	1	1	1	1	1	1	1	1	1	1	1	1	1	1	1	1
30	1	1	1	1	1	1	1	1	1	1	1	1	1	1	1	1	1	1	1
31	1	1	1	1	1	1	1	1	1	1	1	1	1	1	1	1	1	1	1
32	1	1	1	1	1	1	1	1	1	1	1	1	1	1	1	1	1	1	1
33	1	1	1	1	1	1	1	1	1	1	1	1	1	1	1	1	1	1	1
34	1	1	1	1	1	1	1	1	1	1	1	1	1	1	1	1	1	1	1

Table 5: Overview of the profit-loss-account: Calculations according to approach (3)

Practice	Patients p	Proceeds F	Fixed costs K	Variable costs K^V	Total costs $K+K^V$	Profit G	Profit per doctor $\bar{G}$**	Income per doctor $\bar{E}$**
(1)	600	25.095,60	44.134,00	523,80	44.657,80	- 19.562,20	- 19.562,00	438,00
(2)	900	37.643,40	44.134,00	785,70	44.919,70	- 7.276,30	- 7.276,00	12.724,00
(3)	1.200	50.191,30	44.134,00	1.047,60	45.181,60	5.009,60	5.010,00	25.010,00
(4)	1.500	62.739,00	44.134,00	1.309,50	45.443,50	17.295,50	17.296,00	37.296,00
(5)	1.800	75.286,80	53.287,00	1.571,40	54.858,40	20.428,40	20.429,00	40.429,00
(6)	2.100*	87.834,60	66.174,00	1.833,30	68.007,30	19.827,30	9.914,00	29.914,00
(7)	2.400	100.382,40	66.174,00	2.095,20	68.269,20	32.113,20	16.057,00	36.057,00
(8)	2.700	112.930,20	66.174,00	2.357,10	68.531,10	44.399,10	22.200,00	42.200,00
(9)	3.000	125.478,00	66.174,00	2.619,00	68.793,00	56.685,00	28.343,00	48.343,00
(10)	3.300	138.025,80	75.327,00	2.880,90	78.207,90	59.817,90	29.909,00	49.909,00
(11)	3.600	150.573,60	84.480,00	3.142,80	87.622,80	62.950,80	31.476,00	51.476,00
(12)	3.900*	163.121,40	88.214,00	3.404,70	91.618,70	71.502,70	23.835,00	43.835,00
(13)	4.200	175.669,20	89.349,00	3.666,60	93.015,60	82.653,60	27.552,00	47.552,00
(14)	4.500	188.217,00	95.502,00	3.928,50	99.430,50	88.786,50	29.596,00	49.596,00
(15)	4.800	200.764,80	98.502,00	4.190,40	102.692,40	98.072,40	32.691,00	52.691,00
(16)	5.100*	213.312,60	111.389,00	4.452,30	115.841,30	97.471,30	24.368,00	44.368,00
(17)	5.400	225.860,40	111.389,00	4.714,20	116.103,20	109.757,20	27.440,00	47.440,00
(18)	5.700	238.408,20	120.542,00	5.110,10	125.652,10	112.756,10	28.189,00	48.189,00
(19)	6.000	250.956,00	126.695,00	5.238,00	131.933,00	119.023,00	29.756,00	49.756,00

* At this points the form of the practice changed

** Rounded up to full DM amounts

- The results of table 5 altogether reveal that every doctor participating in the practices which have been examined can expect a positive income. In each case the income levels appear to be thoroughl realistic. Thus, for example, the owner of practice (5) with 1800 patients per quarter obtains an annual income of 161.716 DM. By way of a comparison it was established that the average income for ophthalmologists in private practice in 1975, based on an annual number of patients of 8000, amounted to 184.140 DM (Gehb 1977).

- When deciding between a medical position in non-tenured employment in a hospital and the establishment of a practice the positive profit of his own practice is, however, of considerable significance. Thus the foundation of a one-doctor practice with an expected number of patients of 900 and less would, therefore, hardly be economically tenable, whereas with an expected number of patients of 1200 and more it would be advantageous.

In the calculations within the framework of the second optimization variant (4) the number r of the doctors working in the practice (variable 17) is preset and varied in such a way with the number p of patients to be cared for by the practice so that, in order to facilitate a comparison, the number of patients per doctor $\bar{p}$, for the various forms of practice, always amounts to the values 900, 1200, 1500, 1800 and 2100. The parameter-combinations (r, p), based on the numerical evaluation, and their optimal solutions, analogous to the problem formulation (4), are given in tables 6 and 7.

The following aspects can be stressed as new results in contrast to approach (3):

- On account of the restriction of the practice's capacity as a result of the predetermination of the number of doctors r there are parameter-constellations for which acceptable solutions do not exist; in tables 6 and 7 these are marked with a star. It was possible to establish the following capacity boundaries for the preset r-values (Prasiswa 1979): 1931 patients for r=1, 3863 patients for r=2, 5795 patients for r=3 and 7727 patients for r=4.

- The profitability thresholds of the practices examined can be estimated from table 7. The profitability threshold for a one-doctor practice is between 900 and 1200 patients. For the group practices the profitability thresholds are below the number of patients set for these practices. The values of the critical numbers of patients,

Table 6: Overview of the optimal production programme and of the optimal size of an ophthalmology practice with differing forms of practice and numbers of patients: Calculations according to approach (4)

Practice	(1')	(2')	(3')	(4')	(5')	(6')	(7')	(8')	(9')	(10')	(11')	(12')	(13')	(14')	(15')	(16')	(17')	(18')	(19')	(20')
No. of variables \ p	900	1.200	1.500	1.800	2.100	1.800	2.400	3.000	3.600	4.200	2.700	3.600	4.500	5.400	6.300	3.600	4.800	6.000	7.200	8.400
1	972	1.296	0	0	-*	1.944	2.592	1.895	0	-*	2.916	3.888	3.665	0	-*	3.888	5.184	3.790	0	-*
2	0	0	1.620	1.944	-	0	0	1.345	3.888	-	0	0	330	5.832	-	0	0	2.690	7.776	-
3	0	0	0	0	-	0	0	0	0	-	0	0	865	0	-	0	0	0	0	-
4	0	0	0	0	-	0	0	0	0	-	0	0	0	0	-	0	0	0	0	-
5	423	564	705	846	-	846	1.128	1.410	1.692	-	1.296	1.692	2.125	2.538	-	1.692	2.256	2.820	3.384	-
6	0	708	0	0	-	1.062	0	0	0	-	1.593	0	0	1.999	-	0	2.360	0	0	-
7	531	0	885	1.062	-	0	1.416	1.770	2.124	-	0	2.124	2.655	1.187	-	2.124	472	3.540	4.248	-
8	0	540	0	0	-	0	0	0	536	-	1.215	536	0	2.430	-	536	2.160	0	1.072	-
9	405	0	675	810	-	810	1.080	1.350	1.084	-	0	1.084	2.025	0	-	1.084	0	2.700	2.168	-
10	414	552	690	828	-	828	1.104	1.380	1.656	-	1.242	1.656	2.070	2.484	-	1.656	2.208	2.760	3.312	-
11	243	324	405	368	-	486	648	810	468	-	729	468	1.215	0	-	468	1.296	1.620	936	-
12	0	0	0	118	-	0	0	0	504	-	0	504	0	348	-	504	0	0	1.008	-
13	0	0	0	0	-	0	0	0	0	-	0	0	0	1.110	-	0	0	0	0	-
14	585	780	975	1.170	-	1.170	1.560	1.950	2.340	-	1.755	2.340	2.925	3.510	-	2.340	3.120	3.900	4.680	-
15	288	384	480	576	-	576	768	960	1.152	-	864	1.152	1.440	1.728	-	1.152	1.536	1.920	2.304	-
16	900	1.200	1.500	1.800	-	1.800	2.400	3.000	3.600	-	2.700	3.600	4.500	5.400	-	3.600	4.800	6.000	7.200	-
17 (r_1)	1					2					3					4				
18	1	1	1	2	-	1	1	1	3	-	1	1	1	4	-	1	1	2	5	-
19	1	1	1	1	-	1	1	1	1	-	1	1	2	1	-	1	1	2	2	-
20	1	1	1	1	-	1	1	1	1	-	1	1	1	1	-	1	1	1	1	-
21	1	1	1	1	-	1	1	1	1	-	1	1	2	2	-	1	2	2	2	-
22	1	1	1	1	-	1	1	1	1	-	1	1	2	2	-	1	2	2	2	-
23	1	1	1	1	-	1	1	1	1	-	1	1	1	1	-	1	1	1	2	-
24	1	1	1	1	-	1	1	1	1	-	1	1	1	1	-	1	1	1	1	-
25	1	1	1	1	-	1	1	1	1	-	1	1	1	1	-	1	1	1	1	-
26	1	1	1	1	-	1	1	1	1	-	1	1	1	1	-	1	1	1	1	-
27	1	1	1	1	-	1	1	1	1	-	1	1	1	2	-	1	1	1	2	-
28	1	1	1	1	-	1	1	1	1	-	1	1	1	2	-	1	1	1	2	-
29	1	1	1	1	-	1	1	1	1	-	1	1	1	1	-	1	1	1	1	-
30	1	1	1	1	-	1	1	1	1	-	1	1	1	1	-	1	1	1	1	-
31	1	1	1	1	-	1	1	1	1	-	1	1	1	1	-	1	1	1	1	-
32	1	1	1	1	-	1	1	1	1	-	1	1	1	1	-	1	1	1	1	-
33	1	1	1	1	-	1	1	1	1	-	1	1	1	1	-	1	1	1	1	-
34	1	1	1	1	-	1	1	1	1	-	1	1	1	1	-	1	1	1	1	-

* No feasible solution

Table 7: Overview of the profit-loss-account: Calculations according to approach (4)

Prac-tice	Doctors r_1	Patients p	Patients per doctor $\bar{p}$	Proceeds F	Fixed costs K	Variable costs K^v	Total costs $K+K^v$	Profit G	Income per doctor $\bar{G}$**	Profit per doctor $\bar{E}$**
(1')	1	900	900	37.643,40	44.134,00	785,70	44.919,70	- 7.276,30	- 7.276,00	12.724,00
(2')	1	1.200	1.200	50.191,20	44.134,00	1.047,60	45.181,60	5.009,60	5.010,00	25.010,00
(3')	1	1.500	1.500	62.739,00	44.134,00	1.309,50	45.443,50	17.295,50	17.296,00	37.296,00
(4')	1	1.800	1.800	75.286,80	53.287,00	1.571,40	54.858,40	20.428,40	20.429,00	40.429,00
(5')	1	2.100	2.100	* -	-	-	-	-	-	-
(6')	2	1.800	900	75.286,80	66.174,00	1.571,40	67.745,40	7.541,40	3.771,00	23.771,00
(7')	2	2.400	1.200	100.382,40	66.174,00	2.095,20	68.269,20	32.113,20	16.057,00	36.057,00
(8')	2	3.000	1.500	125.478,00	66.174,00	2.619,00	68.793,00	56.685,00	28.343,00	48.343,00
(9')	2	3.600	1.800	150.573,60	84.480,00	3.142,80	87.622,80	62.950,80	31.476,00	51.476,00
(10')	2	4.200	2.100	* -	-	-	-	-	-	-
(11')	3	2.700	900	112.930,20	88.214,00	2.357,10	90.571,10	22.359,10	7.454,00	27.454,00
(12')	3	3.600	1.200	150.573,60	88.214,00	3.142,80	91.356,80	59.216,80	19.739,00	39.739,00
(13')	3	4.500	1.500	188.217,00	95.502,00	3.928,50	99.430,50	88.786,50	29.596,00	49.596,00
(14')	3	5.400	1.800	225.860,40	117.472,00	4.769,70	122.241,70	103.618,70	34.540,00	54.540,00
(15')	3	6.300	2.100	* -	-	-	-	-	-	-
(16')	4	3.600	900	150.573,60	110.254,00	3.142,80	113.396,80	37.176,80	9.295,00	29.295,00
(17')	4	4.800	1.200	200.764,80	111.389,00	4.190,40	115.579,40	85.185,40	21.297,00	41.297,00
(18')	4	6.000	1.500	250.956,00	126.695,00	5.238,00	131.933,00	119.023,00	29.756,00	49.756,00
(19')	4	7.200	1.800	301.147,20	155.391,00	6.285,60	161.676,60	139.470,60	34.868,00	54.868,00
(20')	4	8.400	2.100	* -	-	-	-	-	-	-

*No feasible solution

**Rounded up to full DM-amounts

which mark the profitability thresholds of the practices which have been investigated, are (Prasiswa 1979): 1078 for r=1, 1615 for r=2, 2144 for r=3 and 2693 for r=4. From this it can be seen that the profitablity threshold of the separate forms of practice increases under-proportionally with the rising number of doctors working in the practice.

- Finally with the help of table 7 it can also be shown that, with the same number of patients per doctor $\bar{p}$, the larger the number of doctors working in the practice the higher the profit per doctor $\bar{G}$. If the number of patients per doctor is equated with the work load per doctor this means that with the same work load in a group practice, because the capacity is used better, a higher profit per doctor can be obtained whereas to obtain the same profit in a one-doctor practice the doctor would have to accept a greater work load. This advantage of the group practice does, however, diminish with increasing r. The subject discussed here is illustrated in diagram 2.

If the results of the two optimization variants (3) and (4) are now compared, the application of the methodological consideration for the determination of the optimal size, equipment and organization form of a doctor's practice in the practical case of a specialist practice for ophthalmology has revealed the following:

- By altering the number of patients both approaches have shown that group practices are superior to one-doctor practices because for one thing they lead to a better utilization of the input.

- With the help of approach (4) it could be proved that the advantages of group practices over one-doctor practices are to be found, on the one hand, in the relatively low profitability threshold of group practices and, on the other hand, in the fact that with the same number of patients per doctor the profit per doctor increases with the increasing number of doctors working in the practice.

- In view of the glut of doctors, which has recently been frequently predicted the aspect of the relatively low profitability threshold of group practices, which amongst other things reduces the risk involved in setting up a practice, is of particular importance. If, for example, 900 patients fell upon each doctor, in a one-doctor practice they could not be profitably cared for - see practice (2)

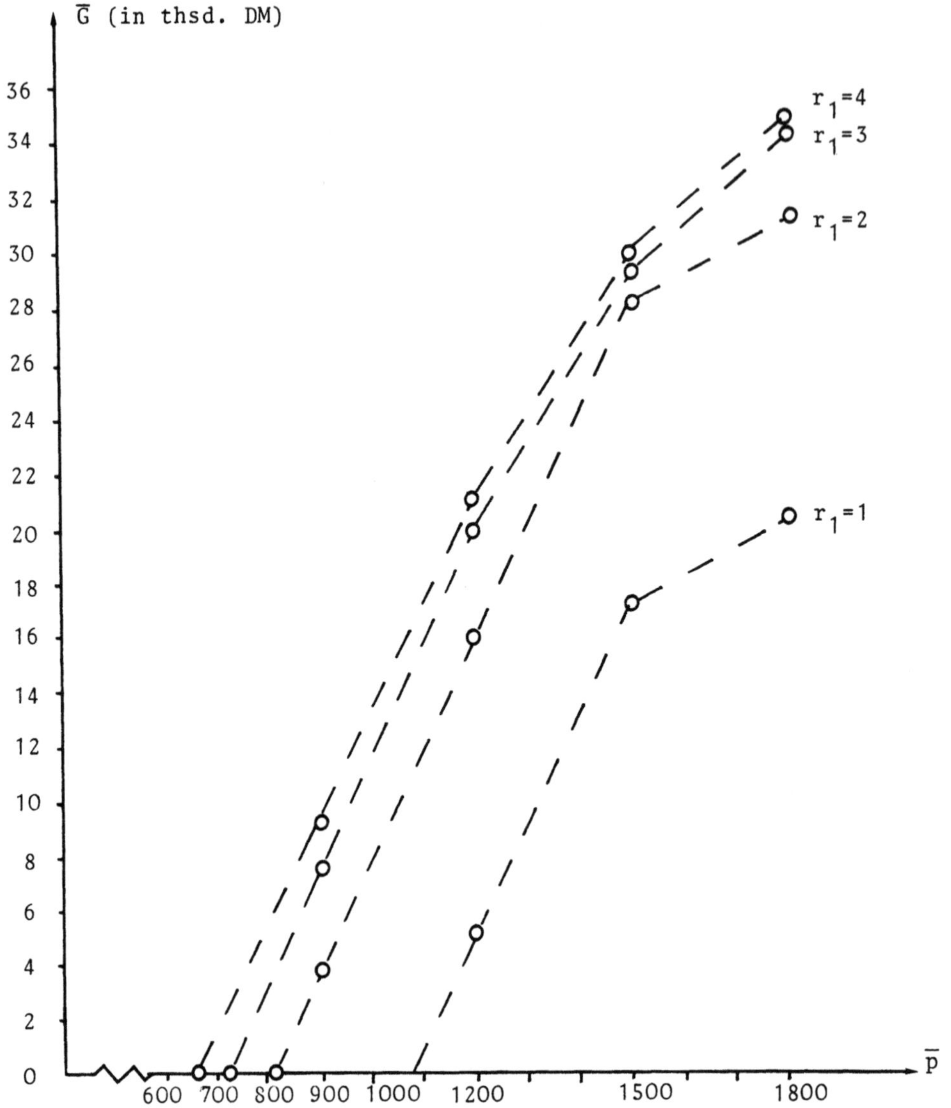

Diagram 2: Lines for the profit per doctor for the different forms of practice dependent on the number of patients

in tables 4 and 5. In a group practice with 2 doctors and altogether 1800 patients to be cared for a profit could, however, be made - compare practice (6') in tables 6 and 7.

- As the two approaches (3) and (4) have differing optimization criteria they generally show different solutions. Thus, for example, with 5400 patients, according to approach (3), with regard to the maximization of the profit, a group practice with 4 doctors with a practice profit of 109.757,20 DM is suggested (practice (17) in tables 4 and 5). According to approach (4), which maximizes the profit per doctor, this number of patients is cared for by a group practice with three doctors with a minimum profit for the practice of 103.618,70 DM (practice (14') in tables 6 and 7). In approach (4) the profit per doctor of 34.540,- DM is, however, considerably higher than that in the optimization variant (3) of 27.440,- DM. If in addition the work load of the individual doctors is considered then, according to the optimal solution of (3), each doctor would have to look after, on average, 1350 patients and, according to that of (4), after 1800. In order to decide finally between the two approaches in the question as to the optimal practice form further non-monetary criteria like spare time (for further education, recreation) would have to be considered. Then each doctor would have to decide whether for 15% more income he is prepared to bear a third higher work load. In the case of a negation the result would be a group practice with four doctors.

4 Final Remarks

In connection with the comments on the results of the calculations in the last section the possible practical uses of the approaches which have been presented have already become obvious. In principle it can be claimed that applying these or similar decision-orientated approaches may be useful in every situation or phase of a practice; whether it is the decision about the establishment of a practice that is due to be dealt with, whether an expansion or reduction of the practice capacity is planned or whether an alteration in the form of the practice or the step by step handover of a practice to a successor is intended. The flexibility required for planning the treatment of such decisions is provided by the formulation of the approaches for the accounting period of a quarter.

The fact that the approaches (3) and (4) are of a more short-term nature and are statically formulated, means that the more long-term character of the decision variables are pushed into the background. This can, however, be justified by the fact that, on account of the normally very long life-span of a doctor's practice, an alternative theoretical investment calculation is subject to considerable uncertainties with regard to the data, which would certainly not simplify the decision making process. The objection that the approaches are based on the assumption that the demand remains constant can be responded to by pointing out that the problem of irregular demand for many specialist groups can be defused to a large extent by adopting the form of an appointment practice.

In view of the prognoses (Lefelmann/Geißler 1978), which are based on the assumption that the number of doctors will rise to between 226.000 and 270.000 by the year 2000 - which would mean that, in comparison with the situation in 1980, the number of doctors could double within a period of twenty years - the practical relevance of such decision making models, as have been presented and applied in this first attempt, will greatly increase.

Literature:

Adam, D.: Krankenhausmanagement im Konfliktfeld zwischen medizinischen und wirtschaftlichen Zielen, Wiesbaden 1972.

Axtner, W.: Krankenhausmanagement, Baden-Baden 1978.

Billerbeck, K.: Kosten-Ertrags-Analyse, Berlin 1968.

Brenner, G.: Die Kostenstruktur in der Arztpraxis, in: Deutsches Ärzteblatt 74, 1977, pp. 2107.

Brockhoff, K., and Rehder, H.: Analytische Planung von Produkten im Raum der Produkteigenschaften, in: Topritzhofer, E. (ed.): Marketing, Neue Ergebnisse aus Forschung und Praxis, Wiesbaden 1978, pp. 327.

Brockhoff, K., et al.: Proceedings in Operations Research, No. 7, Würzburg/Wien 1978.

Dathe, H.N., et al.: Proceedings in Operations Research, No. 6, Würzburg/Wien 1976.

Egle, K.: Wartezeitmodelle und Krankenhausplanung, in: Zeitschrift für betriebswirtschaftliche Forschung 22, 1970, pp. 322.

Feldstein, M.S.: Economic Analysis for Health Service Efficiency, Amsterdam 1967.

Gaede, K.-W., et al.: Proceedings in Operations Research, No. 8, Würzburg/Wien 1979.

Gehb, K.: Umsätze und Einkommen im Durchschnitt, in: Deutsches Ärzteblatt 74, 1977, pp. 2887.

Heinhold, M.: Locations- und Allocationsprobleme bei Krankenversorgungsbetrieben - eine Operations Research Studie, Ph.D. thesis, München 1974.

Herder-Dorneich, Ph., and Kötz, W.: Zur Dienstleistungsökonomik, Systemanalyse und Systempolitik der Krankenhauspflegedienste, Berlin 1972.

Kolesar, P.: A Markovian Model for Hospital Admission Scheduling, in: Management Science 16, 1970, pp. B-384.

Lefelmann, G., and Geißler, U.: Das Ärzteangebot bis zum Jahre 2000, Bonn 1978.

Meyer, M. (ed.): Krankenhausplanung, Stuttgart/New York 1979.

Meyer, M., and Rohde, M.: Zur Bedeutung der Unternehmensforschung für die Krankenhausplanung, in: Betriebswirtschaftliche Forschung und Praxis 23, 1971, pp. 455.

Pfeffer-Küppers, M.E., and Esch, W.: Aspekte der ärztlichen Versorgung in den USA, Stuttgart 1977.

Prasiswa, A.: Die optimale Betriebsgröße einer Arztpraxis, Ph.D. thesis, Hagen 1979.

Smith, W.G., and Solomon, M.B.: A Simulation of Hospital Admission Policy, in: Communications of the ACM 9, 1966, pp. 362.

Part B: Problems in Hospital Planning

Outcome Based Hospital Financing and Decision Oriented Hospital Management

Klaus Hansen

1 Introduction

When designing a hospital reimbursement system, one has to consider simultaneously the public interest of minimizing total cost of the health care delivery system and the individual economic hospital's goal of maximizing the profit. The purpose of this paper is to show that health care financing related to the outcome of hospitals and to the outcome linked costs satisfies both objectives.

Traditionally, health insurers reimbursed hospitals on the basis of reasonable costs. The move from cost based refund to outcome oriented price payment presented health care managers with a budget regardless of costs actually incurred. It encourages hospital management to maximize effectiveness and efficiency. This calls for new management tools to improve the decision making process in hospitals. Therefore the model of and experiences with a decision related information system is discussed in chapter 4 of this paper.

The reimbursement system and the management system are based on the same approach. It is concerned with finding a model for solving the conflict situation between cost minimizing of the whole health care delivery system and profit maximizing of the hospitals. In chapters 2.3.3 and 3.2 it is shown that the solution can be described by a saddle point of a convex programming problem.

Funded by the government of the Federal State of Baden-Württemberg, the outcome oriented reimbursement approach combined with the decision related hospital management system is being applied in a current project.

2 Basic concepts of hospital reimbursement

The principle elements of the pricing process are the method of price setting, the time of pricing and the determination of the unit-of-outcome.

2.1 Method of price setting

Price setting can be based on reasonable and allowable costs. This assumes that the relevant cost information is available and the decision makers really use them. Organizational and goal conflicted problems complicate the hospital refund related to absolute cost determinants.

The price formation can also be the result of a negotiation. Rival demand and rival supply can potentially provide the motivation for hospitals to become more cost effective without sacrificing the quality of medical care. However, the competition and the price mechanism must be regulated in a manner that guarantees the coverage of an adequate health care. In this connection especially attention must be focussed on emergency facilities.

The price charging of an outcome-unit can also be defined based on an exogenous budget. This can be planned at the hospital, regional and/or national level. The apportionment of the global budget depends on refund-units. The problem which remains is to determine those units.

2.2 Time of pricing

The time of pricing is defined by the point in time at which a hospital gets the reimbursement before or after time of performance. Traditionally, most health insurers have reimbursed in retrospect. While this procedure guarantees cover for most hospitals expenditures, it provides disincentive economic effects. Hospital prospective reimbursement systems establish the charge before the period over which the charge is to apply. In this case the risk of variances between actual and refunded costs is with the hospital. Therefore it motivates hospitals to decrease costs.

2.3 Identifying the unit-of-outcome of hospitals

The outcome-unit is the definition of the services hospitals provide. When designing a reimbursement system, it is important to be able to assess the performance of care providers. Outcome has both a quantitative and a qualitative component. Measuring quantitative performance one has simply to add the outcome-units. However, the aggregation of qualitative units of health care is unsolved. Today surrogates and adjunct measures are used to describe the quality of treatment processes.

2.3.1 Hospital outcome-units based on intrahospital performances

In popular opinion the outcome of a hospital are the auxiliary services such as laboratory tests, radiological analyses, clinical examinations and so forth. By recording these performances, one can control and measure the effectiveness of diagnostic, therapeutic and nursing activities. But assuming the true goal of a hospital to be the improvement of the health status of the number of the patients treated, the intrahospital performances are productive factors. So they are input to health care. Intrahospital performances are used with the assumption that they correspond to hospital's outcome. But they have many defects which make them insensitive to significant changes in the health status of patients (Lerner 1973). So it is easy to see that for instance increasing the medications will not increase the patient's health in every case.

2.3.2 Hospital outcome defined as periodical total performance

Finland, France, Ireland, the Netherlands, Sweden and the United Kingdom fund hospitals on the basis of annual budgets. This assumed that the authorities of these countries defined hospital outcome as a time related performance delivered to a region as a whole. The apportionment of the total budget to local health care delivery systems requires periodical and outcome related parameters to calculate the relation between the population and the type of services which must be made available for the different types of patients. The definition of a parameter satisfying these conditions will be discussed in chapter 3.2.

2.3.3 Hospital outcome-units based on treated cases

Many authors (Fetter 1980/1983, Rodrigues 1987, Davis 1987) define the outcome of hospital as the specific goods and services it provides to patients. These include, for example, the x-rays, medication and lab tests ordered by physicians as part of the treatment process as well as nursing care, operating room facilities and certain hotel and social services. In this sense the hospitals input are the labor, material and equipment used in the provision of these goods and services. The specific set of outputs provided to each patient is a "product" of hospitals. Hence, these authors reason, a cost-per-case reimbursement system causes the hospitals to work efficiently.

Let us now discuss an example showing the impact mechanism of full cost pricing per case. For simplicity's sake, we consider a cardiac surgery unit treating only four categories of patients: Aorto-Coronary-Bypass, Aortic-Valve-Replacement, Mitral-Valve-Replacement and Aortic-/Mitral-Valve-Replacement.

Table 1: Predicted and actual number of cases

category of patient	number of cases	
	predicted	actual
Aorto-Coronary-Bypass	250	200
Aortic-Valve-Replacement	175	195
Mitral-Valve-Replacement	160	90
Aortic-/Mitral-Valve-Replacement	100	100

Table 1 shows the predicted and the actual number of treated cases. We assumed that the actual number in two of these categories are less than predicted, in one category the actual number is higher than the predicted one and of the last one the predicted and actual numbers are equal.

Table 2 shows the ready-to-serve-cost and the case-variable costs. Case variable cost can be traced directly to a case. They are those cost which would not exist if this case - hypothetically asked - has not been treated. These case-related costs cover the cost of materials (drugs, electrocardiogram, anesthesia, special diet) and external services (blood infusions, x-rays, lab tests, bacteriological tests, histological examinations, special hotel services). Due to the German so called dual hospital financing law the ready-to-serve-cost cover on the whole staff costs.

Table 2: Ready-to-serve-costs and case related costs

category of patient	ready-to-serve-costs DM	case-related-costs DM
Aorto-Coronary-Bypass	1.45 million	9500
Aortic-Valve-Replacement	1.05 million	15700
Mitral-Valve-Replacement	0.8 million	13000
Aortic-/Mitral-Valve-Replacement	0.56 million	18100

By the aid of the predicted number of cases, the prospective full-cost-prices were calculated (see table 3). The revenue and cost accounting after the period over which the full-cost-rate was applied is presented in table 4. Caused by the variances between predicted and actual number of cases results in a deficit of 0.52 DM (German marks). Attention should be drawn to the fact that the ready-to-serve costs and

Table 3: Calculation of the full-cost-price per case

category of patient	predicted costs	
	total DM	per case DM
Aorto-Coronary Bypass	1.45 mill. + 250 x 9500 = 3.825 mill.	15300
Aortic-Valve-Replacement	1.05 mill. + 175 x 15700 = 3.7975 mill.	21700
Mitral-Valve-Replacement	o.8 mill. + 160 x 13000 = 2.88 mill.	18000
Aortic-/Mitral-Valve-Replacement	0.56 mill. + 100 x 18100 = 2.37 mill.	23700

Table 4: Revenue- and cost accounting

category of patient	revenues DM	costs DM
Aorto-Coronary-Bypass	200 x 15300 = 3.06 mill.	1.45 mill. + 200 x 9500 = 3.35 mill.
Aortic-Valve-Replacement	195 x 21700 = 4.2315 mill.	1.05 mill. + 195 x 15700 = 4.1115 mill.
Mitral-Valve-Replacement	90 x 18000 = 1.62 mill.	0.8 mill. + 90 x 13000 = 1.97 mill.
Aortic-/Mitral-Valve-Replacement	100 x 23700 = 2.37 mill.	0.56 mill. + 100 x 18100 = 2.37 mill.
sum	11.2815 mill.	11.8015 mill.

the case related costs did not change. So the efficiency remains constant. This example shows, that losses can be avoided only, if the predicted number of cases (in the weighted average) is not less than the actual one. As the demand of health care can be described by stochastic processes profit and losses depend on chance event. It misleads hospitals to maximize the number of cases treated in order to avoid deficits. Hence, full-cost-per-case-pricing results in an increased capacity.

As indirect costs are not traceable to a case, the revenues are not cost related. If this criterion is not satisfied, profit and loss do not correlate with the efficiency. We will show that the per case form of payment is a disincentive based system in general.

Let $N_1, N_2, \ldots, N_j, \ldots, N_m$ be the demand on health care (number of cases) of a given hospital's case mix in the time subperiod j. The price of a case is represented by p and K denotes the capacity of treatment (cases per time subperiod). We assume $V(N_1, \ldots, N_m)$ to be the operating costs and F(K) the ready-to-serve-costs per time period.

The profit realized per time period is presented by

(1) $G = \sum_j p\, N_j - V(N_1, N_2, \ldots, N_m) - F(K)$

We assume $G(N_j, K)$ is a convex function.
Let us suppose that the capacity is demand oriented, so that

(2) $K \geq N_j$ for $j = 1, 2, \ldots, m$

must be satisfied. The Lagrange Function has the form

$$L = p \sum_j N_j - V(N_1, N_2, \ldots, N_m) - F(K) + \sum_j u_j\,(K - N_j)$$

As hospital expenditures are reimbursed by the insurance system hospitals cannot influence the price of treatment by quantity variance. So the Kuhn-Tucker conditions (see Krelle/Künzi 1975) (3) - (8) are generated on the assumption

$$\frac{dp}{dN_j} = 0$$

(3) $\frac{dL}{dN_j}\, p - \frac{dV}{dN_j} - u_j \leqq 0$; (4) $N_j\,(p - \frac{dV}{dN_j} - u_j) = 0$;

(5) $\frac{dL}{dK} = - \frac{dF}{dK} + \sum_j u_j \leqq 0$; (6) $K\,(- \frac{dF}{dK} + \sum_j u_j) = 0$;

(7) $\frac{dL}{du_j} = K - N_j \geqq 0$; (8) $u_j\,(K - N_j) = 0$.

If we suppose patients are treated in every time subperiod, so that $N_j > 0$ for all j, (4) implies

(9) $p = \frac{dV}{dN_j} + u_j$

as full cost price per case. It will be noted that in (9) $u_j > 0$ for all j and according to (8) it is seen that

$$K = N_j \quad \text{for all } j.$$

Therefore, if reimbursement is based on full cost pricing , hospitals must operate at full capacity with the effect that emergency facilities are not resourced and the incentive is to maximize the number of patients independent of the medical indication.

3 Reimbursement by case related payment and time related budgeting

We assume that the true goal of hospitals is the improvement of the health status of the number of patients treated. This does not mean that hospitals are not maximizing their profit. To aspire to profit and to avoid losses must be considered as an important element of hospital financing systems. Because of this the reimbursement must satisfy the following conditions.

1. The reimbursement must directly pay the delivered health care. Adjunct measures such as length of stay and number of visits measure the evaluation process or input to health care. These surrogates are used with the implicit assumption that they correlate with outcome measures such as health status, an assumption which is subject to question. For example, an increase in the number of medications may be noxious and not improve care.
2. Health care financing should be related to the outcome linked costs. If a hospital gets more than one unit cost causing for one accounting-unit, the number of accounting-units will increase and in the case of non cost covering per unit the number of accounting units will decrease.

The quantitative and qualitative health care servicing capacity of a region requires the resourcing of staff, beds, laboratories, facilities, organizational structure, etc. As the demand on health care delivered can be described by stochastic processes, the demand on diagnostic, therapeutic and nursing capacities are best handled through the use of probabilities. The projection of hospital ancillary services, such as x-ray units, laboratories, operating rooms, etc. should cover the estimated demand with a safe margin. Case related performances are only produced if this predicted and kept up servicing capacity was really used. Obviously the total hospital outcome is not only case related, but it also renders standby performance. Therefore we defined the primary demand on health care

- to be a case related demand for change in the health status of patients (case treatment) and
- to be a demand for ready-to-serve services in a region with potentially health care-demanding patients (that means for all healthy persons).

From this follows that primary demand oriented health care needs a separate pricing for case treatment and setting a price for ready-to-serve.

3.1 Reimbursement based on patient treatment

We distinguish between quantity and quality of hospital performances. The quantity of performances are the number of patients treated. However, one must evaluate the delivered health care of hospitals with respect to their case mix. This necessitates the classification of patients. Difficulties raising by patient grouping processes shall not be discussed in this paper (cf. Fetter/Freeman 1984,Ohmichi/Miyake 1984,Sanderson 1984). The problem of determining quality of health care is far from being solved. Many authors defined the quality performance of hospitals as the difference between the health status of a patient admitted hospital and leaving it. Left and unsolved is the problem of aggregating a number of measures into a single health index. We suggested the use of simple rates of morbidity, such as the rate of risk of open wound complications, the rate of risk of infantmortality, the rate of risk of anesthesiological complications, etc.

Following the above derived conditions for setting case prices, the case reimbursement should be based on the variable costs per case treated in each patient category. According to (8) the payment per case should be the result of negotiations related to

$$\frac{dV}{dN_j} \quad \text{respectively} \quad \frac{V}{\sum_j N_j} .$$

As mentioned above, these are those costs which would not exist if this case - hypothetically asked - has not been treated. Satisfying

$$p = \frac{dV}{dN_j} \quad \text{and applying (9), the result}$$

$$u_j \geqq 0 \qquad \text{for all } j$$

readily followed. With this, the profit related incentive to increase the hospital's capacity do not take place. Profit can be realized only by decreasing costs.

3.2 Reimbursement based on hospitals potential outcome

Analysing the capacity of a hospital, one has be aware of the fact, that the hospital's potential outcome cannot be measured by the number of beds, staffing level, size of laboratories, operating and recovery rooms, etc., as the effective capacity is above all determined by the quality of management process especially planning and organization. Returning to our assumption that the true goal of hospital is the treatment of patients, its quantitative potential outcome should be measured by the potential number of patients of a given case mix which could be treated per period.

Applying a semi Markov model we will derive the number of patients which could be treated. A hospital can be characterized as a whole series of waiting lines because every station in the complex has the potential of forming queues. As each patient in a hospital must use a bed, we view a ward as a queueing system with a finite number of k parallel channels (beds). All patients demanding health services (unscheduled emergency cases, scheduled hospital patients and those waiting at home) join a single ward's queue. In this way the hospital as a whole is divided in separately queueing systems for each department such as the surgical unit, medical unit, infection unit, etc. drawing into consideration interactions between the departments (see figure 1).

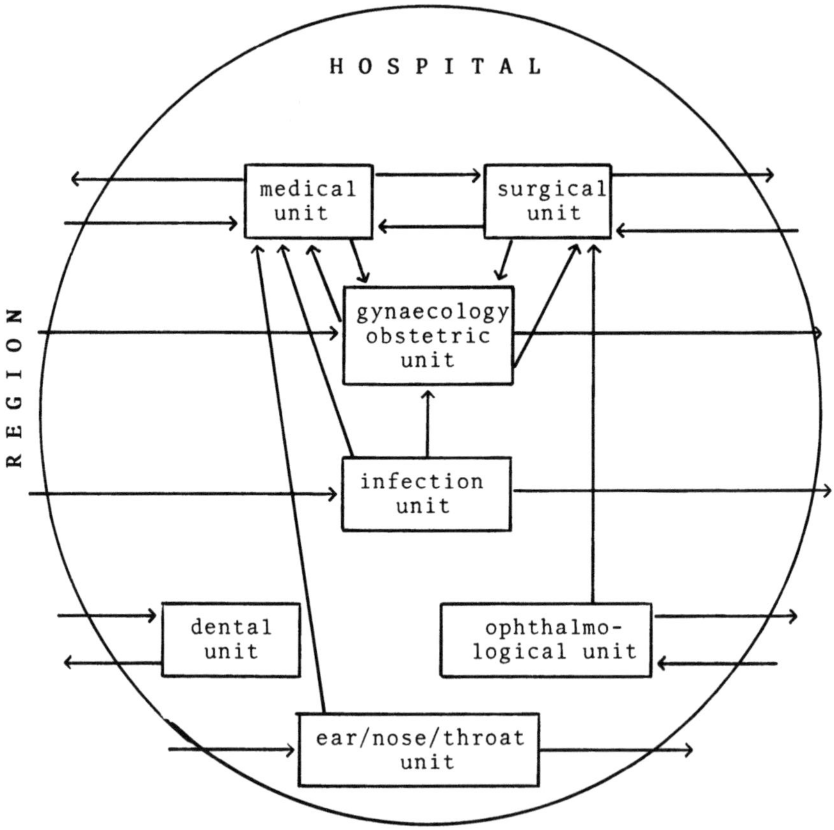

Figure 1: Arriving and servicing processes of a general hospital

To get time dependent solutions, the aid of convolution was used. Let X be the stochastic variable of health care demanding patients of a department, Y that of servicing (treating) and S that of the starting state. For the arrival-service process, then

$$Pr(Z=z_i) = \sum_{z_i=s_i+x_i} p(s_i)\ p(x_i),$$

(10)

$$Pr(Z=z_{i+1}) = \sum_{\substack{z_{i+1}=z_i-y_i \\ z_{i+1}\geq 0}} p(z_i)\ p(y_i|q)$$

where $q = z_i$ if $z_i \leq k$, $q = k$ if $z_i > k$, applies. The relationships (10) apply in general for arbitrary, discrete, independent arrival-service distributions. The average waiting time and length of stay respectively will be denoted d. Considering, the probability that more than one patient may leave the care unit in the interval Δt is negligible, we obtain the following:

$$p(y=0) = 1 - \sum_{j=1,k} [\frac{1}{d}\ \Delta t\ (1 - \frac{1}{d}\ \Delta t)^{k-1}]_j$$

$$p(y=1) = \sum_{j=1,k} [\frac{1}{d}\ \Delta t\ (1 - \frac{1}{d}\ \Delta t)^{k-1}]_j$$

Returning to our assumption that Δt is according to the queueing process small p(y=1) is approximately

$$p(y=1) \approx \frac{k\ \Delta t}{d}$$

and we obtain

(11) $K = \frac{k}{d}$

as the average potential number of patients which could be treated per period.

For an equitable refunding, one has to neutralize the influence of case mix, since the waiting time and the length of stay respectively correspond to the case types treated. Important for the construction of a system of measurement for comparing the relative complexity of different case mixes is the selection of the measure reference from which the difference will be measured. In this approach, as a measure of reference the average treatment pattern for all hospitals being considered in the comparison is taken (see Heinhold/Gaede 1968).

The case mix of hospital i may be expressed in terms of the relative number of patients in each patient class j. The number of cases treated in hospital i will be denoted by n_{ij}, then we get the case mix of hospital i by

$$(12) \quad p_{ij} = \frac{n_{ij}}{\sum_j n_{ij}} \qquad \text{for all } j .$$

Let d_{ijk} be the waiting time and the length of stay of the kth patient respectively in the patient class j in hospital i, then the average waiting time respectively length of stay for each patient class is

$$(13) \quad c_{ij} = \frac{\sum_k d_{ijk}}{n_{ij}} \qquad \text{for all } i,j, \; n_{ij} > 0.$$

We can evaluate the average waiting time and length of stay of hospital i respectively by

$$(14) \quad d_i = \sum_j p_{ij} \; c_{ij} .$$

The case mix of the region is determined by

$$(15) \quad p_{\cdot j} = \frac{\sum_i n_{ij}}{\sum_{i,j} n_{ij}} \qquad \text{for all } j .$$

The average waiting time and length of stay respectively of all cases of the class j for all hospitals are

$$(16) \quad c_{\cdot j} = \frac{\sum_i c_{ij} \, n_{ij}}{\sum_i n_{ij}} \qquad \text{for all } j .$$

We can standardize the average waiting time and the length of stay of hospital i respectively by

(17) $$r_i = \sum_j p_{\cdot j} \; c_{ij} \, ,$$

where $c_{ij} = c_{\cdot j}$, if $c_{ij} = 0$.

This is the average waiting time and length of stay respectively which would be experienced in hospital i if it treated a case mix given by the average case mix for all hospitals being considered in the comparison. This is a neutral adjustment which still allows performance comparisons since all hospitals in the set being compared are treated alike. According to (11) a hospital should be reimbursed related to

(18) $$K_s = \frac{k}{r} \; .$$

Following the condition that health care financing should be based to the outcome linked costs, the ready-to-serve costs should be reimbursed by a time oriented budget, as capacity costs are time related.

In table 5 we present an example of the application of our approach. For the individual hospitals the average waiting time and the length of stay respectively amounts to

$d_A = 9.50$ [days/case],

$d_B = 9.63$ [days/case],

$d_C = 11.71$ [days/case].

For example the ready-to-serve-operating (respect to the case mix treated) of the cardiac surgery of hospital C (28 beds) was

$$K = \frac{28}{11.71} = 2.39 \text{ [patients/day]}$$

or according to a year

$$K' = \frac{28 \times 365}{11.71} = 872.76 \text{ [patients/year]} \; .$$

A hospital must balance a high utilization with the probability of being fully occupied and having to refuse services, especially emergency cases. Whether the unit would have enough capacity depends on the quantity of health care demanded. The relation between supply and

Table 5: Number of cases and length of stay of 3 cardiac surgery units

hospital / category patients	A		B		C	
	number of cases	length of stay	number of cases	length of stay	number of cases	length of stay
Aorto-Coronary Bypass	250	11	200	13	220	14
Aortic-Valve-Replacement	175	9	190	7	40	7
Mitral-Valve-Replacement	160	8	120	8	60	8
Aortic-/Mitral-Valve-Replacement	100	9	50	10	20	7

demand yields to the supply level. Let e be the quantity demanded, then

$$S = \frac{k}{d \cdot e} - 1$$

determines the avarage not-occupied hospital capacity. To illustrate the formula, we consider again hospital C, assuming its average demand to be e = 2.1 cases per day, we get

$$S = \frac{28}{2.1 \cdot 11.71} - 1 = 0.14 = 14\ \% .$$

Whether this up-keep is an adequate capacity to cover the demanded health care, must be decided by those who are responsible for the safety margin of health care. In the Federal Republic of Germany this is the duty of the federal states.

Using the formula (18) we calculate the basis of negotiation for setting the refund for the hospital's C ready-to serve performance:

$$K_s = \frac{k}{r} = \frac{28}{10.17} = 2.75\ [\text{patients/day}]$$

or according to a year, we get

$$K_s' = \frac{28 \cdot 365}{10.17} = 1004.9\ [\text{patients/year}].$$

4 A decision oriented hospital management system

4.1 A general principle of decision oriented hospital management

Corresponding to the outcome oriented hospital reimbursement system we developed a decision oriented hospital management system. It can be viewed as a system of managerial accounting intended to reveal information about the true costs about treating various illnesses and about readiness to operate processes in hospitals. Predetermination of cost, measurement of efficiency, actual presentation of information to management health personnel are examples of the matters dealt with by the costing management system.

The general rule of the developed decision based hospital management tool is to structure both, the complex of hospital performances and the complex of hospital organization according to a strict tree. This is a directed graph containing one root node, no loops and no meshes in which every node is connected to every other node through a chain of arcs. Invoking a strict tree, one can set up a cost center hierarchy which is responsible based. This enables one to implement a hospital information system in which all outputs and their costs are directly traceable to that person, who is responsible for the corresponding decision. Because of this it is an instrument to motivate persons within the hospital organization to make decisions, that follow management goals and allow a better planning for the future.

4.2 Computer based hospital management

As we defined a patient oriented hospital outcome the decision-related costing requires a patient oriented tracing of data performance units. Therefore the environment is an integrated computerized communication application by which data of the areas of a hospital are accumulated and put into the costing system in the daily routine. The system prepares the data and serves all departments of the hospital covering medical patient data, administrative patient data, medical reports and administrative reports. The system is fully integrated. The main part of the system consists of individual patient data registered throughout the stay in hospital. Should the patient be admitted again at a later date, the ward has access to all important data about the patient from previous admissions. Registration itself is always directly related to the individual patients.

Some additional systems were developed which are combined with the centralized computer applications. The laboratory system determines scheduling and sequencing, generates operations planning and covers the communication between the laboratory and the clinical wards. The pharmacy system provides a list of medicine consumption. It also processes the large amounts of data associated with the stocking of medical supplies. Using the medical letter report generator the treating physician can write and send medical letters to the physicians performing the primary care. The personnel management system supplies the scheduling decision process.

The use of EDP in a hospital makes the data transmission easier, better and saves time but only if one develops new modes of information processing. The conventional information processing in hospitals is characterized by a parallelism in the medical area on one side and the administrative area on the other side. One should note of the strong connection between medical data and administrative data. Each medical performance of diagnostic and therapeutic triggers off an administrative performance, perhaps a statistical record or an account. That is why it cannot be reasonable to collect the medical data separately from administrative data. Therefore the essence of the developed hospital information system was to connect the medical sector with the administrative range. The condition is of course that all activity areas are connected by a communication network.

A main part of the internal hospital communication is the informationflow from the wards to the functional areas and back. Performances are demanded by the wards from the functional departments and the results must get back to the wards. Conventional clinical information organization is characterized by a high defect data transmission. Through an EDP-supported communication system errors of communication can be reduced significantly.

The nucleus of the system is the decision related costing. Conciseness is essential to all reports. The periodical routine cost reports are kept to minimum. The hospital information system can however produce special reports. The supervisor of each cost center can ask for case printouts and statistical summaries concerning cost per patient, diagnoses groups, treating phycisians, treating wards, etc. or combination of criteria.

Literature:

Davis, C.K.: The United States Experiences with DRGs, Its Impact on Cost and Quality, Paper presented at the 15th European Health Policy Forum-WHO Meeting, Brussels October 1987.

Fetter, R.B., Shin, Y., Freeman, J.L., Averill, R.F., and Thompson, J.D.: Case Mix Definition by Diagnosis Related Groups, in: Medical Care (Supp) 18, 1980, pp. 1-53.

Fetter, R.B.: A Product Approach to Productivity Improvement in Health Care, Paper presented at the International Economics of Health Care Conference, Paris March 1983.

Fetter, R.B., and Freeman, J.L.: Hospital Management by Diagnosis Related Groups, United States and European Experience, in: van Eimeren, R., Engelbrecht, R., and Flagle, Ch. (eds.): System Science in Health Care, Berlin/Heidelberg/New York/Tokyo 1984, pp. 672-674.

Heinhold, J., and Gaede, K.-W.: Ingenieur-Statistik, München/Wien 1968.

Krelle, W., and Künzi, H.P.: Nichtlineare Programmierung, Berlin/Heidelberg/New York 1975.

Lerner, M.: Conceptualization of Health and Social Well-being, in: Berg, R. (ed.): Health Status Indexes, Hospitals Research and Educational Trust, Chicago 1973, pp. 1-6.

Ohmichi, H., and Miyake, S.: A Diagnosis Related Cost Analysis in Japanese Hospital Care, in: van Eimeren, R., Engelbrecht, R., and Flagle, Ch. (eds.): System Science in Health Care, Berlin/Heidelberg/New York/Tokyo 1984, pp. 675-678.

Rodrigues, J.-M.: Resource Allocation Based on DRGs, Paper presented at the 15th European Health Policy Forum-WHO Meeting, Brussels October 1987.

Sanderson, H.F.: Adapting Diagnosis Related Groups for Use in England and Wales, in: van Eimeren, R., Engelbrecht, R., and Flagle, Ch. (eds.): System Science in Health Care, Berlin/Heidelberg/New York/Tokyo 1984, pp. 679-682.

Special Problems of Resource Planning in Hospitals

Günter Fandel

1 Locational planning in hospitals

1.1 The importance of locational planning in the hospital

Hospitals are service establishments, but from the technical and economic point of view - as far as their organization is concerned - they display many similarities with the production process of industrial firms. The technical, medical and management problems which have to be mastered by them are becoming more and more complex and so one is obliged to apply modern planning and decision-making methods to hospitals (Gierl 1979, Kreß/Welge 1979). The trend in recent years has been to build bigger hospitals in order to be able roughly to amortize the high costs of the necessary medical-technical equipment by means of an optimum rate of capacity utilization. This leads to more stratified internal structures and at the same time makes the operational flow more complicated. The more specialist departments a hospital has means that not only is it more difficult to develop an optimum utilization rate for each of the units radiology, laboratory, and operating area but also the interrelations of these units with one another become more complicated. For this reason it will usually not be sufficient to arrange the organization units or the functional areas along the lines of traditional hospitals. The use of computer-based decision models is now absolutely necessary.

Accurate location distribution in hospitals is one of the most important conditions for an economical production of services, whereby internal locational planning refers to the spatial arrangement of the diagnostic, therapeutic, and nursing service areas and function groups - also called organization units. Using the intensity of communication existing between each of the organization units the best possible lay-out within the hospital must be found. In spite of all the necessary economic considerations the most important rule for the internal operational flow in a hospital is and remains the humanity and efficiency of the medical arrangements. Locational planning will be directly influenced or limited by external data as well as by the hospital's own internal determinants and regulations. External considerations, for example, give rise to the number of wards, consulting rooms and operating rooms, building regulations must be adhered to, the size of the laboratory block and the radiology department must be determined, a decision must be made regarding internal or external maintenance and waste disposal, and it has to be decided whether to have several decentralized facilities for the preparation of beds or a single centralized facility. The run-through times of the various functional groups, movements of patients between the organization units, and the division of the hospital complex into nursing block, housekeeping area, treatment and administration areas can all be counted among the hospital's internal determinants.Fixed and variable organization units can be found within these areas. The hospital's internal regulations are concerned with hygiene, the isolating of particular wards, the division of various areas of activity, the technically required proximity of certain units to one another and the laying down of fixed locations. With these aspects and restrictions in mind it can be seen that basically the same solution methods used in the planning of internal locations in an industrial firm can be applied to locational planning in a hospital. These will be referred to in the following section and then evaluated as to their use in hospitals. Computer-based heuristic procedures are in the foreground.

1.2 Solution methods for internal locational planning

The location models described in the literature can be divided up according to very different criteria (Domschke 1975, Burkard 1975). The basic difference as regards each applied solution method is between analytical and heuristic procedures. Analytical procedures are based on mathematical calculations and permit an exat solution of the problem. They break down very quickly, however, when it comes to practical problems because the time required to solve the problem is too long. Because of this certain approximation procedures - heuristic procedures - are used which, although they do not necessarily lead to an optimum solution, do in fact deliver satisfactory sub-optimum solutions within an acceptable amount of computing time. This type of heuristic procedure can be divided into various classes, opening or construction procedures, exchanging and iterative procedures, as well as combinations of these (e.g. Niedereichholz 1975, Hardeck/Nestler 1974). Whether a solution is optimal or not is often orientated to the minimizing of transport costs or travelling times between the locations.

The characteristic feature of constructive procedures lies in the best possible grouping of the other service areas, one after the other, around a given organization unit (Hardeck/Schmid 1974). In this way plausible starting solutions can be determined. The opening procedures can be differentiated as to whether they have been developed for areas of equal size or of different sizes.

The circulation method (Kiehne 1969), on the basis of the SAT program, works with grid areas of the same size. The solution's construction is based in the main on local contacts, whereby a difference is made between occupied core fields, boundary fields, and free fields. This leads to an extensively occupied relation matrix; the attempt is made to reduce this to a minimum by means of a more compact method of notation. Where the density of occupation of the contact matrix is decreasing and the size of the problem increasing the circulation method is most suitable for finding good solutions, and the increase in time spent computing is relatively low. At the same time difficulties exist where the form of the ground-plan of the rooms is given because the external outline of the connected core of function groups cannot be determined from the start. In addition, fixed organization units are not taken into account.

In contrast to the circulation method the CORELAP procedure (Niedereichholz 1975) combined with the HEROS program does make allowance for the inclusion of areas of unequal size, additional space conditions, and, in its extension, the distribution of the organization units over multi-storied buildings. It consists of an assignment algorithm which, for example, may correspond to the circulation method on the basis of the SAT program, and a segmentation algorithm whereby locational placing begins with the organization unit which displays the most relations with the other organization units. The computing time necessary for this procedure is dependent upon the number of organization units which have to be taken into account. While it is true that data input is not as simple as with SAT, a multi-storied building or a long form can be used here as a basis for considerations as to the choice of location within a firm, and chosen units can be distributed over predetermined locations.

The improvement procedures begin with an arbitrary starting solution.

If this is poor, an attempt is made to bring about an improvement in the objective value by exchanging the locations of two operation units. Within this class of exchanging or iterative procedures there are those too which work with location areas of equal or unequal sizes.

The deterministic exchanging procedure CRAFT (Buffa/Armour/Vollmann 1964) which has often been used as a basis for practical locational problems, and which can be recommended because of its favourable computing time, makes allowance for areas of different sizes and fixed points. On the other hand the exchange of areas is limited. Only equally large or adjoining areas are exchanged in a so-called triple area exchange.The distances between the centers of the various organization units are measured in a right-angled grid network. The final solution is heavily dependent upon the initial arrangement which cannot be removed even with the choice of several alternative starting layouts. A further disadvantage lies in the considerable alteration of the outline of the individual organization units. The LAY program (Hardeck/Schmid 1974), based on the method of the Monte Carlo simulation, works with operating units of equally large size. This can become a disadvantage because of a possible subsequent change in the result for the worse when at the end of the program run-through the standard surfaces have to be replaced by the original sizes of the operating areas. The procedure has, however, several advantages. On the one hand constraints can be brought in in the way of fixed organization units, technically determined proximity of service areas, and rough sizes of these units. On the other hand the possibility exists of getting completely different arrangements within the locational solution by employing different starting random numbers. The quality of the solution depends, as with every simulation procedure, on the amount of computing time necessary for the procedure. The CONUVER program (Baur 1972) is basically a procedure combined from SAT and CRAFT and thus is a combination of a circulation and exchange procedure. While it is true that it delivers good results quickly it must also be said that it contains the disadvantages of both these procedures. Because it makes allowance neither for a long form building nor for fixed points, and CRAFT partially breaks through the ground plan form aimed for this procedure is not a vital extension for the reasons mentioned. Basically it is a combination of two partial optimization procedures. Sauter (1972) and Minten (1972) have developed approximately similar procedures. They, however, employ Vogel's approximation principle for the choice of the organization units which run around the layout core and which are to be placed in such a way as to result in a reduction of the amount spent on transport.

1.3 The application of locational planning to a hospital

1.3.1 General framework

Using the treatment area as an example, because it is the source of the largest amount of costs within the hospital, some of the conditions within the hospital which limit locational planning will be discussed. The types of condition specifically related to hospitals will normally be laid down by special committees consisting of experts and representatives of the hospital staff. As regards the treatment area itself it is assumed that it will be on one level, corresponding to a single-story construction and will be divided into the sub-areas outpatients, radiology, laboratory, sterilization, obstetrics, casualty, and operating theatres.

The outpatients department will normally be placed on the periphery of the treatment area because it is very heavily frequented by visitors from outside. The laboratories and the radiology stations belong in its immediate neighbourhood. These departments must at the same time be just as easily accessible from the operating area. The operating theatres, subdivided into sterile and non-sterile areas, are usually laid down as the fixed organization units in locational distribution. The sterile area has to be centrally placed to protect it from contact from outside. The non-sterile area on the other hand has to be placed at the edge of the treatment area, firstly so that it can be closely linked to the casualty unit, which has perforce to be on the periphery, and secondly in order to separate it from the sterile area. It is practical for the obstetric unit to be directly next to the sterile operating theatres so that the patients can be operated immediately if complications arise. The rooms for changing beds, preparation and waking up must also be directly attached to the operating theatres. The changing-rooms and showers for the staff and the transfer rooms for the operating block have to be taken into account as fixed boundary fields. Similar considerations apply to the intensive care unit. Again, all areas have to have access to the sterilization facilities. In addition, the treatment area has to be so placed within the overall hospital complex that the transport of patients from the nursing block is technically possible and does not cause mental stress. A further problem is the arrangement of the variable organization units such as, for example, lifts for supplies and waste disposal, recreation rooms for staff, storerooms etc.

This brief outline of only a few essential assignment conditions shows just how complicated locational planning in hospital is. In the following section the ability of the abovementioned heuristic procedures to deliver practical solutions will be discussed.

1.3.2 The practicability of a procedure

When planning for a single-story construction only horizontal area arrangements need to be considered; locational planning for a high-rise building, on the other hand, requires a method which can be used for multi-story assignment problems. Common to both types of building is that set areas, fixed organization units, and other boundary conditions specific to hospitals have to be taken into consideration. The ability of a procedure depends now essentially on whether it observes sufficiently such boundary conditions. Those procedures which fail to do this are less practical and will be excluded from further considerations.

The SAT program does not observe place and area conditions and cannot keep safely to a set basic ground form. This is, however, essential for the subdivision of the available areas into the individual function groups. The CRAFT procedure allows the setting of points for the fixed organization units but on the other hand often results in too great an outline alteration for those service stations which have to be positioned In addition, none of the technically necessary proximities so often encountered in the medicial areas of a hospital are taken into consideration. The CONUVER program, a combination of both the above, contains the same disadvantages so that none of the three methods is of use in practical locational planning in a hospital.

In contrast the LAY program, which uses approximate area programming, can place the outpatients department on the periphery of the treatment area and avoids a collision of the organization units of the inpatient areas with the hospital's management areas. Furthermore a multitude of solutions can be achieved using this procedure which show approximately the same objective of minimal transport costs or travelling times. The LAY program offers in this way a considerable amount of flexibility concerning spatial assignment, which is of advantage in the various aspects of economic operation planning. There is, however, the disadvantage that it is not possible to fix the ground-plan of the building. This means that the architect, when planning the ground plan, has to work from a layout which has been declared to be sufficiently optimal. A further disadvantage is that LAY only applies to single-story problems.

These difficulties can be overcome by using the HEROS program in its extended form. It is the only one which can assign the medical organization units over several stories. Because areas of unequal size can be set for the service groups, the desired layout can be kept to and locational regulations can be taken into account, such as, for example, that the radiology and laboratory areas should be easily accessible from the outpatients as well as from the operating block, the HEROS program seems therefore to be the one best suited to produce an optimum hospital layout. The problem of the more difficult data input can be solved by at first using SAT and HEROS simultaneously. Once a general view of possible area distributions has thus been achieved the planner can then feed in further hospital internal boundary conditions and carry on working with HEROS alone.

All types of locational planning for hospitals are seriously hampered by the fact that there is as yet hardly any processed planning data and that the readiness of hospital staff to appreciate the need to collect data is still not in any way pronounced, so that Gierl (1976) felt bound to say that in practice decisions about arranging rooms and appliances in hospitals are the result of the dynamics between architects, doctors and builders. The expositions made in this first section should help to put this group decision process onto a rational basis from the point of view of business planning.

2 Personnel planning in hospitals

2.1 The necessity for and aims of personnel planning

In the first six months of 1980 the sickness insurance organizations in Germany had to pay hospitals 12.2 thousand million DM, whereby the personnel costs alone made up 75% of the total. Hospital staff is expensive and in short supply. Hospitals in the USA decided temporarily to offer $200 to anyone who could find a nurse and persuade her to take a job in the hospital. With this in mind staff planning for a hospital has to decide how many staff will be employed with varying qualifications, in which wards and at which times (Eichhorn 1975, Maas 1977). The objective is to reduce staff costs.

The German literature on this subject contains as yet only a few approaches towards the planning and organization of staff employment in hospitals because economic considerations for hospitals came into play quite late. Since the middle of the 1970s things have changed somewhat: Kim and Meyer (1979) introduced an approach to determining anaesthetic staff requirements, Walter (1979) dealt with scheduling problems for anaesthetists, and Kreß and Welge (1979) demonstrated by means of an example methods of staff planning in the nursing areas of a hospital. In comparison with this, English language articles on the treatment of staffing problems date from the early 1950s; these approaches were, however, mostly macroeconomic in content and concerned themselves basically with questions of supply. Microeconomic approaches in English to staff planning which have as their theme the assigning of hospital staff to tasks or positions on a quantitative, qualitative, temporal and local basis have been published in a concentrated way only since the early 1970s.

The following expositions will provide a short summary of the situation of hospital staff planning, which has its own particular problems compared with staff planning in industrial firms. A hospital is a service establishment with extreme demand fluctuations. While it is true that regularly occurring peaks in demand can be forecast, e.g. as a result of accidents in rush-hours, it will hardly be possible to estimate the demand per time unit with approximately equal use of capacity. In addition, staff allocation in hospitals creates difficulties even when the number of operations is fixed because until now time studies about the performance of doctors' services are hardly available to be analysed and used as generalizations. Furthermore, large reserves of staff are unavoidable because the personnel stock must be so calculated as to guarantee the care of patients even at times of peak demand because of the existing duty to provide care. For rough planning of staffing requirements caused in this way Yett, Drabek, Intriligator and Kimbell (1972) developed a macro- and microeconometric approach to health service staffing policies. Within this framework the management approaches which will be presented here have to supply the fine planning in the hospital service, which can be related to the most varied departments.

2.2 A survey of staff planning models for hospitals in the literature

2.2.1 Determining the optimal supply of doctors for an outpatients department (Schneider/Kilpatrick 1975)

Schneider and Kilpatrick's approach (1975) describes a concept for a solution to the simultaneous treatment of the problems of manpower requirements and manpower use of doctors in an outpatients department. It can be formulated either as a cost model or as a supply model, depending on where the emphasis lies in the planning. The aim of the input-orientated cost variant, given fixed rates of charges for medical treatment and a set number of patients to be treated, is to organize the numbers of staff to be employed and the allocation of equipment for an outpatients department as cheaply as possible, whereby the services to be carried out by the staff have to meet the demand from the patients. The output-orientated supply variant on the other hand aims at maximizing the number of patients who can be treated, with given rates of contribution and an existing supply of medical specialists, whereby at the same time an optimal organizational structure results, in the sense that the solution also provides the optimal assignment of the available staff to the performance of services in combination with the best provision of operating resources for this purpose. Optimizing takes place in both cases with the help of mixed-integer programming. In the simplest case the performance process is represented by the relations which exist between the demand vector of the patients for medical services and the resource vector of the medical staff. Medical treatments can be given by a single person or by teams consisting of doctors, medical assistants and nurses. Medical assistans and nurses belong to the so-called supporting staff; when an individual is active, or a group of supporting staff as a team, they all work under the indirect supervision of a doctor who has ultimate responsibility for the treatment of the patients. The principle of delegating tasks to supporting staff aims on the one hand at the most economical utilization of higher-qualified staff as possible, because of the costs involved. On the other hand the doctors are thus free from routine tasks, but must spend some of their working-hours on supervisory tasks, in particular as direct or indirect supervision of individual staff or teams existing of supporting staff. The extent depends on the services carried out and the qualifications of the respective supporting staff and is registered in the model by means of appropriate constants which at the same time have to take legal regulations and the maintenance of the quality of the treatment into account. Total staff costs, which are to be minimized in the first variant, thus consist of the direct staff working and supervising costs plus those portions of salaries which have no corresponding performance output. When the operation resource costs and the support costs are added the total costs of the outpatients are found, from which income from charges for medical services has to be subtracted. If it proves to be economically significant not to provide certain specialist services in the outpatients the model formulation allows for the provision of these medical services from outside.

In the application examples of the model three medical departments are observed, giving 200 restrictions and 360 variables, so the authors tackle the solution with the help of a computer-based branch-and-bound algorithm. The approach is suitable for the new installation of an outpatients department as well as for the improvement of an existing treatment system of this type. In conclusion several of the most important results will be referred to briefly. In the case in question the approach led to a reduction of around 24% in the total costs; the largest staff savings consisted of 40% by the doctors through the possibilities of their substitution by supporting staff. Medical assistants and nurses can be used increasingly in paediatric departments because many of the routine postnatal and precautionary examinations of healthy children can be delegated to this type of personnel. Altogether, every medical department can show considerable reductions in the number of doctors needed by using supporting staff. Where the number of patients requiring treatment is uncertain part-time staff can be used to provide services. Furthermore, the model can be used as a decision aid for a series of further aspects, e.g. to estimate the effects of the closure of a medical department, to evaluate the use of doctors in obstetrics, gynaecology and paediatrics, to judge the possibilities of using student nurses where there is a temporary scarcity of paediatricians.

2.2.2 Optimal planning of nurse schedules in a hospital (Warner/Prawda 1972)

Warner and Prawda's mixed-integer quadratic programming model (1972) is aimed at the optimal planning of nurse schedules in the nursing wards of a hospital. This staff planning problem consists of a series of part-problems for which an optimal solution is sought. With a given demand for the provision of treatment, which can be expressed by a corresponding matrix of the call for nursing services, the numbers of nursing staff of various professional grades will be determined as well as their distribution over the various hospital wards and working shifts. Four grades of nursing qualifications are brought into action: graduate nurses, registered nurses, nursing aids and ward secretaries. The shifts are divided as usual into day, evening and night shifts. Restrictions as to capacity and minimum requirements of quantitative and qualitative types must be taken into account as regards the nursing staff; minimum requirements as to quantity are especially important in order to be able to keep to the professional and often legally standards of medical and nursing treatment. The assignment problem requires in this framework a complete integer distribution of the nurses. Limited possibilities for substitution among the different categories of nurses are permitted and can be taken correspondingly into account. The aim of the program is to minimize staff scarcity costs caused by a deficit in the utilization of nursing staff set against the call for nursing treatment. In order to quantify these costs it is assumed that the deficiency costs for each nursing grade and each ward and shift show a continuous monotonous decline with a decreasing deficiency until the value 0 is reached with the satisfaction of all demand. In the simplest case this type of cost behaviour pattern can be specified by minimizing the quadratic deviation between demand and supply of treatment expressed in numbers of nurses of each grade, shift and ward for the particular planning period. This procedure has, however, the disadvantage that it does not take into consideration the relative differences in personnel deficiency costs according to nursing grade, ward, and shift. The authors attempt to correct this by a further step bringing in differentiating cost coefficients. The inclusion of the limited substitution between various grades of nurse of the same ward and shift takes place on the basis of conversion rates. The cost weighting and the effect of substitution can be brought in directly in an extended objective function. Difficulties regarding the practical solubility of this model arise because the number of variables and constraints quickly increases dependent upon the number of wards, shifts, and categories of nurses. In a planning period of four days - i.e. 12 shifts - 10 wards, and 4 nursing grades, 2400 variables and 1444 constraints are to be found, which is why the authors propose a division of the initial problem into mixed-integer, quadratic subproblems.

This approach was applied to 6 wards of a general hospital in New Orleans/Louisiana, the 6 wards containig about half of the total of 600 beds in the hospital. The demand for nurses' services in various wards, shifts and grades could be forecasted with 5 - 10% deviation from real demand in the first days of the planning period of two weeks. Thereafter deviations of 20 - 30% occurred. As a result it was found to be more significant to set out a schedule for nursing staff employment twice weekly for a period of 4 and 3 days respectively. The attempt was made to obtain substitution rates and cost coefficients by consulting the administrators and nursing departments. Deviations between the solution values and the actual personnel stock were subjected subsequently to a sensitivity analysis to estimate their effects, whereby, as expected, the more possibilities for substitution allowed the less important was the deficit. By using the model costs under observation in the hospital were be able to be reduced by almost 70%.

The successful employment of this model in other cases is principally dependent upon the ability in each individual case to derive acceptable and plausible values for the model's subjective parameters. Extensions by way of including doctors in the approach go without saying, but can be problematical in that a scarcity of doctors, as far as decisions are concerned, will more than likely not be able to be covered simply and solely by means of short-staffing costs. The advantage of the approach lies above all in that it can be applied to many wards in a hospital. The short-staffing costs for nursing staff are probably difficult to assess in certain circumstances, but can be more readily estimated when staff shortages can be made good by bringing in staff from outside where the costs of their employment are known from the labour market. Where these possibilities for setting off do not exist the esitmate of costs will perhaps have to be regarded as insufficient or too one-sided. There is the further difficulty of formulating and defining the tasks which the individual grades of nursing staff will have to carry out. If the tasks are too narrowly formulated, as a result of job description, possible substitutions are prevented from the start; in the opposite case the criteria for qualification become weak.

2.2.3 Optimal distribution of "standby nurses" from a pool (Trivedi/Warner 1976)

Trivedi and Warner's analytical model of integer programming (1976) has as its aim the optimal distribution of standby nurses from a pool to the different wards according to the actual demand - alongside the nurses assigned to the various wards of a general hospital on a permanent basis and who meet the basic demand for nursing services - so that deviations in peak demand can be met, the necessary personnel stock is not too large, and that nurse employment remains to a certain extent flexible. Especially, answers have to be found to three questions:

- how can the intensity of demand for the employment of an extra nurse in a ward be measured?

- how can this quantity be forecasted for the next 8 hours, in other words for the next shift?

- what technique can help to distribute the standby nurses to the wards so that the forecasted demand is met?

In order to assess the intensity of demand in the different wards regarding the employment of an extra nurse it was assumed that the chief nurse in each ward has enough expert knowledge and experience to guess the demand for additional staff depending on different patient-loads. Measurement of demand was supported by questionnaires. Parallel to this sort of subjective guesswork there were for every ward objective demand influence variables which could be recorded and registered and brought into the considerations. They are concerned with the available nursing-hours in the different grades and the differences in patient-yield as to new admissions, transfers, or postoperative care. From this information an index of intensity of demand was gathered which corresponded to the numerical value entered by the chief nurse on a given scale in the questionnaire.

In order to supply a forecast of demand intensity for each ward at the beginning of each shift using this data a multivariate regressions model was used in which the intensity indices ascertained from the chief nurse were entered as dependent variables. The indicators estimated by the chief nurses can be interpreted as marginal growth rates of nursing staff of different training levels for their wards and shifts. In addition the recorded influence quantities represent the independent variables in the regressions model. Using this as a basis regression equations for each ward and for every grade of nurse had to be worked out which according to their formal structure were assumed to be strict convex decreasing functions, in which the intensity index of demand for an additional unit of a nursing grade is dependent on the available nursing hours of this grade and the respective ward. When all demand intensities for all qualification grades spread over all the wards are added up the total demand index for a shift is arrived at. This has to be minimized by the optimal nurse distribution whereby all the wards in the hospital have to be treated roughly equally so that no extreme solutions for some wards occur.

The division of staff into those nurses who are permanently assigned to a ward and those who belong to the pool as standbys means that the permanent staff to deal with the normal amount of work is fixed from the beginning and that the proper problem consists of making an optimal division of the pool at the commencement of each shift. It has to be borne in mind that because nurses of each qualification level can be substituted for one another each staff allocation to a qualification level not only reduces its demand index but that at the same time the intensity indices of the other qualification levels of the same shift and ward are affected which do not experience any staff alterations. In addition to this the formulation of the model and its application make the following requirements on the solution algorithm appear relevant: it has to be applicable to non-linear monotonous functions of the intensity indices, deliver only integer solution values, and be also able to take account of non-linear restrictions. This is why a modified general branch-and-bound procedure is recommended for solution finding. In the nodes of the branching-tree stand possible starting distributions for pool staff which can then be improved in the run of the algorithm. The question of the sequence in which the qualification levels of pool nurses are assigned to which wards is for the moment left open. At every node a ward is chosen for an allocation which has the largest total demand index of all the wards. This ward is then given a nurse of the level of training for which the demand is most intense. The principle of equal distribution according to intensity of demand is observed by corresponding variance constraints for each ward and qualification.

Trivedi and Warner's approach was used for a period of four weeks in five wards of a hospital and supplied the hospital administration with results which were satisfactory and quickly available. One of the difficulties lies in the subjective assessments of the demand intensity through the chief nurses of the wards. These could possibly be objectified by means of time studies. A further disadvantageous aspect of the problem formulation up to now is that differences from ward to ward in pool nurses' qualification requirements are not taken into account, but it is implicitly assumed that all nursing qualifications can be substituted over all the wards. This can, however, easily be accounted for by means of a corresponding modification of the decision variables and by observance of limited substitution possibilities only.

2.2.4 Nurse scheduling from the point of view of costs (Miller/Pierskalla/Rath 1976)

Miller, Pierskalla and Rath use integer linear programming in order to set up, with the help of their approach, staffing schedules for nurses which have to satisfy a series of criteria. The individual refusal costs, caused by nurses being allowed, within limits, to refuse schedules which are not convenient, go into the objective function alongside the costs caused by the staff of nurses. These total costs have to be minimized, i.e. optimal nursing schedules have to be determined which result in a minimum of refusals with a personnel stock which is as small as possible. The incorporation of the subjective refusal costs into the model distinguishes this approach basically from those problem formulations discussed up to now. The solutions are schedules with sequences of working days and days off for all the nurses in a particular ward or department with a given shift. The planning horizon is from two to eight weeks. In addition constraints have to be taken into account which are to be observed from the point of view of the employer and the employees. These constraints can be divided according to their quality into two groups: in binding and non-binding restrictions. Binding restrictions must be adhered to and define the set of the feasible solution. Non-binding conditions can be violated but then result in costs which appear in the objective function. The hospital itself can often decide which constraints are binding or non-binding from the employer's and the employee's point of view. Binding restrictions include the personal standards of the nurses, qualifications, and regulations on working hours. Non-binding constraints result mostly from planning aspects. For example, the maximum or minimum length of a period of consecutive working days or days off, the number of series of working days and days off, the number of weekends off, and the condition that when possible no weekends are contained in the plans divided into a working day and a day off. Violations of these conditions make up those planning costs described as nurses refusal costs. These costs, weighted together with the personnel stock costs, build the objective function. The authors suggest that the normalized weights between zero and one be chosen with the assistance of a trial-and-error procedure so that both weighted cost components are approximately equal. Optimal rosters are then created by means of a solution algorithm based on the principle of iterative plan improvements. For this purpose feasible nurse schedules are used as starting solutions and corrected successively in such a way that the binding restrictions are fulfilled and the refusal costs, or the total costs, are reduced.

Initial experiences with this suggested solution concept for the derivation of optimal nurse schedules were gained through its intensive application to a day shift in a ward of a hospital with 800 beds. The hospital had collected previous preferences of individual nurses for different rosters and these together with the values for the minimum and the desired staff were entered into the algorithm as starting data. The rosters thus gained were then compared with past rosters. The comparison showed that the rosters created with the help of the algorithm were easily able to meet the required job demand. In 50% of the cases the target amount and the actual amount were identical and in 90% of the cases the deviations were so minimal that they could safely be ignored. A control of the rosters as to staff dissatisfaction or rather the refusal costs implied by this led to the findings that the rosters could hardly be improved. In 44% of the cases the roster with the minimum costs was found and in 88% of the cases the rosters were among the top 10%. The rosters developed by the algorithm, however, displayed more continuous periods of 2 - 3 days off one after the other than the rosters put together formerly by the hospital administration, and the number of split weekends was considerably reduced.

The model can be extended so as to include the employment of part-time staff and the possibility of rotating shifts. A weak point, however, are the subjective refusal costs of the nurses with unsatisfactory schedules. This type of emotional component can have a disarranging effect on the quantification of costs. On the other hand the authors contend that the model is so realistic that it can cope with every type of roster pattern and staff attendance conditions and that it can be used for many different hospitals with varying policies.

2.2.5 The matrix method of duty scheduling for nurses (Aft/Watt/Thomason 1975)

With the help of the heuristic procedure of the matrix method Aft, Watt and Thomason (1975) attempt to organize duty rosters for nurses in hospital wards satisfactorily so that in the course of time periods of consecutive days off for the staff are distributed as equally as possible over the days of the week. This type of distribution is of particular interest for hospital departments and medical staff faced with weekend duties. These have to be parcelled out among the staff along with the normal shifts on a rotatory basis in such a way as to be regarded by the employees as fair. This cannot be achieved on a short-term planning basis; long-term duty roster rotations hold out more promise of success. Even if it is true that fewer staff are required at weekends and that many part-time workers prefer weekend work staff in those wards which require daily duty cannot have each weekend off. Furthermore the terms of collective agreements have to be observed as well as the individual wishes of staff regarding shifts and hours of work contingent upon their personal circumstances.

The matrix method starts with the total demand for a grade of staff distributed over the different working-days of the week and expressed in man-days and contrasts this with the staff in the same accounting units. Manpower requirements for the carrying out of tasks and functions can be met by different types of the same category of personnel. Full-time staff, senior staff, and part-time staff may be used. Only full-time staff are included in the rotating schedules because it is assumed that an optimal planning of the days off for senior staff and for part-time staff already exists; for the former by reason of their five-day week and for the latter because they have chosen their own working days, otherwise they can be treted in the same way as full-time staff. In addition, the number of full-time staff who do not wish to take part in the rotating schedules but prefer fixed working-days can be determined for certain working-days in the week. These can then be subtracted from the total number off full-time staff to give the number of full-time staff for whom rotating schedules have to be prepared. In general it is accepted that the maximum number of consecutive working-days for those staff whose duty rotas are created in longer rotation cycles by means of the matrix method will not exceed seven and that the periods of days off will be two or three days which will lead to an average five day week. In order to achieve a fair distribution of days off over the different days of the week it is appropriate to make the length of the cycle of rotating schedules as long in weeks as there are full-time staff taking part in the rotation; the cycle therefore has one week per rotating full-time worker. The cycle must always be planned well ahead of time in order to give staff sufficient time to allow for their own plans. Starting with the first employee the corresponding blocks of 2 or 3 days off are rotated over the days of the week and this pattern is repeated successively for the following off-duty employees so that their off-duty blocks begin on the same day or one day later and so that manpower requirements for each working day are covered. In this way each employee is treated fairly over the period of the cycle, i.e. each receives the same number of weekends off. An arrangement which is fair in the long-term is benefitted even more when the sequence of employees is changed from cycle to cycle, so that the first employee in the first cycle is placed at the back of the queue of rotating employees in the next cycle.

The matrix method supplies very useful solutions for rotating schedules in continuously occupied wards and balances employee interests satisfactorily over the period of time. A further advantage lies in the simple planning procedure with employee participation as to whether they wish to take part in the rotation or whether they wish to have any particular day off. The flexibility necessary for increased manpower requirements or emergencies is achieved with the assumption that all employees within a grade under observation can be substituted for one another and that enough qualified staff are available.

A disadvantage of the method is that it can only be used for one type of employee, which means that each type of employee must be planned for separately. Combinations of employee groups with different qualifications and limited substitution possibilities cannot be planned. Furthermore additional days off, for holidays, sickness or further training, cannot be taken into account. The approach can only be used for one shift per day, so that distortions in manpower utilization caused by disadvantageous shifts remain outside the discussion. The method could be extended, indeed, to include these situations. Substitution between different types of employee can be brought into account when working out the planning data in that the difference between available and required employees is corrected through the utilization of other types of employee. The other disadvantages can be eliminated by using a similar computer program from Morrish and O'Connor (1972).

2.2.6 Approaches based on queueing theory

In developing manpower planning models for hospitals a number of authors has fallen back on findings based on queueing theory. The question here is mostly how the capacity utilization of a medical services centre or hospital department should be when there is a conflict with the reasonable waiting times of the patients. Further aspects can be the average length of a queue measured in the number of patients in the line and the amount of time they spend in the system. In this context it is assumed that the arrival times of the patients are Poisson distributed and the treatment times exponentially distributed. Often only one services centre is considered with one or several service stations. In the event that the servicing system of the hospital under observation has several service centres joined to one another via the process of the output of medical services, the migratory movements of the patients between these centres are described by matrices of transition probabilities. In order to arrive at the total manpower demand in this type of service system, information is needed about the number, the type, and the sequence of the required performances, the length of the treatment and nursing times and the efficiency of the equipment and working areas. The number and type of hospital services called for can be estimated using past experience values. Controlling or rather smoothing out manpower requirements by means of hospital admission policies is limited because now and then the treatment of emergency patients has to be included. Staff loads in the different wards thus prove to display great variations in the course of time.

The problem of how many operating teams, nurses and beds should be available in an intensive care unit so that a manpower or bed scarcity does not cause too many emergency cases to be turned away or make the queue too long is handled by Meyer, Hansen and Klausmann (1975) with the help of an approach based on queueing theory. For emergency patients the probability of having to join a queue on arrival is minimized. At the same time, however, care must be taken that manpower costs in this area are not unreasonably high. A favourable way of solving this conflict might be to take a nurse at short notice from the pool when an emergency case comes in. Schmidt (1980) developed another approach for the surgical ward of a hospital and differentiated between admission and occupancy policies for urgent and non-urgent cases. Fandel and Schmidt's contribution to this book gives a comprehensive account of this from an algorithmic and application point of view. Kim and Meyer (1979) deduce the risk to patients in the event that not enough anaesthetists are available in an operating theatre by using the queueing theory. Kao (1974) describes the stochastic run-through of heart patients in a hospital on the basis of semi-Markov processes. The required amount of manpower can be gathered from the amount of time the patients spend in the service centres. Hegemann (1986) used the queueing theory to design an optimal capacity and running off plan for the diagnostic area of a hospital. This is the first time that an approach of this sort with a service system with more than one service centre has been introduced where at the same time findings exist concerning the exponential distribution of the types of examination in the diagnostic stations. Fandel and Hegemann's article in this book gives an application orientated version of this analysis.

3 Inventory problems (of easily perishable goods) in hospitals

3.1 Some general aspects

Inventory problems with easily perishable goods are found in two areas in hospitals: the storage of blood plasma and radio-isotopes. Hospitals store plasma for the different blood groups in blood banks. The plasma usually has a limited shelf-life of about 35 days. A certain amount of plasma for each blood group has to be available for emergencies. This leads to the hospital and the doctors taking exaggerated precautions concerning the storage and standards of blood plasma. Consequently there is high wastage of blood plasma caused by the expiry of the time-limit for use. Different types of radio-isotopes are used in hospitals for diagnostic purposes. These radioactive substances are delivered in chemical solutions for medical use. The perishableness is therefore twofold. On the one hand the chemical solution, like blood plasma, has only a limited shelf-life, about 14 days in the case of a solution with the radio-isotope Jod-131. On the other hand radio-isotopes are subject to radioactive disintegration which is vital for its use; the half-life of Jod-131 is 8.04 days. These laws mean that there is a permanent shrinkage of stock. The circumstances described here give a rise to an examination of the inventory systems in use and their optimal organization.

Such inventory systems display different characteristic features. The goods which are to be stored have to be divided into groups for which demand varies exceedingly. In the case of the blood bank it is the plasmas of the various blood groups and in the other case the different radio-isotopes. The demand for the goods is stochastic. It cannot therefore be fixed with certainty but can only be described by probability distributions. Where Jod-131 is concerned, for example, the empirical distributions of the daily demand can be approximated by means of normal distributions (Gierl/Schläger 1979). Where demand is stochastic deficiencies can never be completely eliminated. One of the following ways of proceeding will come into question, depending on requirements: treatment will be postponed, e.g. where radio-isotopic diagnosis is concerned, or demand will be met in the short-term by carrying out special activities as for blood transfusions in emergency cases, whereby an extreme increase in costs will be accepted.

The essential characteristic is the perishableness of the stored goods. This can be defined by a maximum permitted storage period or by the laws of radioactive disintegration. It may be assumed that an order will be followed by delivery the same day. Radio-isotopes are delivered by a pharmaceutical firm and blood plasma comes either from a regional blood bank, another hospital or from a blood donor. One of the peculiarities of blood banks in hospitals is the system of reserving blood plasma. Doctors are able to reserve blood plasma for the treatment of their patients. The reserved amounts are either used up or returned to the non-reserved stock after a period of time. This reservation system can be regarded as an inventory in front of the consumption process.

To sum up, inventory problems considered here can be interpreted from a management point of view as multi-product inventory problems with stochastic demand and subdepots or reserved stocks (Klausmann/Martin 1979).

The following criteria for the optimization of stocks can be found in the relevant literature:

- the shortage rate, i.e. the share of stock deficiencies in the total consumption,

- the expiry rate, expressed as the amount of total stock lost as a result of the lapse of time,

- the average age of the stored goods on use.

This last criterium is a medical one and plays an important part where blood plasma is concerned. With increasing age the medical value of the plasma decreases. From an economic point of view it must be assumed that this criterium is sufficiently accounted for by the restriction of the maximum period of storage. The first two criteria correlate negatively with one another. This leads to the usual difficulties of decision situations with multiple objectives. The problem can be simplified if the shortage and expiry rates can be expressed in cost quantities.

The costs which have to be considered when planning inventory systems for easily perishable goods in hospitals are:

- procurement costs,

- costs for medical consumption,

- storage costs - these include the costs of tying up capital and expiry costs -,

- shortage costs.

Procurement costs include the costs of ordering and any forwarding costs which may be billed. The costs for medical consumption are the procurement prices of those goods which are actually used for medical purposes. Storage costs consist of the capital tying up costs, i.e. interest calculated on the capital tied up in the stored goods, and the expiry costs. The expiry costs are to be understood as the procurement prices of the goods lost through exceeding the maximum storage period or through radioactive disintegration. Shortage costs accrue in various ways according as to how the deficiencies are treated. If the occurrence of a deficiency is dealt with by postponing a patient's treatment for a day the costs of the longer hospital stay are to be assessed. In the other case the shortage costs are caused by the extra-budgetary short-term procurement of the missing goods.

The objective quantity is then the sum of these costs for medical goods, whereby a maximum shortage rate is given as a restriction.

The time of ordering and the amount ordered are decision variables for inventory models. The amount ordered is dependent on target stocks according to which inventory policy is used. In the following descriptions of hospital inventory problems presumed stocks are in the foreground as decision variables. Analytic methods and simulation models can be used as planning processes. The analytical treatment of this type of inventory system with stochastic demand, shortages caused by disintegration laws, and subdepots gets complicated very quickly. For this reason simulation models are preferred in the literature on the subject. Planning inventory systems for hospitals can then be carried out as follows. Firstly, heuristic methods are used to look for solutions for stockkeeping which appear to be of use. These include, for example, the choice of inventory policy and organizational aspects. It is obvious that when storing easily perishable goods the optimal organization of stock arrivals and issues must correspond to the FIFO principle; those goods stored first must be used first. The heuristically determined solution can then be compared using a simulation model as regards the costs relevant to decision-making.

3.2 Particular inventory problems

3.2.1 Storing a radio-isotope (Gierl/Schläger 1979)

Gierl and Schläger (1979) consider a nuclear-medical laboratory in which the radio-isotope Jod-131 is stored along with other radioactive substances. A probability of 95 % for meeting any demand is given. The aim is to minimize the costs which consist of those listed in the previous paragraph. Shortage costs accrue as a result of a postponement of treatment. The price per theoretical productive activity of the radio-isotope varies according to the day on which the order is given. An (s,Q) policy is used for the stockkeeping; the probable demand of each following working day serves as the order limit s. Using the demand of the current working day as a basis a check is made as to whether the remaining stock will cover the demand for the following day. If this is not the case an order process is put into motion. The amount ordered will arrive on the morning of the following day. The ordered amount Q is varied during the simulation.

For the purpose of this analysis the distribution of the daily demand is examined empirically. By that one receives week-day specific normal distributions, which are statistically proven. The order limit and amount are now varied in the simulation runs. One after another the mean value of each distribution, the mean value minus the standard deviation, and the mean value plus the standard deviation are chosen as order limits - expressed in units of the assessed demand for the following working day. Activities of 1.25×10^{-4} Ci (Curie), 2.5×10^{-4} Ci, 5×10^{-4} Ci, 10^{-3} Ci and 2×10^{-3} Ci are considered as order quantities. The mean value of each distribution proves to be the cost optimal order limit. This means that the order limit s in the (s,Q) policy is fixed according to the day on which the order is placed.

As regards the dependence of costs from the amounts ordered the expected relations emerge with most types of costs. The procurement and shortage costs decrease and the expiry costs increase when the amount ordered is increased. As expected the total costs run in a u-form, dependent on the amount ordered. The activity 10^{-3} Ci emerges as the amount ordered which causes minimum total costs. Thus the order limit and amount are determine for the specific constellation of data.

3.2.2 Stockkeeping in a hospital blood bank (Klausmann/Martin 1979)

The subject under examination is the blood bank of a hospital with stochastic stock arrivals. The blood bank is stocked up by telephoning names on a list of blood donors whose arrival at the following day is stochastic. The reservation system in use in the hospital is also worthy of examination. The amount of time plasma spends in reserved stocks until it is consumed or taken out of the reserve is stochastic. An exaggerated reserving practice is a typical weak point of blood bank systems; this is analysed in the simulation approach. The main point is to expose the connection between the shortage rate and the expiry rate for the individual groups of blood plasma. The hospital under observation used an (S,T)-type policy. Because blood donors are called in every day the order period is T = 1 day. Apart from this presumed stocks S are given for each blood group to be stocked up by means of daily donations. The amount of presumed stocks S is a variable in the simulation model.

A series of discrete distributions was determined empirically for the treatment of the stockkeeping system. These distributions describe the week-day demand for plasma, the length of the reservations, the time difference between making the appointment and the arrival of the blood donor, and the frequency of the blood groups of the plasma in stock. The last aspect helps to divide the types of blood group into classes for the simulation, whereby five classes of blood group types are formed, and the division is carried out so that demand is practically the same for blood group types of the same classes. In each class 30 simulation runs are carried out for each of three different presumed stock levels. Each run delivers a shortage rate and an expiry rate. With a given class and a given presumed stock the average shortage rate and expiry rate are brought into relation with each other. The simultation runs are then modified so that the time spent as reserved plasma by stock which is not used but sent back to total stock is reduced by one day.

The results of the simulation show impressively just how the expiry rate decreases when reservation policy is altered in the manner described. In contrast to this the effect on the shortage rate is not great. Both effects lead to a decrease in costs. From an economic point of view it seems to be advisable to influence the doctors with the aim of shortening the reservation time of plasma which is later no longer needed. Further economically justified recommendations for actions can hardly be deduced from the results of the simulations as there is no explicit consideration of costs. In contrast to this, suggestions for the choice of presumed stocks can be justified from the point of view of medical provisions when, for example, a uniform shortage rate for all blood group types is aimed at.

3.2.3 The constitution of a regional blood bank system (Page 1979)

In contrast with the situation described in the previous section the case now under consideration is that of several hospitals being supplied from a central blood bank. It is reasonable to accept that simultaneous planning by all the hospitals involved will lead to additional possibilities for rationalization. As far as cooperation of the hospitals and the central blood bank is concerned let the following be assumed: blood donors come to the blood bank to donate blood when they want to do so; they are given appointements only in scarcity situations. The blood bank supplies the individual hospitals on a regular basis. Where deficiencies exist unscheduled deliveries will take place. Where the blood bank is not able to meet deficiencies the hospitals will support each other on a basis of reciprocity. Only in exceptional cases will the hospitals work directly with their own blood donors.

The aim when planning the blood bank system is to minimize the costs per each blood plasma used in the hospitals. The costs consist of the procurement, stockkeeping, expiry, and shortage costs together. Shortage costs accrue when a blood plasma can be found neither in a hospital depot nor in the blood bank system as a whole. The shortage costs in hospital depots consist of the number of unscheduled deliveries multiplied by the costs of these deliveries. The shortage costs in the system as a whole are given by the number of immediate blood donations necessary to cover deficiencies multiplied by the corresponding costs.

The regional stockkeeping system described here is quite complicated and so plans for such a scheme cannot be characterized simply by specifying a particular stockkeeping policy. On the contrary, the point of the simulation is to compare certain heuristic procedures as to their costs. As far as the suggested policies are concerned presumed stocks are of importance for the individual hospitals which are varied in the framework of the simulation model. An inventory factor giving the relationship of the presumed stock to the average weekly demand is equivalent to the specification of an amount of presumed stock.

Page suggests the following heuristic procedure for the planning of the stockkeeping system:

(1) the hospitals must keep to the FIFO principle strictly when using blood plasma.

(2) presumed stocks are laid down for the blood bank and the individual hospitals. The presumed stock for the blood bank is to be regarded as a safety stock for the system as a whole whereas the presumed stocks for the hospitals are based on individual demand. The daily scheduled delivery of plasma to the hospitals takes place step-by-step. At first each hospital receives the plasma it has ordered for the day. Minimum stocks in the hospitals are replenished should they fall below a percentage of the presumed stocks. A further allotment of the reserves available in the blood bank to top up the presumed stocks takes place only to those hospitals which would receive deliveries anyway; this qualification is aimed at reducing transport costs as a share of procurement costs. The policy of scheduled deliveries does not affect unscheduled deliveries in emergencies.

(3) In order to match the production of plasma to demand a procedure for making appointments for blood donors will be introduced. On each working day the probable stock per blood group is assessed for the same day in the following week: the calculation includes

the figures for actual stock on hand as well as estimates for expiry, consumption of plasma and new stock arrivals. As many blood donors are then called in for that day in the following week as are necessary to bring the assessed amounts of stock up to the required amounts.

(4) A recycling process is introduced in order to make further improvements in the system: blood plasma is redistributed among the hospitals. Plasma superfluous to requirements can be redistributed as well as older plasma for a hospital whose requirements are so great that it is less than likely that the expiry date will be reached. To avoid transport costs only those hospitals will take part in the redistribution system which would have received deliveries on that day anyway.

The basis of the system is empirical data from the existing blood bank system; the necessary parameters and distributions could be worked out or estimated. Simulation runs are carried out using the real system and then with the four additional systems gained by extending the real system step-by-step with modifications (1) - (4) of the heuristic procedure. In addition simulation runs were used in which the inventory factor was varied.

The results show that each of the proposed measures contributes to cost reductions. The recommendation for action is, therefore, that the heuristic model of the stockkeeping system described here be realized. The optimal inventory factor and the optimal levels of presumed stocks can be read directly from the second series of simulation runs. The optimal inventory factor in the concrete case reads 1,25, i.e. optimal presumed stocks are about 25% higher than the average weekly demand.

Literature:

Aft, L.S., Watt, J.R., and Thomason, C.Y.: Scheduling 7-Day Weeks Poses Equity Problems, in: Hospitals, September 1, 1975, pp. 93-96.

Baur, K.: Betriebsmittelzuordnung bei der Fabrikplanung, Ph.D. thesis, Stuttgart 1972.

Buffa, E.S., Armour, G.C., and Vollmann, T.E.: Allocating Facilities with CRAFT, in: Harvard Business Review 42, 1964, pp. 136-158.

Burkard, R.E.: Heuristische Verfahren zur Lösung quadratischer Zuordnungsprobleme, in: Zeitschrift für Operations Research 19, 1975, pp. 183-193.

Domschke, W.: Modelle und Verfahren zur Standortbestimmung, in: Zeitschrift für Operations Research 19, 1975, pp. B13-B14.

Eichhorn, S.: Krankenhausbetriebslehre, Vol. I, Stuttgart/Berlin/Köln/Mainz 1975.

Gierl, L.: Partialmodelle der Ablaufplanung im Krankenhaus auf empirischer Grundlage, Ph.D. thesis, Erlangen/Nürnberg 1976.

Gierl, L.: Simultane Patientendurchlaufplanung für mehrere Leistungsstellen, in: Meyer, M. (ed.): Krankenhausplanung, Stuttgart/New York 1979, pp. 196-205.

Gierl, L., and Schläger, W.: Planung der Lagerhaltung des Radioisotops Jod-131, in: Meyer, M. (ed.): Krankenhausplanung, Stuttgart/New York 1979, pp. 185-195.

Hardeck, W., and Nestler, H.: Aus der Praxis der Layoutplanung mit EDV, in: Wt - Zeitschrift für die industrielle Fertigung 64, 1974, pp. 95.

Hardeck, W., and Schmid, M.: Rechnerunterstützte Raumplanung - eine praktische Anwendung des Verfahrens von Günther - Working Paper No. 2 , Nürnberg 1974.

Hegemann, H.: Kapazitäts- und Prozeßplanung in der klinischen Diagnostik, Berlin/Heidelberg/New York/Tokyo 1986.

Kao, E.P.C.: Modeling the Movement of Coronary Patients within a Hospital by Semi-Markov-Processes, in: Operations Research 22, 1974, pp. 683-708.

Kiehne, R.: Innerbetriebliche Standortplanung und Raumzuordnung, Ph.D. thesis, Wiesbaden 1969.

Kim, H., and Meyer, M.: Zur Ermittlung des Personalbedarfs in der Anästhesie, in: Meyer, M. (ed.): Krankenhausplanung, Stuttgart/New York 1979, pp. 207-221.

Klausmann, H.-S., and Martin, H.: Systemanalyse und Simulation einer Krankenhausblutbank, in: Meyer, M. (ed.): Krankenhausplanung, Stuttgart/New York 1979, pp. 234-246.

Kreß, O., and Welge, Ch.: Personalplanung im Pflegebereich, in: Meyer, M. (ed.): Krankenhausplanung, Stuttgart/New York 1979, pp. 142-153.

Maas, H.-J.: Zielsetzung und Zielerreichung im Krankenhaus, Bochum 1977.

Meyer, M., Hansen, K., and Klausmann, H.-S.: Mathematische Planungsverfahren II, Essen 1975.

Miller, H.E., Pierskalla, W.P., and Rath, G.J.: Nurse Scheduling Using Mathematical Programming, in: Operations Research 24, 1976, pp. 857-870.

Minten, B.: Anpassung einer optimalen Maschinenzuordnung an vorgegebene Gebäudeabmessungen, in: Wt - Zeitschrift für die industrielle Fertigung 62, 1972, pp. 289-293.

Morrish, A.R., and O'Connor, A.R.: Cyclic Scheduling, in: Hospitals, February 16, 1970, pp. 66-71.

Niedereichholz, Ch.: Heuristische Verfahren der transportkostenoptimalen Betriebsmittelzuordnung, in: Zeitschrift für Betriebswirtschaft 45, 1975, pp. 725-742.

Page, B.: Ein Simulationsmodell zur optimalen Versorgung von Krankenhäusern mit Blutkonserven durch einen regionalen Blutspendedienst, in: Meyer, M. (ed.): Krankenhausplanung, Stuttgart/New York 1979, pp. 110-123.

Sauter, T.: Optimale Zuordnung von Werkzeugmaschinen in einer Fertigungshalle mit vorgegebener Gebäudeabmessung in einer Richtung, in: Wt - Zeitschrift für die industrielle Fertigung 62, 1972, pp. 213-216.

Schmidt, E.: Zur Planung des Bettenbestandes von Krankenhäusern, Ph.D. thesis, Hagen 1980.

Schneider, D.P., and Kilpatrick, K.E.: An Optimum Manpower Utilization Model for Health Maintenance Organizations, in: Operations Research 23, 1975, pp. 869-889.

Trivedi, V.M., and Warner, D.M.: A Branch and Bound Algorithm for Optimum Allocation of Float Nurses, in: Management Science 22, 1976, pp. 972-981.

Walter, B.: Einsatzplanung für Anästhesisten, in: Meyer, M. (ed.): Krankenhausplanung, Stuttgart/New York 1979, pp. 222-233.

Warner, D.M., and Prawda, J.: A Mathematical Programming Model for Scheduling Nursing Personnel in a Hospital, in: Management Science 19, 1972, pp. 411-422.

Yett, D.E., Drabeck, L., Intriligator, M.D., and Kimbell, L.J.: Health Manpower Planning: An Econometric Approach, in: Health Services Research 2, 1972, pp. 134-147.

Approaches to the Planning of the Optimal Supply of Beds in Hospitals

Günter Fandel and Erhard Schmidt

1 Introduction

Since the end of the World War II public health has accounted for a steadily increasing share of the GNP. The increase in expenditure in the Federal Republic of Germany has lead to a "costs explosion" in public health being discussed and the State being forced to take measures to stop this development. Between 1962 and 1976 alone there was an increase of 652% in expenditure on public health (Fritz 1977).

Hospital nursing costs in particular developed in a similar way to the total expenditure on public health; of all the areas of public health hospitals hold a leading position when it comes to the allotment of costs. Hospital running costs are distributed on average as follows (Deutsches Ärzteblatt, p. 1347):

staff costs	71.4%
medical costs	13.1%
food	5.7%
water/energy/fuel	3.0%
managing and administration	2.9%
miscellaneous	3.9%.

Staff costs can even reach 80% of the total costs in larger hospitals and university clinics.

It can be seen that almost 90% of the total costs in a hospital are fixed costs. Where the capacity of the hospital is fixed these costs are, in practice, linked to the number of beds and accrue independently of the number of patients who are actually treated. The solution of the problem of determining the optimum capacity of a hospital is therefore not only important for the prevention of unnecessary capital expenditure; moreover, the solution can be of just as much importance from the perspective of the prevention of unnecessary subsequent costs for those hospitals which were built on too large scale with permanently accruing fixed costs. The examination into the supply of beds in existing hospitals and the respective optimal organization of this supply is, therefore, of great significance. Approaches towards a solution of this problem will be illustrated on the basis of a survey in the following pages, and their suitability for bringing the decision situation under control will be discussed.

In the framework of these inquiries it will be assumed that the factors of the demand for the hospital beds of different medical faculties are given and known. These include in the main the hospitalization frequency of in-patients, the duration of their stay, and the degree of utilization of the beds. Here it is possible that wards with the same patient-yield (i.e. the number of patients arriving for, and receiving treatment) and the same average duration of stay can have differing bed supplies according to how the patient-yield is divided into urgent and non-urgent cases. Close attention will be paid to this additional aspect in the following statements; it is important as regards the varying suitability of the approaches because the admission policies of a hospital towards urgent and non-urgent patients have a decisive influence on the planning of the bed supply. From the point of view of time the first priority is the treatment of the urgent cases. Urgent cases, where possible, should not be sent away immediately upon arrival because all available beds are occupied. Non-urgent cases on the other hand can be allotted to a queue, whereby a reasonable waiting time will have to be determined. While urgent cases demand a reserve capacity, the formation of queues of non-urgent patients serves to make deviations in demand more steady and to enable the organization of a continuous production of hospital services with a view to a satisfactory full use of the capacity.

If the non-admission rates for urgent cases and the average waiting time for non-urgent cases are to be used as a yardsticks for achievement in hospital planning based on a quantitatively optimal supply of needs, the efficiency principle demands that the supply of needs regarded as necessary, expressed through an upper bound for non-admissions and average waiting periods, should be realized with the lowest capacity possible. Which non-admission rates and which average waiting period is then translated into reality in the actual running of the hospital depends on the admissions policy chosen; the determining of this policy precedes the planning of the supply of beds. For this purpose various possibilities for the different treatment of urgent and non-urgent cases will be discussed. A critique of these approaches gives rise to the development of a new recommendation of a solution to the simultaneous determination of the optimal amount of beds and emergency beds for a hospital. The principle for the solution and its algorithm will then be demonstrated by means of a practical case. To sum up, the following premises will be used for further discussion on the basis of the relations which have already been outlined:

1) The problem of the determination of the optimal size of a hospital is equivalent to the problem of the determination of the optimal number of beds.

2) The patient-yield is made up of the group of urgent and the group of non-urgent cases. The group of urgent cases is granted priority in the admissions policy.

3) The chief objective of the hospital's governing body is the best possible provision of hospitals services for the population from the point of view of economic efficiency.

2 Methodical possibilities for describing the running of a hospital service

2.1 Important elements of the description

In order to be able to follow the running of a hospital from the point of view of timing and so to arrive at conclusions for the determination of the optimal bed supply, the most important elements, those defining capacity and its fulluse, will be commented upon on more detail, and will be described with mathematical and statistical methods. The most important elements are (Egle 1970):

1) The number of hospital beds and if necessary the establishment of that portion of the beds reserved for urgent cases, either on a priority basis or exclusively;

2) The total number of urgent patients; urgent cases are only rejected when all beds, including the emergency beds, are occupied;

3) The total number of non-urgent patients; these will be admitted when beds other than those reserved for urgent cases and emergencies are free; in all other cases they will be refused admission or put onto a waiting-list;

4) The duration of stay of those cases which are treated.

2.1.1 The number of hospital beds and of the beds reserved for emergencies

The number of hospital beds and of those reserved for urgent cases can be represented by natural numbers. In the following n stands for the total number of available beds and n_1 for the emergency beds, i.e. $n_1 < n$ always holds.

The number n_1 can, in practice, be made up of a number of normal beds, i.e. beds which are usually to be found in the wards, and of emergency beds, i.e. additional beds which are set up in rooms and corridors when all other beds are occupied. Because this latter type of emergency bed is not positively rated, for socio-political and medical reasons, the quota of normal beds in n_1 is adjusted so that normally a regular bed is available for an urgent case and so that emergency beds will only have to be set up in extraordinary situations such as catastrophes and epidemics etc.

2.1.2 Patient-yield as a stochastic process

The number of patients coming to a hospital daily to ask for admission is, according to experience, subject to deviations; this applies equally to urgent and non-urgent cases. These deviations cannot be predicted exactly. On the contrary, the number of patients has to be described with the help of random variables. If t stands for the time and if $I \subseteq \mathbb{R}^+$, then $X(t)$ can be interpreted as the number of patients arriving in the period of time t, and $(X(t))_{t \in I}$ as a stochastic process. If, in addition, the conditions

(1) $\quad X(t) \geq 0$ for each $t \geq 0$,

(2) $\quad X(t + \tau) - X(t) \geq 0$ for all $t, \tau \geq 0$

are fulfilled - as is the case in reality - the arrival process of the patients can be described as a flow (Neumann 1977). A Poisson process with the arrival rate λ is assumed here as a special flow describing the numbers of patients with the variance and expected value

$$E(X(t)) = Var\ (X(t)) = \lambda t.$$

The number of occurences of most of the illnesses which have to be treated in hospital can be quite well approximated with the help of the Poisson arrival process; this has been shown by various empirical studies (Esogbue/Singh 1976, Meyer/Schläger 1975). The Poisson process is most often employed in literature to describe patient-yield when factors are decisive for the ill-health of a person which are usually not at the same time factors in the ill-health of another person. This enables these illnesses to be recognized as independent of the illnesses of other people; this means that the illnesses have to be regarded as completely independent events which occur singly and suddenly for the hospital and thus correspond very well with the character of a Poisson process. In this case the frequency of occurence of such illnesses in the hospital's catchment area can be presumed to be Poisson distributed (cf Adam 1972).

Because it is to be presumed of all the observed illnesses that they occur approximately corresponding to the Poisson process, the process resulting from the collection of several types of illness can itself be regarded as a Poisson process because two Poisson processes together form again another Poisson process. For the purposes of this article it is sufficient for the present to divide all the illnesses into urgent and non-urgent cases. Two Poisson arrival processes are observed: for urgent cases with the arrival rate λ_1 and for non-urgent cases with the arrival rate λ_2. The arrival rate corresponds to the expected patient-yield in each period of time.

2.1.3 The duration of stay

A patient's duration of stay begins with his hospitalization and ends with his discharge, transfer to another hospital, or with his death. The duration of stay can be regarded as a random variable which has a statistical distribution as its basis. Different possibilities for description present themselves hereby.

The description of the duration of stay as an exponentially distributed random quantity has as its basis the hypothesis that the departures from the hospital represent a Poisson process just as much as the arrivals do, i.e. it is assumed that the number of departures is Poisson distributed with the parameter and expected value μ. The plausibility of this hypothesis is supported by empirical studies. The close connection between exponential and Poisson distribution has also lead to exponentially distributed treatment times forming the basis of many assessments, because the waiting systems for Poisson arrivals and departures, which are often used in the assessments, are those which have up to now been most closely examined.

A distribution which includes exponential distribution as a special case is shown in the Erlang distribution (Sasieni/Yaspan/Friedman 1959). The advantage of the Erlang distribution lies in the fact that through the chances for variation of two parameters for existing empirical data quite good theoretical distribution functions can be found. On the other hand there is the disadvantage that the employment of the Erlang distribution leads to more complex mathematical models, and thus finding solutions becomes more difficult.

2.2 The hospital as a service unit

The hospital can be regarded as a service station which is approached by customers, here patients, who are then attended to and then pass out of the system. Usually the customers arrive at irregular time intervals; because the capacity of the service station is usually not large enough to cope with all these deviations and to attend to all customers immediately upon arrival, queues usually form. An analysis of the events in this type of service station with the help of the mathematical tool of the queueing theory suggests itself here.

The hospital, or rather its departments, can then be described as service stations with n parallel servicing channels, whereby n is the number of beds. Parallel servicing channels means that the beds are usually interchangeable as far as their utilization is concerned. The patient is not concerned which of the n beds he is given on admission; when a bed is assigned to him he keeps it for the duration of his stay in the hospital. The beds are, therefore, not linked as service stations one after the other. If it is further assumed that the number of arrivals and the number of departures are in each case Poisson distributed, the hospital, better, its departments, can be regarded as an M/M/n waiting system with a Markov arrival process, a Markov servicing process and n service stations.

In the following will be denoted by

- λ the arrival rate of the patients
- μ the clearance rate per bed
- n the number of beds in the hospital or ward respectively
- p_j the stationary probability of a Markov process which indicates that j patients are in the servicing system, i.e. are in the queue or being treated.

If there are j patients in the hospital and in the queue it is said that the system is in the state j.

The stationary probabilities p_j can be determined dependent on n, λ, and μ. They read

$$p_j = \frac{\rho^j}{j!} p_0 \text{ for } j \leq n,$$

$$p_j = \frac{\rho^j}{n!n^{j-n}} p_0 \text{ for } j \geq n,$$

with

$$\rho = \lambda/\mu$$

and

$$p_0 = \frac{1}{\sum_{j=0}^{n-1} \frac{\rho^j}{j!} + \frac{\rho^n}{(n-\rho)(n-1)!}} .$$

3 Models of different admission policies

3.1 Simple decision models

3.1.1 A decision model exclusively for urgent cases

First of all a ward will be considered which only admits urgent cases; a queue of patients cannot, therefore, exist. If all beds are occupied an incoming urgent case must be rejected. The decision model helps to arrive at the smallest number of beds by which the probability of loss does not exceed a definite tolerance level v.

Because no queue is to be observed

$$\sum_{i=0}^{n} p_i = 1$$

$$p_o = 1 - \sum_{i=1}^{n} p_i = \left(\sum_{i=1}^{n} \frac{\rho^i}{i!}\right)^{-1}$$

$$p_n = \frac{\rho^n}{n!} p_o$$

must be valid.

p_n stands for the probability that all beds are occupied and that an incoming urgent case has to be rejected (Egle, 1970); p_n, therefore, indicates the probability of loss.

The decision problem then reads, given ρ and V

$$\min \{n \mid p_n(n) \leq V\} = n^*.$$

Because the rejection of urgent cases is judged very negatively on medical and socio-political grounds the probability of such a case will be held to a minimum by adjustments to n.

3.1.2 Decision models for exclusively non-urgent cases

3.1.2.1 A decision model with an unlimited queue

Patients belonging to the non-urgent group stand out because a waiting time is expected of them before they are treated; of course the reasonableness of the length of time spent waiting is limited by the generally prevailing conceptions of what is right. These conceptions can be allowed for in the model by setting definite tolerance values for the mean length of the queue or the mean waiting time which may not be exceeded.

For the mean length u of the queue

$$u = \frac{\rho^{n+1}}{(n-1)!(n-\rho)^2 \sum_{j=0}^{n-1} \frac{\rho^j}{j!} + (n-\rho) \cdot \rho^n}$$

is valid, and for the mean waiting time w

$$w = u/\lambda$$

holds.

Tolerance limits U and W can be laid down for u and w respectively. These limits may not be exceeded by an allowed solution (Egle 1970). The decision model then reads:

$$\min \{n | u(n) \leq U\} = n^*$$

or

$$\min \{n | w(n) \leq W\} = n^*.$$

Because

$$u = \lambda w$$

for

$$U = \lambda W$$

the same result is obtained in both variants.

3.1.2.2 A decision model with a limited queue

In the foregoing section an arbitrarily long queue of patients was allowed; the expected value of the length of that queue was not to exceed a maximum limit U. In practice, however, patients are rejected when the queue or the time spent waiting as a result of the queue exceeds a definite value; they then have to go to another hospital.

Supposing that to join a queue of the length s can just be reasonably excepted of a patient; if an incoming patient comes to a queue of the length s he will be rejected. The probability that a patient must be rejected is then p_{n+s} with

$$p_{n+s} = \frac{\rho^{n+s}}{n!n^s} p_o$$

$$p_o = 1/(\sum_{i=0}^{n} \frac{\rho^i}{i!} + \sum_{i=n+1}^{s} \frac{\rho^i}{n!n^{i-n}}).$$

Those patients who are not rejected then have the following average waiting time w_s:

$$w_s(n) = \sum_{j=0}^{s} \frac{j+1}{n\mu} p_{j+n} = \frac{1}{n\mu} \frac{\rho^n}{n!} p_o \sum_{j=0}^{s} (j+1) \frac{\rho^j}{n^j}$$

$$= \frac{\rho^n(s\rho^{s+1} - (s+1)\rho^s n + n^{s+1})}{(n-1)!\mu(n-\rho)^2 n^{s+1}} p_o .$$

If the rejection or loss probability p_{n+s} is not to exceed the value V and the average waiting time w_s of the admitted patients is not to exceed the value W, the following optimization problem exists, where λ,μ, and s are given:

$$\min \{n | p_{n+s} \leq V \text{ and } w_s(n) \leq W\} = n^*.$$

3.2 Models for the simultaneous registration of urgent and non-urgent cases

3.2.1 Problems of the simultaneous registration of urgent and non-urgent cases

The simple decision models deal exclusively with one single patient-type only. Many hospitals wards, however, are characterized through the treatment of urgent and non-urgent cases together. In order to set up decision models for these wards which meet their practical requirements it is necessary to consider simultaneously both types of patients and their different attributes affecting the running of the hospital.

To do this it is necessary to devide the patient-yield into urgent and non-urgent cases. This differentiation then results in two different arrival processes. Furthermore, the fact that urgent cases cannot wait for treatment has to be taken into account. This means that these patients either have to be admitted immediately or to be sent to another hospital.

The simultaneous consideration of both types of patient leads to much more complex models in comparison with the basic models illustrated in the earlier sections. The effects of both arrival processes on the running of the hospital are difficult to register because the arrival process of one type of patient has an influence on the service process of the other type of patient. For example, urgent cases get preferential treatment over the waiting non-urgent patients, so the principle "first come - first served" is ignored and the time spent waiting by the non-urgent patients is longer.

In the literature on the subject there are various procedures illustrated which all aim at the simultaneous consideration of urgent and non-urgent types of patient. These procedures are mostly built on the queueing theory, the theory of Markov chains, and the theory of simulation. The procedures are partly contained in the models on the determination of the number of beds and partly in models on the determination of an optimal admission policy. The models on the determination of an optimal admission policy are not only interesting as a study of the procedures for simultaneous consideration of both types of patient which they recommend. There is also a close connection between the problems "determination of the number of beds" and "determination of an admission policy", a connection which will be investigated briefly in the following paragraphs.

3.2.2 The connection between admission policy and the number of beds

Models on the determination of an optimal admission policy proceed on the assumption that there is a fixed number of beds and a given arrival process for urgent cases on which the hospital administration has no influence. The admission process for non-urgent cases is then the action variable, or, if that has been determined, the action variable is the number of beds reserved for urgent cases.

If the optimal admission policy for patients of the non-urgent sort found in this way is compared with the actual number of these patients, it can then be decided whether the number of beds used as a basis for the determination of the optimal admission policy is sufficient or not. The direction and size of any necessary variation in the number of beds follow from this comparison; with the help of an iterative procedure the optimal number of beds draws nearer. The optimal number of beds is then the same as the minimum number of beds necessary to cope with the numbers of non-urgent cases brought about by the optimal admission policy.

The control procedure can, of course, be varied in such a way as to bring in, for example, the loss quota of non-urgent cases as a criterium. Other restrictions can also be built into this procedure.
The relationship of the admission policy and the number of beds is definite because the admission policy is the essential part of the determination of the number of beds. An admission strategy underlies, mostly indirectly, every model for the determination of the number of beds. This is why the model for the determination of the admission policy are not just of interest for the studies of the procedures for the simultaneous consideration of urgent and non-urgent cases which they contain, the material content is also of interest.

3.2.3 Young's models

In his two models Young (1966) sees the hospital as a service system with n service stations, whereby n is the number of beds in the ward under consideration. The beds are grouped in the system as parallel service stations, i.e. a patient occupies the same bed for the whole course of his treatment; beds are available to incoming patients as they become free. Young has two types of patient under consideration. The first group consists of the urgent cases (type 1); these cannot be rejected by the administration if beds are free. The number of admissions of this type of patient clearly represents a stochastic process.

Non-urgent cases constitute the second group (type 2); the hospital administration decides on their admission. If the hospital administration does not interfere in the arrival process the number of admissions of this type of patient also constitutes a stochastic process, otherwise the arrival rate of this group is deterministic. This procedure is justified by the assumption that this group of patients consists of non-urgent cases who can be expected, on medical grounds, to put up with a refusal of admission.

Model I: the number of admissions of non-urgent cases as an action variable

In his first model Young (1966) examines the effect the admissions rate of non-urgent patients, as an action variable for the hospital, has on the state of the system.

Let n denote the number of beds in the ward under consideration. The duration of stay of a patient is described by an exponentially distributed random variable with the expected value $1/\mu$; no distinction between types of patient is made for the duration of stay. The intermediate arrival times of the non-urgent patients follow an Erlang distribution defined by the parameters k and λ_2, whereby $k \in \mathbb{N}$ applies.

Through the description of the intermediate arrival times as Erlang distributed random variables the above-mentioned hypotheses concerning the admission of patients of type 2 can be taken into account in the model. If the hospital administration has laid down a fixed number of daily non-urgent admissions, the intermediate arrival times of the non-urgent cases will be represented through the Erlang distribution with λ_2 and k, $k = \infty$, whereby λ_2 equals the fixed number of daily admissions of patients of type 2. If the number of daily admissions of non-urgent patients is a random number, the intermediate arrival time will be represented through the Erlang distribution with λ_2 and k, $1 \leq k < \infty$, whereby λ_2 stands for the expected value per day.

The hospital is unable to influence the admission number of patients of type 1; if beds are free the arrival rate equals the admission rate and is only dependent on chance. For this reason Young presupposes that the number of type 1 patients admitted daily is Poisson distributed with the parameter λ_1, and the intermediate arrival time is exponentially distributed with the parameter $1/\lambda_1$, respectively. In addition Young bases his considerations on the following assumptions (1966):

1. The state of the system is defined as the number of occupied beds.

2. The arrival processes of the urgent and non-urgent cases are independent of one another and are also independent of the state of the system.

3. Patients faced with a fully-occupied ward on arrival are sent away. This means that there is no waiting-list for admission to hospital.

Let i denote the number of occupied beds, p_i the probability that i beds are occupied. According to Young this gives the following result:

$$p_i = \frac{\rho^i \rho^{-\rho}}{i! \sum_{j=0}^{n} \rho^j \rho^{-\rho}/j!} ,$$

with $$\rho = (\lambda_1+\lambda_2)/\mu .$$

By inserting different values λ_2 the alterations in the state of the system can be examined; in this form model I constitutes an explanatory model. With the help of the probabilities p_i constraints can be formulated, as in 3.1 above. If n, λ_1 and μ are given, the optimal admission policy for non-urgent cases can be determined.

It can be established that the results of the derivation are independent of the choice of the parameter k of the Erlang distribution (Kolesar 1970), i.e. the results are independent of whether the number of admitted non-urgent patients is deterministic or whether it is brought into the model I as a random quantity whose intermediate arrival time is Erlang distributed with the parameter k, $1 \leq k < \infty$. This makes the application of the model much easier because the difficult task of estimating the parameter k does not have to be carried out, and only the parameter $1/\lambda_2$ for the representation of the number of admissions of non-urgent patients has to be determined. Simplicity is altogether the greatest advantage of model I; with only four input values, namely, λ_1, λ_2, μ, and n, whereby determination of the values of n as the number of occupied beds presents no problems at all, Young is able to register the classification of the

patient-yield into urgent and non-urgent cases, a classification which is important in practice. Model I can serve the hospital administration as an aid to decision-making in the running of the hospital or of a ward in that they can examine the effects of variations in the model of the quantity λ_2, which they control, and then, according to the values they place on the lossrates, they can then determine the optimal values for λ_2, and thus for the number of patients of type 2 who are to be admitted on average.
Furthermore, model I can also serve as a preparation for decision-making in the planning of the number of beds required for a hospital or for a ward, whereby n is then the decision variable. λ_1 is estimated using comparable existing data, λ_2 is gained from the admission strategy for non-urgent patients which is to be used in the later running of the hospital or ward, respectively. λ_2 can, of course, be estimated using existing data, just as much as λ_1, or this estimation can serve as a basis for the fixing of a deterministic quantity. With the help of this quantity n can be so dimensioned that the loss rate corresponds to the conceptions of the planners, e. g. by not exceeding a definite tolerance level. This restriction can be expressed in model I, for example, by laying down that the probability p_n, i.e. the probability that all beds are occupied and that new patients must be rejected, may not exceed a definite value.

In spite of the fundamentally possible application of this model I its employment in practice meets with considerable difficulties. The question whether all constituent facts important in practice are contained in the model, and whether their influence in reality is also expressed in the model must be answered in the negative:

1. That a waiting-list for non-urgent cases is not considered does not correspond with reality. In order to make the process of satisfying the demand for those hospital services which are determined by random numbers of incoming patients at least partially steadier, it is necessary to put those patients onto a waiting-list whose illnesses do not need to be treated immediately. On the other hand upper tolerance levels must be laid down for the length of the time to be waited. Exceeding these tolerance levels must be regarded as no longer reasonable.

2. The very nature of things precludes the existence of a waiting-list for urgent cases. On the contrary, beds are usually kept free in order to keep the probability that an urgent patient will have to

be rejected down to a minimum. These free beds may only be occupied by urgent cases; if all other beds are occupied, non-urgent cases must go in a queue. This state of affairs, observed in practice, does not come into play in model I. Consequently Young differentiates between urgent and non-urgent cases but only as regards the character of the arrival flow. No priority is granted to the urgent patients as regards service; if all beds are occupied - and up to full occupation no difference is made - urgent cases are rejected just as non-urgent ones are. The equal treatment of both types of patient is expressed in the result of the derivation, in the way that the arrival rates λ_1 and λ_2 only appear in the term $\rho = (\lambda_1 + \lambda_2)/\mu$; a change in λ_1 has, therefore the same effect as a change in λ_2.

3. The possibility given by Young's model I of fixing deterministically the intermediate arrival times of non-urgent patients, and thus the number of these patients to be admitted per unit of time (day), leads to the following conclusion: in order to be in a position to admit daily a fixed number of patients of type 2 the patient-yield of this type must be considerably higher than the fixed admission number, because of the non-existent waiting-list, so that this number, in spite of random variations, can definitely be admitted every day. This means that a substantial number of patients requesting admission must be rejected. However, this state of affairs can only be realized, at most, in a private clinic, which has to work to make a profit and whose costs for non-utilized capacity are very high. A public hospital cannot take over the above admission strategy because its declared objective is to supply the population of the catchment area with hospital services.

Model II: the number of reserved beds as an action variable.

With model II Young attempts to counter the criticism in point 2 above by reserving from n beds available for occupation $n - B$, $B \in \{0,1,\dots n\}$, beds for urgent patients. This means that if at least B beds of the n beds are occupied, type 2 patients requesting admission will be rejected. The number of admissions of patients of this type is now dependent upon the number of beds available for them, and indeed Young assumes that in the event that $x < B$ beds are occupied exactly $B - x$ patients of type 2 will be admitted the following day. By means of this admission strategy the number of occupied beds never falls below B, because a possible fall in the number of occupied beds below B would be immediately prevented by the admission of patients of type 2.

Whereas the number of admissions of non-urgent patients is fixed deterministically - although it is depent on the occupied beds - the admission process of urgent patients is displayed, as in model I, by a Poisson process; as in the first model the service time is regarded as a random variable which follows the exponential distribution.

Let p_i again stand for the probability that i beds are occupied; Young (1966) then reaches the following conclusion

$$p_{B+x} = \rho^x p_B \; B!/(\rho+x)! \quad \text{with } x = 1,2,\dots,n-B,$$

whereby

$$p_B = \frac{\rho^B}{B!\; e^{\rho} \sum_{k=0}^{n-B} \rho^{B+k} e^{-\rho} (B+k)!}$$

and $\rho = \lambda_1/\mu$.

The admission strategy for non-urgent cases is now determined by the fixing of the quantity B. By varying B the effect of an alteration in the number of beds reserved for urgent cases can be examined. Furthermore, the model can be used, given B, λ_1 and μ, to determine the optimal number of beds, for example, by means of the following optimization instruction:

$$\min \{n | p_n(n) \le V\} = n^*.$$

In model II Young has, in contrast to model I, taken account of the fact that urgent patients must have priority over the non-urgent cases by reserving a number of beds solely for patients of type 1. The admission strategy for patients of type 2 is no longer constant in model II, but is conditional on the number of beds available for patients of this type. A further advantage of this admission policy lies in the guarantee that the number of empty beds never exceeds n - B. Through a corresponding variation of the quantity B a desired minimum of capacity utilization can be realized. Furthermore, the patients B - x of type 2 who are to get a bed are in fact guaranteed to get one.

In spite of this improvement as regards the first model fundamental areas for criticism remain which were commented upon in the discussion of the first model. Further points for criticism arise as well.

Just as in the first model, no queue for non-urgent cases is allowed for in model II. This considerably limits the usefulness of the results gained from the model for practical purposes.

The criticism of the deterministic fixing of the number of admissions of non-urgent cases, which was only directed at a section of the utilization possibilities of the first model, is in modell II directed at the whole range of possibilities. It is true that a constant number of the type 2 patients to be admitted daily is not given in modell II, but because of $0 \leq B - x \leq B$ perhaps B type 2 patients must be admitted, the demand for hospital beds from type 2 patients must be so large, because of a non-existent queue, that at all times the admission of B patients of type 2 is possible for every day. However, because, on average, a lot fewer than B type 2 patients can be admitted daily the relationship between the demand of the group 2 patients and the numbers admitted has changed for the worse as regards model I; i.e. with the underlying admission strategy in the second model even more type 2 patients have to be rejected than with the constant admission number possible in model I. If, on the other hand, the demand of type 2 patients for hospital beds is not high enough to allow the admission at any time of B type 2 patients, the values of the model's input quantities $B - x$ can no longer be actually realized, so that the model delivers incorrect results for practical operation. Apart from that, the realization of the minimum capacity employment is no longer guaranteed.

The incongruity between the patient-yield of type 2 and the number of patients of this type actually admitted could be lessened if, instead of the supposition that patients who are rejected are lost to another hospital, it is supposed that patients rejected on one day are part of the patient-yield on the following day; in this way a reserve is built up which makes sure that there are always enough patients to be admitted. Thus there is a kind of queue which cannot be quantified in the model; because of this, restrictions such as a reasonable waiting time and reasonable queue length cannot be fed in.

In conclusion it can be said that Young's models are only of importance in hospitals in which the maximization of profits is the highest objective and for which the maximal provision of hospital services for the population plays no part, or only a secondary one.

3.2.4 Kolesar's model

Kolesar (1970) combines in his model the method of linear programming with the theory of the Markov processes. The actual decision problem is formulated as a linear optimization problem into which the supposition is fed, as a constraint, that the state of the system, i.e. the number of occupied beds, is a Markov chain.

Kolesar differentiates between serval quantities from which the state of the system is deduced. Let

X_t = the number of occupied beds in the period t,
n = the number of existing beds,
i.e. $X_t \leq n$.

At the same time Kolesar distinguishes between two types of patient, the urgent cases (type 1) and the non-urgent (type 2). The arrival process of the urgent cases A_t occurs with a definite probability distribution; i.e. let

$$P(A_t = j) = a_j, \qquad t = 0,1,..... \quad j = 0,1,..... \; .$$

The distribution is, therefore, stationary in time. The arrival process does not need to follow a definite probability distribution, e.g. the Poisson distribution; the values a_j can be determined empirically.

The number of the patients to be admitted who belong to the non-urgent group is in period t the deterministic quantity S_t which is fed into the model as a decision variable. This must be optimized with regard to the expected state of the system, i.e. the following dependence exists:

$$\text{for } X_t = i \quad \text{holds: } S_t = k(i), \qquad i = 0,1,...,n.$$

The departures from hospital, through release, transfer and death, are denoted by D_t for the period t; D_t is hereby a random variable and is dependent on the degree of occupancy in the hospital or the ward. This dependence can be so represented:

$$P\,(D_t = j\,|\,X_t = i) := d_{ij}, \qquad i,j = 0,1,\ldots,n, \quad t = 0,1,2,\ldots.$$

D_t is, like A_t, a stationary random process. The values for d_{ij} can be estimated from empirical data.

Using the quantities A_t, S_t, D_t, and n the state of the system can be depicted as a Markov chain.

For X_{t+1}

$$X_{t+1} = \min\,\{n,\ X_t - D_t + A_t + S_t\}, \qquad t = 0,1,\ldots.$$

is valid, because $X_t \leq n$.

Transition probabilities can now be deduced from this relation:

$$g_{ij}^{k} = P\,\{X_{t+1} = j\,|\,X_t = i,\ S_t = k\} \qquad i = 0,1,\ldots,n, \quad j = 0,1,\ldots,n, \quad k = 0,1,\ldots,n-i.$$

g_{ij}^{k} states therefore the probability that the state of the system will change from i to j, provided that k non-urgent cases are admitted. For $j<n$

$$g_{ij}^{k} = \sum_{n=0}^{j-i-k} a_n d_{i,j-i-k-n}$$

is obtained; for $j = n$

$$g_{in}^{k} = \sum_{j=n-i-k}^{\infty} \sum_{n=j} a_n d_{i,n-j}$$

is valid.

By employing the values a_j and d_{ij} the transition probabilities can be calculated.

Let X_t be a Markov chain, p_{ij} the transition probability from state i to state j, and R the decision rule from which X_t is dependent (here $R \approx S_t$). With

$$\pi_j\ (R) = \lim_{t\to\infty} P\{X_t(R) = j\,|\,X_o(R) = i\}$$

a general optimization problem can be formulated:

$$\sum_{j=0}^{n} c_j \pi_j(R) \longrightarrow \max$$

(v)

$$(1) \quad \sum_{j=0}^{n} a_{ij} \pi_j(R) = b_i, \qquad i = 1,2,\ldots,m,$$

$$(2) \quad \pi_i - \sum_{j=0}^{n} \pi_j(R)\, p_{ji}(R) = 0, \quad i = 0,1,\ldots,n,$$

$$\sum_{j=0}^{n} \pi_j(R) = 1,$$

$$\pi_j(R) \geq 0, \qquad j = 0,1,\ldots,n.$$

The constraints (1) depict arbitrary limitations, the constraints (2) require the observance of the conditions for Markov chains.

Let R show the admission strategy for non-urgent cases; R can then be formally registered through conditional probabilities:

$$s_{jk} = P(S_t = k \mid X_t = j), \qquad j = 0,1,\ldots,n, \quad k = 0,1,\ldots,n-1;$$

s_{jk} are, therefore the decision variable, to be determined optimally, which state implicitly which number k of non-urgent cases is to be admitted when j beds are occupied. Normally

$$s_{ji} = 1 \quad \text{for one } i \in \{0,1,\ldots,n-j\} \text{ and}$$

$$s_{jk} = 0 \quad \text{for } k \neq i;$$

is valid, i.e. the number of patients of the non-urgent type who are to be admitted is clearly stated for every state $X_t = j$.

In general

$$\sum_{k=0}^{n-j} s_{jk} = 1$$

is always valid.

Let

$$x_{jk} := s_{jk}\pi_j(R), \qquad \begin{aligned} i &= 0,1,\dots,n, \\ k &= 0,1,\dots,n-j, \end{aligned}$$

then, because of

$$\pi_j \sum_{k=0}^{n-j} s_{jk} = \sum_{k=0}^{n-j} x_{jk} \implies \pi_j = \sum_{k=0}^{n-j} x_{jk}$$

the following linear optimization problem is obtained from (v):

$$\sum_{j=0}^{n} c_j \sum_{k=0}^{n-j} x_{jk} \longrightarrow \max$$

$$\text{(v')} \quad \begin{aligned} &(1) \quad \sum_{j=0}^{n} a_{ij} \sum_{k=0}^{n-j} x_{jk} = b_i, \qquad i = 0,1,\dots,m, \\ &(2) \quad \sum_{k=0}^{n-1} x_{ik} - \sum_{j=0}^{n} \sum_{k=0}^{n-j} x_{jk} g_{ji}^{k} = 0, \qquad i = 0,1,\dots,n, \end{aligned}$$

$$\sum_{j=0}^{n} \sum_{k=0}^{n-j} x_{jk} = 1,$$

$$x_{jk} \geq 0, \qquad \begin{aligned} j &= 0,1,\dots,n, \\ k &= 0,1,\dots,n-j. \end{aligned}$$

The s_{jk} can then be calculated from the relation

$$s_{jk} = x_{jk} / \sum_{i=0}^{n-j} x_{ji}.$$

Specific optimization models can be formulated from the general optimization problem through a corresponding arrangement of objective function and constraints.

a) Maximizing the use of capacity

The objective function of a model for the maximization of the use of capacity, with the constraint that the probability of being rejected should not exceed a certain tolerance limit, consists of the expected value of the state of the system E(X(t)), which is to be maximized. It holds

$$E(X(t)) = \sum_{j=0}^{n} j \, \pi_j(R) = \sum_{j=0}^{n} j \sum_{k=0}^{n-j} x_{jk}.$$

The constraint that the probability of rejection should not be too high is registered by Kolesar in that the probability that all beds are occupied - meaning that a new arrival has to be rejected - does not exceed a certain limit. The optimization problem

$$\max E(X(t))$$
$$x_{n0} \leq b$$

is thus obtained.

b) Minimizing the number of rejections

A further example of how the general optimization problem can be carried over into a specific optimization problem is shown by the problem of minimizing the number of rejections, whereby the minimum use of capacity is to be taken into consideration:

$$\min x_{n0}$$

$$\sum_{j=0}^{n} j \sum_{k=0}^{n-j} x_{jk} \geq b.$$

In this way diverse specific optimization models can be deduced from the general optimization problem.

The most important aspect of Kolesar's model is its wide range of application. A multiplicity of specific optimization models can be deduced from the general model according to which immediate problem is to be analysed. The admission strategy is more flexible than that of Young's models. In Kolesar's model an optimal admission number for patients of type 2 is calculated for each state of the system. Young's second model had, it is true, an admission number B - x, dependent on the state of the system, but this only had the objective of keeping the minimum number of occupied beds to B: in Kolesar's model the admission strategy is optimized as regards the objective function and the constraints.

A great advantage of Kolesar's model lies in the fact that no specific probability distributions are imputed to the input quantities which define the Markov chain; the quantities must only be stationary as to time. The model's scope is, therefore, hardly limited. On the other hand, there is the difficulty with the empirical calculation of the values a_j and d_{ij} which is a disadvantage.

Nevertheless there are several areas for criticism, as in the case of Young's models, which are valid here as well. Kolesar does not allow for a queue for patients of type 2; furthermore, no places are reserved for urgent cases. In addition, the rejection of admission of an urgent case is not estimated to be worse than that of a non-urgent case. The position in the model of the urgent case must, therefore, be improved.

3.2.5 Egle's model

Egle (1970) also considers a hospital ward in which urgent as well as non-urgent cases are treated. He starts with an admission policy in which the priority for the urgent cases is incorporated as follows:

If beds are free, no differentation between urgent and non-urgent cases is necessary; every incoming patient is admitted when beds are free. If all beds are occupied, and the incoming patients have to wait in a queue, the order "first come - first served" has to be altered so that newly-arrived urgent cases go to the top of the queue and thus receive treatment before the non-urgent cases when beds become free.

This admission policy would, however, also mean that urgent cases would have to wait, even if for a shorter period of time than the non-urgent cases. Egle therefore assumes that the urgent cases at the top of the queue are given emergency beds where they can receive the necessary treatment. They wait there until regular beds are free for them.

This assumption enables waiting times for urgent cases to be excluded. The planning objective is now to fix the supply of beds in the ward so that the mean waiting time for non-urgent cases does not exceed a defined standard value.

Egle bases his considerations on two different Poisson arrival flows, one for urgent cases with the expected value λ_1, and the other for non-urgent cases with the expected value λ_2. He regards the treatment time as an exponentially distributed random quantity with the parameter μ for both groups of patients.

Egle obtains the following result for the mean waiting time w for non-urgent cases:

$$w = \frac{P}{\mu^2 (n-\rho)\ (n-\rho_1)}$$

with

$$\rho = (\lambda_1 + \lambda_2)/\mu,$$

$$\rho_1 = \lambda_1/\mu,$$

$$P = \sum_{i=n}^{\infty} p_i,$$

i.e. P is the probability that non-urgent cases will have to wait.

The influence of the arrival rate of the urgent cases on the waiting time of the non-urgent cases is made evident by the expression $(n - \rho_1)$ in the denominator. For $\lambda_1 \rightarrow n\mu$ the waiting time w is infinite, i.e. the total treatment capacity μn is occupied exclusively by urgent cases. In order to make the treatment of non-urgent cases possible

$$\lambda_1/\mu < n$$

must be valid.

The decision problem then reads:

$$\min \{n \mid w \leq W\} = n^*$$

with W as the tolerance limit for the waiting time.

In contrast to Young and Kolesar Egle takes waiting-lists for non-urgent cases, which do, of course, actually occur in practice, into consideration in the form of queues. Apart from this the group of urgent cases is granted genuine priority. In spite of this priority, however, Egle's admission policy fails to convince completely. Egle attempts to neutralize the contradiction between the two opposite elements of the admission policy - on the one hand placing even urgent cases in a queue, even if they are placed at the head, and on the other the elimination of the waiting time for urgent cases - by assuming the existence of emergency beds. Egle hereby shifts one part of the problem onto the problem of the determination of the supply of emergency beds, without, however, going into it more closely; when the results from his model are converted into practice Egle simply says that an "adequate emergency bed capacity" must be provided.

The role of the emergency beds is overtaxed in the model. If a high use of capacity is aimed for, i.e. if the ward is quite often fully occupied, it will fairly often happen that urgent cases have at first to occupy emergency beds. This is not in keeping, however, with the intention that emergency beds are only to be made up for extraordinary and unforeseeable events. It would be better, therefore, to say that a sufficiently large number of regular beds is available for emergencies; the model will then deliver a decision rule for one section of the regular beds only, namely for those beds which are also open to non-urgent cases.

Because urgent patients who find all the beds occupied have, according to the model, to wait in a queue for their admission to a regular bed, their treatment has not yet started in the model, although, in practice, they are already being treated and nursed in the emergency bed. The treatment time only begins in the model when a regular bed is free for the urgent patient; the treatment time in the emergency bed is ignored. The waiting time in the model for urgent cases is, therefore, too long; this error is reflected by the waiting-time assessed for the non-urgent cases, which is also too long.

3.2.6 The simulation model from Smith and Solomon

With the simulation of different admission strategies Smith and Solomon attempt to discover the admission strategy which makes admissions as constant as possible, i.e. which brings about a daily number of admissions with few deviations and a predetermined use of capacity.

Two types of patients are observed. The first group is distinguished by being admitted although they had not made an appointment; for example, urgent cases. The second group consists of patients who have been promised a bed for a particular date; it is presumed that these patients will be admitted into hospital exactly two weeks after being assured of a bed by the hospital administration. The number of assurances which may be given daily is calculated by means of the respective underlying admission strategy. Smith and Solomon run through three admission strategies:

Strategy 1: a certain percentage of the number of those released today is noted.

Strategy 2: the number of those released today, plus or minus a constant number, is the same as the assurances.

Strategy 3: a fixed number, independent of the number of releases, is noted.

The number of assurances exactly two weeks ago is the basis for the number of admissions today. As not all the patients sent for actually turn up at the hospital this number is multiplied with a percentage which states how many of the patients sent for do in fact turn up.

The running of the hospital is simulated for a whole year. For every month an average number of the daily incoming patients in group 1 and a monthly percentage of those patients in group 2 sent for and actually arriving is worked out from the values observed in the previous hospital year.

In diagram 1 the simulation of the hospital's working system for one day is illustrated by way of example using strategy 1 or 2 as a basis. At the start of the day 1052 beds are occupied and 1053 at the end of the day.

The average degree of the utilization of capacity and the deviations in the daily admissions can be calculated using the values gathered over the 365 days.

A comparison of the simulations of the three admission strategies has shown that strategy 3 is optimal: this results in utilization of capacity which is practically equal to that desired, and the number of patients admitted daily is at the same time subject to the fewest deviations of all three strategies.

The objective criteria contained in Smith and Solomon's simulation model are the achieving of a desired maximum performance as regards bed-occupation and the most constant number of daily admitted patients which is possible. While the objective of realizing a capacity occupation presents no problems, the problem of how to make the number of admissions more constant appears to be at least over-emphasized. Certainly, a constant, steady number of admissions is desirable for the running of the hospital but should remain a secondary objective. The main objectives should be the maximum use of capacity from the point of view of costs and the best possible care of the population from the point of view of services.

While it is true that the admission strategy which is the best for the purposes of the underlying objective target can be established by means of the simulation model from the set of the tested admission strategies, it is none-the-less true that this solution is subject to a certain arbitrariness through the choice of the admission strategies which are to be tested; the best of the observed strategies is not necessarily the optimal admission strategy.

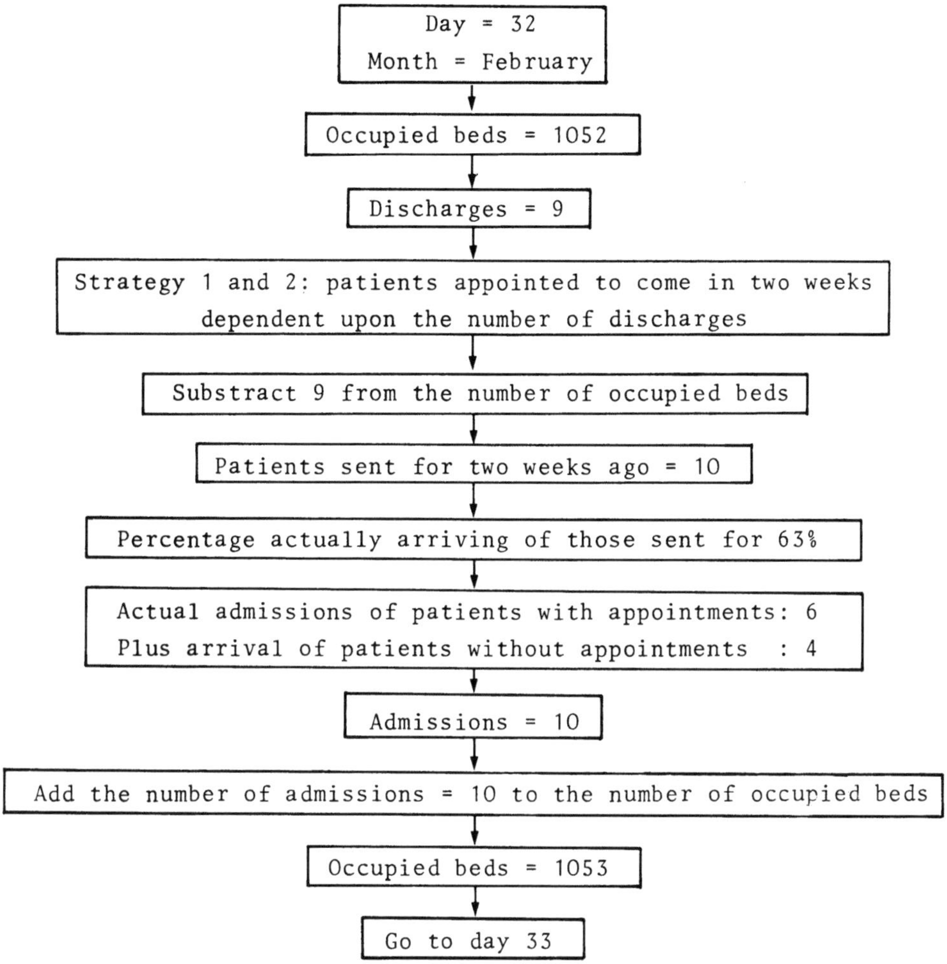

Diagram 1: Flow diagram for Smith and Solomon's simulation model

In order to define the best admission strategy each individual strategy must be calculated with different values, e.g. for strategy 1 with different percentages for the number of discharges; for strategy 2 different constant additions to and subtractions from the number of discharges; and for strategy 3 different fixed numbers of admissions. It is true that these possibilities are reduced because to a certain extent it can be estimated which values would lead too far away from the desired use of capacity, but the volume of calculations is nevertheless still quite large.

This model is unsuitable as an aid in the planning of the number of beds needed because it cannot be judged whether strategy 3 is the best solution for a bed-supply other than that assumed in the model.

3.2.7 A model for the determination of the optimal number of reserved beds

In contrast to Young's second model Esogbue and Singh (1976) do not attempt to present the number of beds to be reserved for urgent cases but to determine it in an optimization process.

The arrival process of the urgent cases describes a Poisson process with the parameter λ_1 and, correspondingly, the arrival process of the non-urgent cases also describes a Poisson process with the parameter λ_2. The periods spent in the hospital are exponentially distributed random variables with the parameters μ_i, $i = 1,2$. The bed-supply is preset and equal to N. n is the number of beds from N whose occupation means that only urgent cases will be admitted. After the derivation and solution of differential and difference equation systems the stationary probabilities

$$P_{j,j_2} \text{ with } j \leq N,\ j_2 \leq j,\ j_2 \leq n,$$

are obtained, i.e. that j of the N beds are occupied and of these j patients j_2 are non-urgent cases. Urgent cases are rejected when all N beds are occupied; non-urgent patients must go to another hospital when n of the N beds are occupied. The probability V_2 that a non-urgent patient will be rejected amounts to:

$$V_2 = \sum_{j=n}^{N} \sum_{j_2=0}^{n} P_{j,j_2}.$$

For the probability V_1, that an urgent patient will be rejected

$$V_1 = \sum_{j_2=0}^{n} p_{N,j_2}$$

is valid.

If c_2^i, $i = 1,2$, stands for the penalty costs for rejecting a patient of type i and c_1 for the costs per unit of time of an empty bed, the costs K_V of the rejections are:

$$K_V = c_2^1 v_1 \lambda_1 + c_2^2 v_2 \lambda_2$$

and the costs K_B of the empty beds:

$$K_B = \begin{cases} c_1 \sum_{j=n+1}^{N} \sum_{j_2=0}^{n} (N-j) p_{j,j_2} & \text{for } j > n, \\ c_1 \sum_{j=0}^{n} \sum_{j_2=0}^{j} (N-j) p_{j,j_2} & \text{for } j \leq n, \end{cases}$$

while $K = K_V + K_B$ stands for the total costs K.

The objective is to determine n so that the costs are minimized, i.e.

$$K(n) \longrightarrow \min.$$

The solution for the treatment of urgent cases appears in this model to be the best of all the models illustrated up to now. By fixing the quantities c_2^1 and c_2^2 the rejection of urgent and non-urgent cases can be valued differently. The reservation of a part of the bed-supply for urgent cases must be an element of a useful admission strategy.

Esogbue and Singh's model can be criticized for not allowing any waiting times for non-urgent cases; if n of the N beds are occupied, non-urgent patients seeking admission are rejected. This does not correspond with the conditions found in reality.

3.2.8 Conclusions

An analysis of the approaches described shows that Esogbue and Singh's and Egle's models deliver the most serviceable results. In Egle's model the influence of the arrival process of the urgent cases on the waiting times for the non-urgent cases is convincingly deduced, while Esogbue and Singh are the only one who place the problem of the reservation of beds for urgent cases in the centre of the examination. The weakness of Egle's model lies in not considering the problem of the emergency bed capacity; on the other hand, Esogbue and Singh ignore queues and waiting times for non-urgent cases which are found in practice.

In the following section a model for the simultaneous fixing of the optimal supply of beds and emergency beds will be presented. The considerations will start on the basis of the underlying admission strategy found in Esogbue and Singh's model, with the exception that non-urgent cases will be placed on a waiting-list in the event that all available beds are occupied. As many non-urgent cases will be admitted daily as beds which they are allowed to occupy become free, except when there are not enough patients on the waiting-list to occupy the free beds.

4 A model for the simultaneous determination of the optimal supply of beds and emergency beds

4.1 A sketch of the decision approach

Schmidt (1981) was the first to formulate the model here under consideration. It starts with the following deliberations.

When there is a relatively large number of empty beds the undifferentiated admission of urgent and non-urgent cases presents no problems, as there are always enough beds available. Only when the supply of regula beds is exhausted is a differentiation between the admission of urgent cases and that of non-urgent cases necessary in order to be able to give priority to the urgent cases. This priority is to be guaranteed by a certain number n_1 of beds which are reserved exclusively for urgent cases. The hospital ward is then characterized by the number n of regular beds which may be occupied by urgent or non-urgent cases, and by the additional number n_1 of beds reserved exclusively for urgent cases. The n_1 beds are only used by the urgent cases when the regular beds are all occupied.

If all n_1 emergency beds are occupied a new urgent case must be rejected, and the patient will have to be accommodated in another hospital. The loss quota is worked out through the number of urgent cases turned away.

If a non-urgent case finds all the regular beds occupied he then joins a queue; a member of the queue can only be treated when all n_1 reserved emergency beds are free and in addition one of the n regular beds becomes free. The order on the queue of non-urgent cases is "first come - first served".

The objective of the decision model is to minimize the two quantities n and n_1, whereby political targets as regards the admissible average queue or waiting time for non-urgent cases as well as the loss quota of the urgent cases must be considered as constraints.

4.2 Determining the probabilities for the states of the system and the occupation of emergency beds

Starting points are two Poisson distributed arrival processes for urgent and non-urgent cases with the parameters λ_1 and λ_2. Let the duration of stay follow the exponential distribution with the parameter μ and let it be equally distributed for both types of patient.

The system is then in the state Z_t^i when the following is true:

at time t there are exactly i of the n regular beds occupied for $i = 0,1,\dots,n$;

or: at time t all regular beds are occupied and in addition there is a queue of i-n non-urgent cases for $i = n+1, n+2,\dots$.

For the states Z_t^i, $i = 0,1,\dots,n-1$, it is true that neither a queue of urgent patients exists nor is one of the n_1 emergency beds occupied. If a state Z_t^i, $i = 0,1,\dots,n-1$, exists this also gives information as to the occupancy of the emergency beds.

For a state Z_t^i, $i = n, n+1,\dots$, all possibilities for emergency bed occupation are, in principle, within reach. If all n regular beds are occupied the following incidents can occur:

a) $j = 0,1,\dots,n_1$ of the n_1 emergency beds are occupied in addition to the regular n beds;

b) $m = 0,1,\ldots$ non-urgent cases are waiting to be given an unoccupied regular bed.

The incidents above are not mutually exclusive, on the contrary, incidents from each of a) and b) occur together at a definite point in time.

For Z_t^i, $i = 0,1,\ldots,n-1$, the incidents $j = 0$ from a) and $m = 0$ from b) occur per definition each with the probability of one; in order to characterize the state Z_t^i as regards emergency bed occupancies it is sufficient for $i = 0,1,\ldots,n-1$ to state the number of occupied regular beds. If, however all n regular beds are occupied, every possible combination of incidents from a) with those from b) can occur. In order to be able to use the theory of the Markov processes, a definite characterization of the system is necessary. To do this the total problem will be divided into two subproblems:

First subproblem
At this level all relevant constituent facts for the non-urgent cases are looked at, as far as they need to be considered in dependence upon the results derived from the second subproblem. In the first subproblem, therefore, the effects of the entry parameters n, n_1, λ_1, λ_2, and μ on the treatment and waiting processes of the non-urgent cases will be examined. Essentially, the issue here is the deduction of the stationary probability distribution p_i, $i \in \{0,1,\ldots,n,n+1,\ldots\}$, whereby, independent of time t

p_i, $i = 0,1,\ldots,n-1$, may denote the probability that i of the regular beds are occupied;

p_n, $i = n$, may denote the probability that n regular beds are occupied, but that no queue of non-urgent cases exists;

p_i, $i = n+1, n+2,\ldots$, may denote the probability that all regular beds are occupied and in addition a queue of the length i of non-urgent cases exists.

Second subproblem
Relevant facts for the urgent cases must be depicted using the knowledge gained from the first subproblem, i.e. the stationary probabilities $s_j|Z_t^i$ independent of time t are to be determined that j of the n_1 emergency beds are occupied, provided that the system is in the state Z_t^i.

Because they are closely interlaced the both subproblems can only be solved simultaneously.

Because of basic processes constitute Poisson processes and thus homogeneous Markov processes, all combination processes from the basic processes are homogeneous Markov processes. As a solution p_i, $i \in \{0,1,\ldots, n,n+1,\ldots\}$, of the stationary probability distribution for Z_t^i and s_j, $j \in \{0,1,\ldots,n_1\}$, of the stationary probability distribution for the emergency bed occupancy process the following is obtained:

$$p_i = \frac{\rho^i}{i!} p_0, \qquad i \in \{1,\ldots,n-1\},$$

$$p_n = \frac{\rho^n}{n! s_0} p_0,$$

$$p_{n+1} = \frac{\rho^n \rho_2^i}{n! n^i s_0^{i+1}} p_0, \qquad i \in \{1,\ldots.\},$$

$$s_j = \frac{n! \rho_1^j}{(n+j)!} s_0, \qquad j \in \{1,\ldots,n_1\},$$

with

$$\rho = \lambda/\mu,$$
$$\rho_1 = \lambda_1/\mu, \qquad \lambda_2 < \mu n s_0,$$
$$\rho_2 = \lambda_2/\mu, \qquad \lambda = \lambda_1 + \lambda_2,$$

and

$$p_0 = 1/(1 + \sum_{i=1}^{n-1} \frac{\rho^i}{i!} + \frac{\rho^n}{n!\ s_0 - (n-1)!\rho_2}),$$

$$s_0 = 1/1(1+n! \sum_{j=1}^{n_1} \frac{\rho_1^j}{(n+1)!}).$$

The condition $\lambda_2 < \mu n s_0$ states that the expected value of the arrival process of the non-urgent cases must be smaller than the expected value of the service process when n regular beds are fully occupied, which are determined for non-urgent cases. Where n regular beds are fully occupied the amount of $\mu n s_0$ of the total service capacity is for the benefit of the non-urgent cases. If the arrival process of the non-urgent cases exceeds this service capacity an infinite long queue of non-urgent cases ensues, which is not very meaningful.

4.3 Formulation of the decision model

It is now possible, using the probabilities p_i and s_i, to develop and estimate certain criteria which can be built into the decision model as restrictions. For costs reasons the attempt will be made to minimize the hospital's bed-supply. This minimization must not, however, lead to patients having to put up with situations which are regarded by current opinion as unreasonable. These impossible conditions express themselves in the form of unreasonably long queues and unreasonable waiting times for non-urgent cases, and in too many rejections of urgent cases. In the decision model, therefore, values are present for the length of the queue, the average waiting time, and the rejection quota which are still just acceptable.

$$u = \frac{\rho^n \rho_2}{(n-1)!(ns_0-\rho_2)^2} p_0$$

is valid for the average length u of the queue for non-urgent patients.

The average waiting time w is

$$w = \frac{\rho^n}{\mu(n-1)!(ns_0-\rho_2)^2} p_0 .$$

Between u and w the relation

$$u = \lambda_2 w$$

applies.

From this relation follows: if the same average length u of the queue emerges for n, n_1, λ_1, λ_2, μ and $\bar{n}$, $\bar{n}_1$, $\bar{\lambda}_1$, $\bar{\lambda}_2$, $\bar{\mu}$ with $\lambda_2 < \bar{\lambda}_2$ then

$$w = \frac{u}{\lambda_2} > \frac{u}{\bar{\lambda}_2} = \bar{w}$$

is valid.

The smaller the quota of non-urgent cases is, i.e. the higher the quota of urgent cases by constant average queue length, the longer the non-urgent patients have to wait. This fact expresses that a non-urgent patient must expect that urgent cases will be given preference during his waiting time. That part of the waiting time which occurs as a result of urgent cases being given priority is all the longer, the larger the share of service capacity is which is given over to urgent cases.

If all regular beds are occupied the probability that all n_1 emergency beds are also occupied equals s_{n_1}. Altogether, therefore

$$v = s_{n_1} \sum_{i=n}^{\infty} p_i$$

is valid for the probability v that all emergency beds are occupied, i.e. that an incoming urgent patient will have to be rejected; the probability corresponds to the loss quota.

The absolute number of the rejected urgent cases per unit of time equals

$$\lambda_1 v ,$$

i.e. after an average $1/(\lambda_1 v)$ units of time one urgent patient will be rejected.

The decision model can now be formulated with the derived quantities. Let W stand for the still just admissible average waiting time for the non-urgent cases and for the just admissible loss quota for the urgent cases. Let W, V, λ_1, λ_2, and μ be given. The following decision problem then arises:

$$\begin{aligned} &\min\ n + n_1 \\ &\quad w \leq W , \\ &\quad v \leq V . \end{aligned}$$

4.4 Solution procedure

The minimum bed supply, which still just fulfills the constraints, is determined by a search algorithm.

Initial value for the supply of regular beds is

$$n^* = \min \{n \mid n > \rho_2\}$$

and for the supply of emergency beds

$$n_1 = 0$$

All the values n, $n < n^*$, are not suitable for the solution, as they lead to an infinitely long queue for the non-urgent cases.

The pair (n, n_1) is to stand for the input values in each case; the first input then reads:

$$(n^*,0).$$

In accordance with the formula derived in section 4.3 w and v are computed for the input $(n^*,0)$. If the conditions

$$w \leq W,$$
$$v \leq V$$

are fulfilled $(n^*,0)$ is the desired solution.

If not, the supply of beds is increased by one. Here there are two possibilities to consider:

a) the regular bed supply n^* is increased by one to n^*+1, or
b) the number of emergency beds n_1 is raised from zero to one.

The total supply of beds in both cases amounts to n^*+1. Each of the pairs $(n^*+1,0)$ and $(n^*,1)$ which fulfil the constraints represents a solution. While the solution as regards the total supply of beds is, therefore, always unique, the division of the bed supply into regular and emergency beds is not always unique.

If no solution has been found with the total supply of beds n^*+1 the supply is further increased until a solution has been found. With a bed-supply of n^*+i beds there is a total of i+1 possibilities for the division of i additional beds into regular and emergency beds. In principle, therefore, i+1 pairs must be examined as to their compliance with the constraints. The following theorem (Schmidt 1981, p. 123) enables the amount of calculation necessary to be reduced:

> if the relation $w \geq W$ is valid for a pair $(n+k,m)$, the relation $w > W$ is valid for all pairs $(n+k,m')$ with $m' > m$.

Economically this theorem means: by increasing the supply of emergency beds with otherwise equal entry data the rejection quota v becomes smaller, because the treatment capacity for urgent cases is increased. On the other hand, the waiting time w is made longer by an increase in the supply of emergency beds. The treatment capacity for non-urgent cases becomes smaller, because fewer urgent cases are rejected, and these additional admissions for urgent cases are pushed into the queue in front of the non-urgent cases waiting there.

The advantage for the numerical application lies in all pairs $(n+k', m')$ with $m' > m$, $k' < k$, being excluded from further considerations, if the relation $w \geq W$ is valid for a pair $(n+k,m)$. The number of calculations is thus reduced.

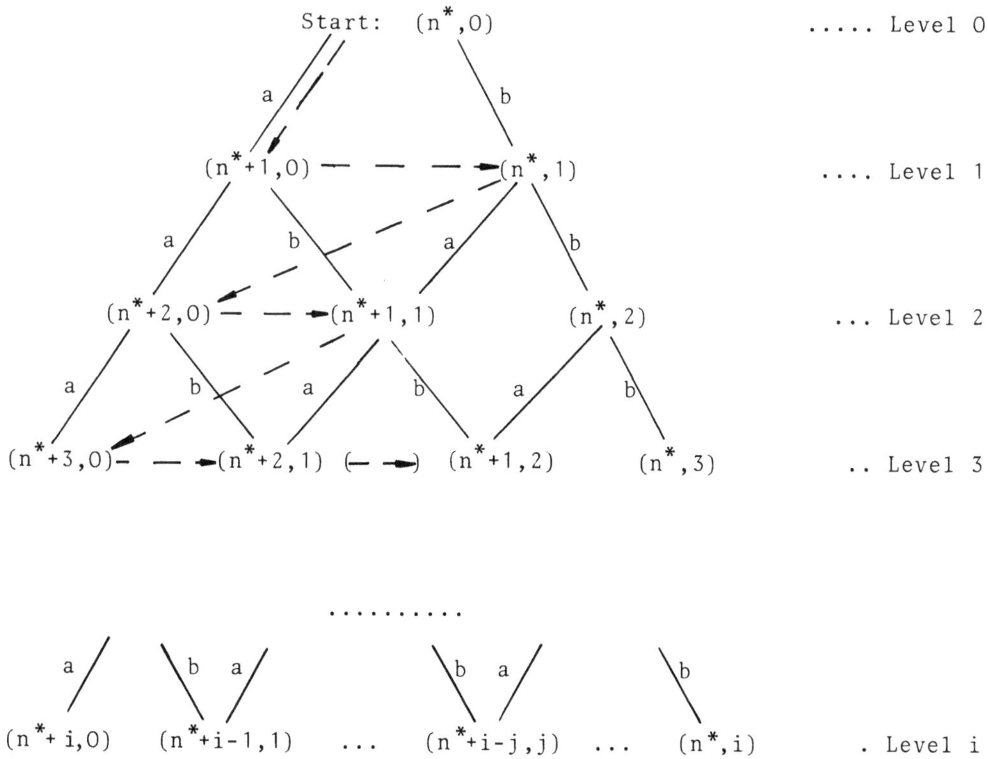

Diagram 2: Search tree for the solution of the decision problem

Diagram 2 shows the possibilities for the division of a gradually increased bed supply. The a-lines mean an increase in the regular bed supply of 1, the b-lines an increase in the emergency bed supply of 1. Each of the pairs on the left is connected with the initial value $(n^*,0)$ by a-lines only; the pairs on the right are reached by the b-lines. All other pairs are connected with the initial value $(n^*,0)$ by at least one a-line and one b-line respectively. The iterative approach to the optimal solution is shown by the dotted lines. The two pairs $(n^*+3,0)$ and $(n^*+2,1)$ may show the elements of the solution set. The following relations underlie the tracing of the dotted lines:

Pair	Relation
$(n^*,0)$	$w \leq W$ and $v > V$
$(n^*+1,0)$	$w < W$ and $v > V$
$(n^*,1)$	$w > W$ or $v > V$
$(n^*+2,0)$	$w < W$ and $v > V$
$(n^*+1,1)$	$w > W$ and $v \gtreqless V$
$(n^*+3,0)$	$w < W$ and $v \leq V$
$(n^*+2,1)$	$w \leq W$ and $v < V$
$(n^*+1,2)$	$w > W$ and $v < V$

In general the following rules for the search algorithm can be obtained from the example:

1. Work out the relations for the pairs of a level from left to right.

2. Jump to the next level either when the previous level has been worked out (see levels 0 and 1), or when the relation $w > W$ occurs for the first time for a pair (n, n_1) on the previous level (see level 2); in the latter case all further points on the decision tree are superfluous which provide for n or fewer regular beds.

3. If the relations $w \leq W$ and $v \leq V$ occur on a level together for the first time, the solution lies completely on this level. The level is worked further until $w > W$ is valid (cf. pair $(n^*+1,2)$ on level 3); this pair no longer belongs to the solution set.

Rule 2 shows that it is expedient first of all to calculate the average waiting time w for each pair; because if $w > W$ is true a calculation of v is unnecessary, because a jump must be made to the next level in any case.

Rule 3 states that the solution of the total bed-supply is unique, the splitting into regular beds is not unique.

Diagram 3 shows the algorithm for a solution of the problem of the total bed-supply and its division into regular and emergency beds. In this n^* means the least necessary supply of regular beds as may be required from the actual state of the procedure; correspondingly, $\bar{n}$ states the total bed supply. According to rule 2 n^* and $\bar{n}$ are each increased by 1 when the relation $w > W$ turns up on a level; $\bar{n}$ is increased apart from that when the relevant points of a level have been worked out. Relevant points of a level are the pairs which have not been excluded by reason of the conclusions reached in accordance with rule 2.

If a solution has been found the total bed supply is thus unique. There are, however, other ways of apportioning beds which are also conceivable as solutions, apart from the first one found. Because the total bed supply has to be minimized all optimal solutions must lie on one level. All pairs lying on a level on which an optimal solution has been found, and which also fulfill the both constraints, are also themselves optimal solutions. Therefore, if the first optimal solution has been found, the level is worked further to the right until the relation $w > W$ turns up for a pair. This pair is no longer an optimal solution; the relation $w > W$ applies to all pairs on this level which stand further to the right, so that these pairs cannot be optimal solutions and there is no need to calculate them.

4.5 A case study on the optimal supply of beds and emergency beds

The determination of the optimal supply of beds and emergency beds in a hospital ward will be demonstrated by means of an example.

Let the patient-yield of a ward in a surgical hospital amount to 0.52 urgent patients per day, and 3.52 non-urgent patients per day; let the average duration of a stay in the ward be about 14 days (Jahresbericht 1977 des Städtischen Krankenhauses Frankfurt/Höchst); i.e.

$$\lambda_1 = 0.52; \quad \lambda_2 = 3.52; \quad \mu = 1/14.$$

The following constraints shall apply: the average waiting time for non-urgent cases may not exceed $W = 14$ days; the rejection quota for urgent cases may not be more than $V = 1.5$ %.

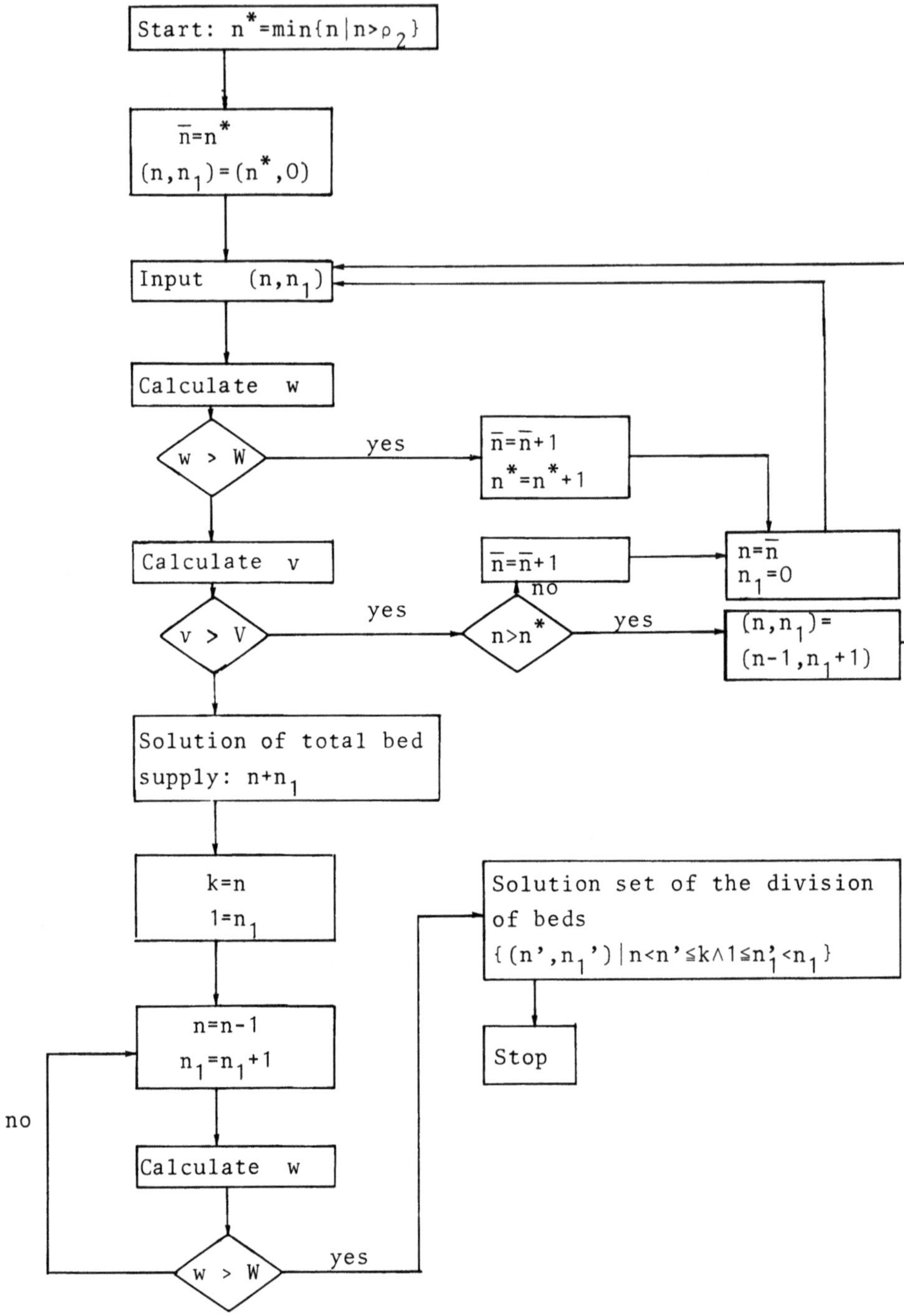

<u>Diagram 3:</u> Solution algorithm for the problem of the bed supply

The minimum supply of beds must be found which can satisfy the demand while fulfilling the requirements laid down in the constraints; in addition, the optimal division of the total bed-supply into regular beds, which can be occupied by both types of patient, and emergency beds for the use of urgent cases only, has to be stated.

The iterative approximation to the optimal solution can be followed in table 1.

$(n,n_1) = (50,0)$ is chosen as initial value because

$\min \{n | n > 3.52 \cdot 14 = 49.28, n \in \mathbb{N}\} = 50.$

The bed supply (50,0) results in an average waiting time of 18.23 days, and a loss quota of 93.78 %. Both constraints are therefore violated. The bed supply must therefore be increased.

The bed supply (51,0) keeps inside the upper limit for the average waiting time, but the loss quota is much too high. The pair (50,1) does not have to be assessed along rule 2, because a regular bed supply of 50 beds is in any case insufficient.

The next pair is (52,0). The loss quota is still above the permitted upper limit, while the constraint for the waiting time is fulfilled. In accordance with rule 1 the calculation continues with the pair (51,1).

Reserving a bed for urgent cases worsens the position of the non-urgent cases enormously, because the preferential treatment of the urgent cases now comes into play. An urgent case pushes itself in front of the waiting non-urgent cases and thus reduces the service capacity $\mu s_0 n$ for the non-urgent cases. For the pair (52,0) $s_0 = 1$ and therefore $\mu s_0 n = 3.71 > \lambda_2 = 3.52$, for the pair (51,1) $s_0 = 1-s_1 = 1-v$ and therefore $\mu s_0 n = 3.2 < \lambda_2 = 3.52$, i.e. the pair (51,1) has an arrival process for the non-urgent cases greater than the service process for these patients; this means an infinitely long waiting time for the non-urgent cases.

Following rule 2, the next pair is (53,0).

The process just described carries on the same way until pair (56,1) is reached. For the first time a finitely long waiting time for the non-urgent patients is achieved with just one emergency bed; the constraint

Table 1: Loss quota v and average waiting period w dependent on n and n_1 for $\lambda_1 = 0.52$, $\lambda_2 = 3.52$, and $\mu = 1/14$

n	n_1	v	w
50	0	93,78	18,23
51	0	85,44	6,95
52	0	77,46	3,99
51	1	12,30	∞
53	0	69,85	2,63
52	1	12,10	∞
54	0	62,63	1,86
53	1	11,90	∞
55	0	55,82	1,37
54	1	11,70	∞
56	0	49,43	1,03
55	1	11,50	∞
57	0	43,47	0,79
56	1	10,71	35,04
58	0	37,96	0,61
57	1	9,07	8,35
59	0	32,90	0,47
58	1	7,63	4,14
57	2	1,22	18,60
60	0	28,28	0,37
59	1	6,36	2,47
58	2	1,00	6,40
61	0	24,10	0,29
60	1	5,27	1,60
59	2	0,82	3,40
58	3	0,12	6,78

for the average waiting time is, however, not yet fulfilled. It is to be noted that the transition from pair (57,0) to pair (56,1) leads to a reduction in the loss quota through the reservation of one bed for urgent cases from 43.47 % to 10.71 %; on the other hand, there is at the same time a steep increase in the waiting time, because non-urgent patients only get a chance when the emergency bed is unoccupied and in addition a regular bed becomes free.

Adherence to the maximum permissible loss quota is achieved for the first time by pair (57,2); because the average waiting time is still too long the optimal solution has not yet been reached.

The pair (58,2) fulfills for the first time both constraints and is thus an optimal solution; this pair is, in fact, the only optimal solution, because the neighbouring pair (57,3) will lead to an average waiting time for non-urgent cases which is too long, because the pair (57,2) already violates this condition.

The ward under observation should, therefore, contain 60 beds; of these beds two should be reserved exclusively for the use of urgent cases, i.e. these beds will only be occupied when all the other 58 are occupied and urgent cases arrive. A non-urgent patient will only be given a bed when two of the 60 beds are free for the admission of possible emergency cases and in addition there is one unoccupied bed.

If the ward is laid in this way it would mean that about 1 % of the urgent cases would have to be sent to another hospital, and the non-urgent cases would have to wait on average 6.4 days until they were given a bed; the probability that a non-urgent patient would have to wait is 76.2 %, and there are on average 23 patients on the waiting-list.

The optimal solution has a degree of capacity utilization of 94 %. The actual bed supply in the surgical ward was 63 and they were utilized to 89.3 %.

Literature:

Adam, D.: Krankenhausmanagement im Konfliktfeld zwischen medizinischen und wirtschaftlichen Zielen, Wiesbaden 1972.

Axtner, W.: Krankenhausmanagement, Baden-Baden 1978.

Egle, K.: Wartezeitmodelle und Krankenhausplanung, in: Zeitschrift für betriebswirtschaftliche Forschung 22, 1970, pp. 322.

Esogbue, A.O., and Singh, A.J.: A Stochastic Model for an Optimal Priorit Bed Distribution Problem in a Hospital Ward, in: Operations Research 2 1976, pp. 884.

Fritz, K.: Möglichkeiten der Kostendämpfung im Krankenhaus, in: Deutsches Ärzteblatt, 1977, p. 1543.

Jahresbericht 1977 des Städtischen Krankenhauses Frankfurt/Höchst.

Kolesar, P.: A Markovian Model for Hospital Admission Scheduling, in: Management Science 16, 1970, pp. B-384.

Meyer, M., and Schläger, W.: Ablaufplanung im Krankenhaus mit Hilfe von Operations-Research-Modellen, in: Mertens, P. (ed.): Die Unternehmung in ihrer gesellschaftlichen Umwelt, Wiesbaden 1975, pp. 121.

Neumann, K.: Operations Research Verfahren, Vol. 2, München/Wien 1977.

Sasieni, M., Yaspan, A., and Friedmann, L.: Operations Research - methods and problems, New York/London/Sydney 1959.

Smith, W.G., and Solomon, M.B.: A Simulation of Hospital Admission Policy in: Communications of the ACM 9, 1966, pp. 362.

Tätigkeitsbericht der Bundesärztekammer 1976/77: Arzt und Krankenhaus, in: Deutsches Ärzteblatt, 1977, pp. 1346.

Young, J.P.: Administrative Control of Multiple-Channel Queuing Systems with Parallel Input Streams, in: Operations Research 1, 1966, pp. 145.

On Capacity Planning of Diagnosis Systems in Hospitals

Günter Fandel and Holger Hegemann

1 Object and course of the investigation

In the last twenty years hospitals have developed into cost and investment intensive service enterprises confronted with a rising pressure of costs. Apart from an enormous expansion in personnel costs the reasons can be seen in a higher equipment with apparatus based on the rapid developments in the medical-technical progress and the therewith attendant and fast increasing demand for hospital services.

Aspects of medical necessity and effectiveness are decisive for the production of health services in hospitals; but this process must be reviewed on the basis of efficiency considerations as well. This follows from the mere fact that a hospital must be regarded as a consumer oriented facility having to provide certain medical services efficiently by combining different production factors. Although some methodical and legal deliberations have already been made in this direction, the German hospital system does not yet satisfy those economic criteria being already fulfilled in other industrialized nations. In this context the fact is characteristic, that hospital management was not represented at the health economy congress of the Verein für Socialpolitik 1985 by a particular study group.

This argumentation applies correspondingly to the diagnostics being of central significance to the service production in hospitals. For, this subsystem is claimed as the first service area by the patients and the examination results received hereby give important orientation marks for the following therapy and care.

The authors are especially indebted to the former medical director, Dr. Klaus Pieper, and the team of doctors of the diagnosis system at the General Hospital of Hagen City for having made possible the empirical study carried out in this context.

The inexpedient allocation of medical staff and equipment especially in the diagnostics would lead to considerable differences in the load degrees of the different diagnostic service units and to increased waiting times for patients in front of the diagnostic rooms. The latter would entail a retardation of the following therapy and care. In order to avoid such misallocations and their consequences capacity planning in the clinical diagnostics on the basis of the methods of operations research is indispensable.

So far, only subsystems of the clinical diagnostics have been analyzed in the literature by means of network-planning-technique (Fleck 1977, Taylor/Keown 1980), queueing theory (Bailey 1954, Taylor/Templeton 1980) and simulation (Carruthers 1970, Gierl 1976, O'Kane 1981, Revesz/Shea/Ziskin 1972). The above mentioned problem, however, can only be solved by a central capacity planning including the interdependencies existing in the form of patients' ways among the single diagnostic units of a hospital. In addition, under instrumental aspects it must be objected, that the network-planning-technique does not allow the consideration of the patient's arrival behaviour in the diagnostic area and that the simulation as a method without the quality of convergency will remain inferior to the queueing theory as long as the special planning situation allows the application of this exact method.

Consequently, a queueing model, which shall describe the structure of the diagnostic system and the diagnosis process by means of patients flows as close to reality as possible, is chosen as the basis for the analytical investigations to be carried out within the scope of capacity planning. In contrast to the approaches in the literature, in which only single diagnostic rooms or units and actually only one patient flow were objects of the model considerations, here however two modifications are necessary. On the one hand, the entire approach demands that a network-oriented total system of the diagnostics is taken as the basis. On the other hand, attention has to be paid to the fact that this general system is passed through by two patient streams simultaneously resulting from the examination processes of out-patients and in-patients. With regard to the management and optimal configuration of such systems it can be demonstrated, though, that the queueing models well-known from the literature (Gross/Harris 1974, Jackson 1963) can also be extended easily to such a generalized problem situation under certain assumptions (Hegemann 1985).

The queueing model for capacity planning presented in the following can be applied to the planning of measures for constructing new or extending old buildings in the clinical diagnostics of hospitals. At the same time, it allows to reveal weaknesses within existing diagnosis systems by means of system indices like patients' waiting times, load degrees of the apparatus and the length of the queues and to show alternatives for an improvement of the capacity structure of the diagnosis area. Thereby the long-term optimal capacity structure is often characterized by waiting times of patients in front of diagnostic service units not exceeding a given reasonable limit and reaching a possibly high load degree for the single examination rooms as well as for the total diagnostic system.

Finally, the methodical reflections will be exemplified for the diagnosis system of the General Hospital of Hagen City, which contains 650 beds. Thoughts on rationalization are in the foreground of the application-oriented statements. It will appear, that simple organizing measures concerning the rearrangement and fusion of diagnostic service units can reduce the average patients' waiting times by more than 20% and allow an increase in the expected load degree of the total diagnosis system by 18%.

2 Queueing theoretical description of a diagnosis system

2.1 An outline of the diagnostics and their particularities

Beside therapy, care, and medical education and research the diagnostics are part of the medical area of a hospital, which is differentiated from the economic and administrative area containing mainly management tasks. The numerous relations possibly existing between the diagnosis system and other subareas of a hospital are not object of the reflections. The considerations rather concentrate on the diagnostics as a system, their system elements and the interdependencies occurring among them as well as on the derivation of suitable system indices characterizing the quality of the diagnosis system under economic aspects. The diagnostics possess their external relations in the flows of out-patients and in-patients entering, passing through and leaving the diagnosis system for reasons of diagnosis on the initiative of private doctor's practices or by order of the care and therapeutical departments of the hospital.

The diagnostics can be viewed as the totality of all those activities necessary for the production of a diagnosis; so these activities delineate the way to a diagnosis. Under system analytical aspects the diagnostics are usually divided into the sections X-ray diagnostics, laboratory diagnostics, function diagnostics, and endoscopy (Eichhorn 1976, pp. 281), which themselves can be subdivided into single service units or diagnosis rooms. In these service units being elements of the diagnosis system single diagnostic services are produced in the form of examinations by combining medical personnel, diagnostic equipment and means of medical needs as resources. The medical staff consists of doctors, medical-technical assistants, medical helpers as well as, occasionally, laboratory assistants and operating nurses. The actual diagnosis generally emerges from the composition of such individual diagnostic services in different service units; so the diagnosis ensues within the scope of a diagnostic process or is its result, respectively.

Within the diagnosis system the service units, generally united in departments under the disciplinary responsibility of a head physician, are connected by the flows of in-patients and out-patients and the information flux accompanying them. These flows result from the diagnoctic processes arranged by doctors of the different medical departments in dependence of the sickness of the individual patient to set up the diagnosis. These processes, normally different for every patient, can be seen as disease-specific parts of the total diagnostic process because of their disjunctive connection of individual diagnostic examinations. Usually they are not fixed a priori, but are mostly made concrete by the doctors during the examination. So the patients' ways via the diagnostic service units, essentially determining the internal relation structure of the total diagnosis system, must be considered as stochastic.

It is obvious to understand the diagnosis system as a waiting system and therefore to make it accessible to a queueing theoretical analysis. The diagnostic rooms can be interpreted as service stations, the patients are the traffic units, the waiting-room is the queue, and the flows of the out-patients and in-patients correspond to the traffic streams. Thus it is possible to describe the formal structure of the diagnosis system as a discrete, dynamic, stochastic, and open system by the number of diagnostic service units, the stochastic arrival behaviour of the out-patients and in-patients, the stochastic examination times in the service units as well as by the stochastic patients' ways with the transition probabilities from one service unit to the next. This, however, is not possible in the scope of a conventional queueing model; on the contrary, two extensions are necessary. Firstly, it has to be taken into account that the demand flow consists of two partial streams. Secondly, the stochastic structure of the diagnosis processes being dependent on the patients' ways has to be regarded. Whereas directly usable clues can be found in the queueing theoretical literature for the first modification, which can be taken over as results here, the necessary second modification is mastered by adding the GERT network-model (Pritsker/ Happ 1966, Neumann/Steinhardt 1979) to the queueing model in order to conceive realistically the stochastic arrival processes in the form of patients' ways. To a certain extent, both planning procedures are combined by including the exclusive-or-branchings known from the GERT model and therewith the transition probabilities of the patients between the diagnosis rooms into the queueing theoretical model construction. On this basis realistic system indices can be determined for the total diagnosis system giving information about how well the single service units are coordinated and allowing secure statements about the service quality and the efficiency of the total diagnosis system and its partial elements.

In order to judge about the efficiency and service quality of a queueing system diagnostics the following system indices for the single service units i, $i=1,\dots,N$, as well as for the total system are of interest:

(1) The expected waiting time of a patient in front of a diagnostic room and in the total system; it may be denoted by $E(V_{q_i})$ and $E(V_q)$.

(2) The expected time a patient spends in a service unit and in the total system; it is indicated by $E(V_i)$ and $E(V)$.

(3) The expected number of waiting patients in a service unit and in the total system; it is expressed by $E(L_{q_i})$ and $E(L_q)$.

(4) The expected number of patients in a service unit and in the total system; it is symbolized by $E(L_i)$ and $E(L)$.

(5) The expected load degree of a service unit and of the total system; it will be denoted by ξ_i and ξ.

These indices serve also as a basis for changes in the capacity structure of a diagnosis system to be carried out eventually.

Among these system indices the expected waiting time of a patient and the expected load degree of the service units and the total system are relevant with regard to health policy. These two criteria, which are to be minimized or maximized, are in conflict with each other being known from analogous areas of industrial production as the dilemma of scheduling. In the field of health policy this conflict is mostly solved in the way that the load degrees are maximized under the constraint that the waiting times do not exceed socially reasonable limits.

2.2 Formal description of the model of a diagnosis system

2.2.1 Premises

The queueing theoretical analysis to be carried out later on is based on the following premises:

(P 1) The out-patients and in-patients arrive at the diagnosis system from outside one by one; the arrival processes are Poisson processes with the intensities λ_o^a (for the out-patients) and λ_o^s (for the in-patients), i.e. the interarrival times are exponentially distributed with the parameters λ_o^a and λ_o^s. The subindex zero indicates the outside of the diagnosis system as the source and sink of the patients flows.

(P 2) The number of potential patients, who can enter the diagnosis system, is regarded as unlimited.

(P 3) The patients remain in the queue of the respective diagnostic service unit they joined after their arrival up to the beginning of the examination.

(P 4) The examinations of the patients in the respective diagnosis rooms take place individually and are not dependent on the arrival processes.

(P 5) The examination times of the diagnostic actions in the service units are exponentially distributed with the parameters μ_i, $i=1,\dots,N$.

(P 6) An examination once started will be finished without interruptions.

(P 7) Breakdown periods of the equipment are not considered.

(P 8) The diagnosis system consists of N service units; each diagnostic service unit i, i=1,...,N, can be composed of $n_{p_i} \in \mathbb{N}$ parallel and identical diagnostic rooms.

(P 9) If a patient has once left a diagnostic service unit i, he cannot enter it immediately again, i.e. the transition probability r_{ii} is equal to zero for all $i \in \{1,...,N\}$.

(P 10) The ways of patients from a service unit i to a service unit j are independent of each other for all $i, j \in \{1,...,N\}$, $i \neq j$.

(P 11) Times needed for the ways between service units may be neglected.

(P 12) The way of a patient through the diagnosis system is free of cycles; so he enters each service unit once at most.

(P 13) Waiting-room capacities in the diagnostic service units are unlimited.

(P 14) Patients enter the diagnosis rooms according to the service discipline "first come - first served" (FCFS).

(P 15) There are two independent sources of the flows of out-patients and in-patients.

The premises (P 1) and (P 5) were backed by the results of the empirical study - that will be reported later -, so that their supposition which can also be found in the literature is of no problem. In addition (P 5) allows the arbitrary joining or separation of diagnostic examinations without changing their distribution character. This is relevant for an eventual organizational rearrangement of diagnostic examinations necessary to reach an optimal capacity structure; that will be discussed more detailed below.

(P 9) and (P 12) exclude backward loops which would contradict (P 4). Otherwise the arrival processes in front of the service units would no longer be Poisson processes (Walrand 1982, Malamed 1979a, 1979b); this quality, however, is decisively necessary for the following analysis. Moreover, (P 12) was backed by the empirical study.

2.2.2 The formal model of a general diagnosis system and its characteristics

Under the premises stated above the diagnosis system can be understood as a network-type queueing system of $N \in \mathbb{N}$ service units i, i=1,...,N, arranged in parallel or in series, which is run through by q=2 different patient flows as graphically demonstrated in figure 1.

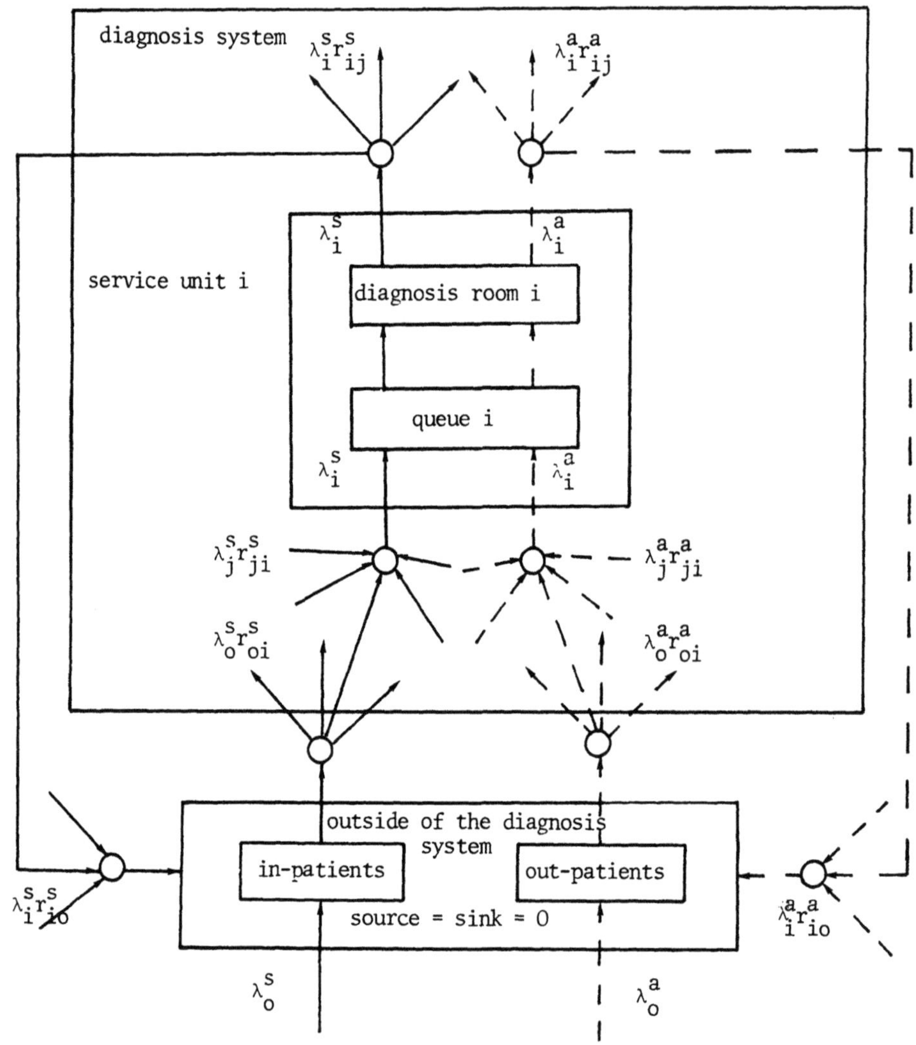

Figure 1: The diagnosis system as a queueing system

In this connexion

- λ_i^a, λ_i^s and λ_j^a, λ_j^s, respectively, indicate the flows of out-patients and in-patients going to and leaving the outside of the diagnosis system and the diagnosis service units in the diagnosis system with i, $j \in \{0,\ldots,N\}$.

- r_{ij}^a, r_{ij}^s and r_{ji}^a, r_{ji}^s, respectively, indicate the transition probabilities of the out-patients and in-patients from unit i to unit j and vice versa with i, $j \in \{0,\ldots,N\}$, $r_{ij}^a = r_{ji}^a = r_{ij}^s = r_{ji}^s = 0$ for i=j (premise (P 9)) and

$$\sum_{j=0}^{N} r_{ij}^a = \sum_{j=0}^{N} r_{ij}^s = 1, \quad i=0,\ldots,N.$$

On account of the premises (P 1), (P 5), (P 8), (P 13) to (P 15) the diagnosis system can be typified extending Kendall's notation (Kendall 1953) by the queueing model M/M/N/∞/FCFS/2; the first two symbols indicate that the distributions of the patients' interarrival and examination times are Markovian. If there is only one diagnostic service unit with one diagnosis room or n_p parallel diagnosis rooms, one gets the well-known model typifications M/M/1/∞/FCFS/2 and M/M/n_p/∞/FCFS/2, respectively.

Furthermore the general diagnosis system is characterized by the fact, that a branching of the patients' flows in the meaning of an exclusive-or-knode appears behind the outside of the diagnosis system and every diagnosis room and that a fusion or a superimposition of several patients flows occurs in front of every diagnostic service unit and the outside of the diagnosis system. According to the patient's type these flows are ordered in out-patients and in-patients. Because of the following three basic theorems all (partial) flows of out-patients and in-patients within the diagnostic system are Poisson processes.

Theorem 1 (Burke 1956, 1972):

The departure processes of an M/M/1/∞/FCFS/1- and an M/M/n_p/∞/FCFS/1-queueing system being in equilibrium are Poisson streams and have the same intensities as the arrival streams.

Theorem 2 (Klimow 1979):

The composition of c independent Poisson streams with the intensities $\lambda_1,\ldots,\lambda_c$, $c \in \mathbb{N}$, is again a Poisson stream with intensity $\lambda = \lambda_1+\ldots+\lambda_c$.

Theorem 3 (Ferschl 1964):

If the mobile units of a Poisson stream with the intensity λ are stochastically distributed over $c \in \mathbb{N}$ partial streams in such a way that subsequently a unit is within the partial stream i with the probability r_i $(i = 1,\ldots,c)$, then the c partial streams are Poisson streams each with the intensity $r_i\lambda$.

This fact is of advantage for the following parts of the analysis. On the one hand it is possible to determine the arrival rates λ_i in front of the single diagnostic service units just by means of the transition probabilities r_{ij}^a and r_{ij}^s together with the total arrival rates λ_0^a and λ_0^s. On the other hand this firstly allows to analyze the single diagnostic service units seperately by applying queueing theoretical considerations and to describe their efficiency by means of indices before, in a second step, one obtains the indices of the total diagnosis system from the combination of the indices of the single diagnostic service units.

Now, $\lambda^a = (\lambda_0^a,\ldots,\lambda_N^a)^T$ may denote the vector of the arrival rates of out-patients and $\lambda^s = (\lambda_0^s,\ldots,\lambda_N^s)^T$ that of in-patients, and

$$R^a = \begin{pmatrix} 0 & r_{01}^a & \cdots & r_{0N}^a \\ r_{10}^a & 0 & \cdots & r_{1N}^a \\ \cdot & & & \cdot \\ \cdot & & & \cdot \\ \cdot & & & \cdot \\ r_{N0}^a & & \cdots & 0 \end{pmatrix} \quad \text{and } R^s = \begin{pmatrix} 0 & r_{01}^s & \cdots & r_{0N}^s \\ r_{10}^s & 0 & \cdots & r_{1N}^s \\ \cdot & & & \cdot \\ \cdot & & & \cdot \\ \cdot & & & \cdot \\ r_{N0}^s & & \cdots & 0 \end{pmatrix}$$

may indicate the so-called routing matrices of the out-patients and the in-patients with the corresponding transition probabilities. Then the relations

$$\lambda^a = {R^a}^T \lambda^a,$$

$$\lambda^s = R^{s^T} \lambda^s,$$
$$\lambda = \lambda^a + \lambda^s = R^{a^T} \lambda^a + R^{s^T} \lambda^s$$

are obviously valid. If λ_0^a and λ_0^s are known it is easily possible to calculate the flow intensities λ_i, λ_i^a and λ_i^s needed for the analysis from these equation systems by means of the transposed routing matrices of the transition probabilities. In case the single diagnostic service units and the total diagnostic system are in equilibrium, i.e.

$$\lambda_i^a + \lambda_i^s < \mu_i \text{ and } \lambda_i^a + \lambda_i^s < n_{p_i} \mu_i, \text{ respectively,}$$

holds for every service unit with only one or n_{p_i} parallel diagnosis rooms, one obtains from the equations the queueing theoretical indices concerning the single diagnostic service units and the total system as mentioned in paragraph 2.1 and compiled in table 1. A single service unit corresponds - as already explained - to an M/M/1/∞/FCFS/2- or an M/M/n_p/∞/FCFS/2-model. Furthermore, the total system M/M/N/∞/FCFS/2 is also to be differentiated whether the number of parallel, identical diagnosis rooms of every service unit is arbitrary (n_{p_i} arbitrary) or whether every service unit consists of only one diagnosis room ($n_{p_i} = 1$ for all i=1,...,N). As for the derivation of the indices one may be directed to the references Little (1961), Ferschl (1964), Gross/Harris (1974), Lemoine (1977), and Hegemann (1985).

3 The diagnosis system of the General Hospital in Hagen City

3.1 Structure, operating parameters and indices

The diagnostic system of the General Hospital in Hagen City comprises five departments: function diagnostics, sonography, endoscopy, computer tomography, and X-ray diagnostics, which are divided into twelve service units with one diagnosis room each. Under queueing theoretical aspects it is an M/M/12/∞/FCFS/2-model whose structure referring to number and designation of the service units, their services, staff and apparatus is shown in table 2. The relevant examination times in the service units are between 8:00 am and 4:00 pm with the X-ray diagnostics being manned 24 hours a day by a medical-technical assistant at least, though.

The parameters of the arrival processes of the out-patients and in-patients at the twelve diagnostic service units - important for the pro-

Table 1: Indices of the single service units and the total diagnosis system

indices	single service unit M/M/1/∞/FCFS/2	single service unit $M/M/n_p/\infty/FCFS/2$	total system M/M/N/∞/FCFS/2, $n_{p_i}=1\ \forall i$	total system M/M/N/∞/FCFS/2, n_{p_i} arbitrary
expected waiting time $E(V_{q_i})$ resp. $E(V_q)$	$\frac{\rho_i}{\mu_i(1-\rho_i)}$	$\frac{1}{\lambda_i^a+\lambda_i^s}\cdot\frac{\rho_i^{n_{p_i}+1}}{(n_{p_i}-1)!(n_{p_i}-\rho_i)^2}p_{o_i}$	$\frac{1}{\lambda_o^a+\lambda_o^s}\sum_{i=1}^{N}\frac{\rho_i^2}{1-\rho_i}$	$\frac{1}{\lambda_o^a+\lambda_o^s}\sum_{i=1}^{N}\frac{\rho_i^{n_{p_i}+1}}{(n_{p_i}-1)!(n_{p_i}-\rho_i)^2}p_{o_i}$
expected indwelling time $E(V_i)$ resp. $E(V)$	$\frac{1}{\mu_i(1-\rho_i)}$	$\frac{1}{\lambda_i^a+\lambda_i^s}\left(\rho_i+\frac{\rho_i^{n_{p_i}+1}}{(n_{p_i}-1)!(n_{p_i}-\rho_i)^2}\cdot p_{o_i}\right)$	$\frac{1}{\lambda_o^a+\lambda_o^s}\sum_{i=1}^{N}\frac{\rho_i}{1-\rho_i}$	$\frac{1}{\lambda_o^a+\lambda_o^s}\sum_{i=1}^{N}\left(\rho_i+\frac{\rho_i^{n_{p_i}+1}}{(n_{p_i}-1)!(n_{p_i}-\rho_i)^2}p_{o_i}\right)$
expected number of waiting patients $E(L_{q_i})$ resp. $E(L_q)$	$\frac{\rho_i^2}{1-\rho_i}$	$\frac{\rho_i^{n_{p_i}+1}}{(n_{p_i}-1)!(n_{p_i}-\rho_i)^2}p_{o_i}$	$\sum_{i=1}^{N}\frac{\rho_i^2}{1-\rho_i}$	$\sum_{i=1}^{N}\frac{\rho_i^{n_{p_i}+1}}{(n_{p_i}-1)!(n_{p_i}-\rho_i)^2}p_{o_i}$
expected number of patients in the system $E(L_i)$ resp. $E(L)$	$\frac{\rho_i}{1-\rho_i}$	$\rho_i+\frac{\rho_i^{n_{p_i}+1}}{(n_{p_i}-1)!(n_{p_i}-\rho_i)^2}p_{o_i}$	$\sum_{i=1}^{N}\frac{\rho_i}{1-\rho_i}$	$\sum_{i=1}^{N}\rho_i+\frac{\rho_i^{n_{p_i}+1}}{(n_{p_i}-1)!(n_{p_i}-\rho_i)^2}p_{o_i}$
mean load degree ξ_i resp. ξ	ρ_i	$\frac{\rho_i}{n_{p_i}}$	$\frac{1}{N}\sum_{i=1}^{N}\rho_i$	$\frac{1}{N}\sum_{i=1}^{N}\frac{\rho_i}{n_{p_i}}$

$$\rho_i=\frac{\lambda_i^a+\lambda_i^s}{\mu_i}\qquad p_{o_i}=\frac{1}{\sum_{n_i=0}^{n_{p_i}-1}\frac{\rho_i^{n_i}}{n_i!}+\frac{\rho_i^{n_{p_i}}}{(n_{p_i}-1)!(n_{p_i}-1)}}$$

Table 2: Structure of the diagnosis system

area	room	services	executive personnel	important equipment
function diagnostics	function diagnostics 2 (FCT 2)	long-term-ECG resting-ECG rhythm-ECG pacemaker check phonocardiogram apexcardiogram carotid pulse curve orthostasis-ECG oscillogram	1 or 2 medi-cal-technical assistants (and 1 doctor)	1 long-term ECG computer 1 ECG apparatus 1 ultrasonic doppler apparatus
	function diagnostics 3 (FCT 3)	exercise-ECG echocardiogram pulmonary function test dye-dilution	1 medical-technical assistant and 1 doctor	1 ECG apparatus 1 echocardiograph 1 spirometre 1 dye-dilution apparatus
sono-graphy	sonography (SONO)	sonographic examination of the abdominal organs	1 doctor	1 sonographic equipment
endoscopy	endoscopy (ENDO)	gastroscopy colonoscopy ERCP esophageal dilation organ biopsy laparoscopy endoscopic sclerosizing of varices rectoscopy proctoscopy	1 or 2 medi-cal-technical assistants and 1 or 2 doctors	1 operating table and different endoscopes
computerized tomography	computerized tomography (COMP)	abdominal CT spinal CT cerebral CT pancreatic CT thoratic CT kidney CT liver CT pelvic CT	2 medical-technical assistants (and 1 doctor)	1 computer tomograph
X-ray diagnostics	X-ray diagnostics 1 (X 1)	fluoroscopy and roentgenogram of all parts of the body upper gastro-intestinal series barium enema phlebography esophagus ERCP fistulography	1 medical-technical assistant and 1 or 2 doctors	1 Bucky table

Table 2 (continued)

X-ray diagnostics	X-ray diagnostics 2 (X 2)	arthrography myelography (otherwise as in X 1 but without phlebography)	1 medical-technical assistant and 1 doctor	1 Bucky table
	X-ray diagnostics 3 (X 3)	chest X-ray (2 levels) trachea cervical spine paranasal sinuses	2 medical-technical assistants	1 Bucky wall tripod
		tomography of all regions of the body drip infusion cholecystography drip infusion pyelography		1 Bucky table
		panoramic picture of the upper and lower jaw bones		1 status-X-apparatus
	X-ray diagnostics 4 (X 4)	renovasography arteriography of of arms and legs lymphangiography aortography	1 medical-technical assistant and 2 doctors	1 AOT changer
	X-ray diagnostics 5.1 (X 5.1)	bones cholecystography after intravenous injection thorax (inclined)	1 medical-technical assistant	1 Bucky table
		chest X-ray (2 levels) paranasal sinuses abdomen trachea spine (up-right-position)		1 Bucky wall tripod
	X-ray diagnostics 5.2 (X 5.2)	bones pyelography by intravenous injection function of articulations (knee or ankle) *Scheuba*	1 medical-technical assistant	1 Bucky table
	X-ray diagnostics 6 (X 6)	mammography pneumocystography galactography roentgenogram of the soft tissues of the hands	1 medical-technical assistant	1 mammomat

cess structure of the diagnosis system - as well as the distribution of examination times in the service units and the routing matrices of the transition probabilities have been investigated within a three-week-period on the basis of diagnosis processes of more than 1,700 out-patients and in-patients by means of a self-recording-method of the medical personnel working in the diagnostic system. Table 3 contains the intensities of the arrival flows and the examination rates. Hereby the outside of the diagnostic system is called 0. Then the routing matrices R^a and R^s follow. From these quantities one can calculate the indices of the single service units and the total diagnosis system according to the relations shown in table 1; they are compiled in table 4. Among these indices the expected waiting times of the patients $E(V_{q_i})$ and $E(V_q)$ as well as the load degrees ξ_i and ξ are of special interest for the further considerations.

3.2 Weak point analysis of the diagnosis system

Looking at the indices listed up in table 4 the great differences in the load degree ξ_i of the single diagnostic rooms come up as the first weak point of the diagnosis system of the General Hospital in Hagen. Whereas the load degree of the computerized tomography reaches about 70% and is therefore rather high, the load degrees of the X-ray rooms 2, 5.2 and 6 reaching 13.7%, 25.5% and 6.2% as well as of the sonography reaching 13.6% must be called very low. Furthermore, the considerable differences between the X-ray rooms 1 and 2 equipped nearly identically are especially remarkable.

High divergencies can also be stated for the patients' waiting times $E(V_{q_i})$. A patient in front of the computerized tomography and X-ray room 4 must wait for his examination up to one hour on average, whereas the examination starts mostly immediately in the sonography, in the X-ray rooms 3 and 6 and in the function diagnosis room 2.

The analysis of the indwelling times $E(V_i)$ shows extremely high values for the computerized tomography and the X-ray rooms 1, 2 and 4. In the X-ray rooms the long indwelling times must be attributed to the relatively long examination times, whereas the long indwelling time of nearly 1 1/2 hours in the computerized tomography can be explained by the large part of waiting times.

Comparing the waiting times with the load degrees one meets the well-

Table 3: Arrival and examination rates of the diagnostics

room	i	λ_i^a	λ_i^s	λ_i	μ_i
Outside of diagnostics	0	0,089444	0,153750	0,243194	-
FCT2	1	0,017083	0,065694	0,082777	0,193742
FCT3	2	0,007639	0,008889	0,016528	0,058173
SONO	3	0,001806	0,013611	0,015417	0,113483
ENDO	4	0,005357	0,010863	0,016220	0,042030
COMP	5	0,015667	0,010111	0,025778	0,037263
X 1	6	0,003889	0,013889	0,017778	0,037890
X 2	7	0,001667	0,001111	0,002778	0,020243
X 3	8	0,019722	0,050417	0,070139	0,207512
X 4	9	0,002222	0,000278	0,002500	0,008520
X 5.1	10	0,025417	0,032917	0,058334	0,112965
X 5.2	11	0,004861	0,005556	0,010417	0,040794
X 6	12	0,003472	0,000694	0,004166	0,066869

$$R^a=(r^a_{ij})=\begin{bmatrix}
0 & 0,185 & 0,005 & 0,014 & 0,060 & 0,172 & 0,033 & 0,019 & 0,160 & 0,025 & 0,254 & 0,054 & 0,019 \\
0,472 & 0 & 0,415 & 0 & 0 & 0 & 0 & 0 & 0,106 & 0 & 0,008 & 0 & 0 \\
0,764 & 0 & 0 & 0 & 0 & 0 & 0 & 0 & 0,200 & 0 & 0,036 & 0 & 0 \\
1,000 & 0 & 0 & 0 & 0 & 0 & 0 & 0 & 0 & 0 & 0 & 0 & 0 \\
0,949 & 0 & 0 & 0,051 & 0 & 0 & 0 & 0 & 0 & 0 & 0 & 0 & 0 \\
0,947 & 0,009 & 0 & 0 & 0 & 0 & 0 & 0 & 0,044 & 0 & 0 & 0 & 0 \\
1,000 & 0 & 0 & 0 & 0 & 0 & 0 & 0 & 0 & 0 & 0 & 0 & 0 \\
0,917 & 0 & 0 & 0 & 0 & 0 & 0 & 0 & 0,083 & 0 & 0 & 0 & 0 \\
0,775 & 0,021 & 0,007 & 0,007 & 0 & 0,014 & 0,021 & 0 & 0 & 0 & 0,063 & 0 & 0,092 \\
1,000 & 0 & 0 & 0 & 0 & 0 & 0 & 0 & 0 & 0 & 0 & 0 & 0 \\
0,951 & 0 & 0 & 0,005 & 0 & 0 & 0,022 & 0 & 0,022 & 0 & 0 & 0 & 0 \\
0,914 & 0 & 0 & 0 & 0 & 0 & 0 & 0 & 0,086 & 0 & 0 & 0 & 0 \\
0,640 & 0 & 0 & 0 & 0 & 0 & 0 & 0 & 0,080 & 0 & 0,280 & 0 & 0
\end{bmatrix}$$

$$R^S=(r^S_{ij})=\begin{bmatrix}
0 & 0{,}232 & 0{,}033 & 0{,}065 & 0{,}063 & 0{,}050 & 0{,}060 & 0{,}005 & 0{,}261 & 0{,}001 & 0{,}196 & 0{,}032 & 0{,}002 \\
0{,}841 & 0 & 0{,}049 & 0{,}011 & 0{,}002 & 0{,}013 & 0{,}002 & 0{,}002 & 0{,}061 & 0 & 0{,}015 & 0{,}004 & 0 \\
0{,}953 & 0 & 0 & 0 & 0 & 0 & 0{,}016 & 0 & 0{,}031 & 0 & 0 & 0 & 0 \\
0{,}735 & 0{,}133 & 0 & 0 & 0{,}031 & 0{,}010 & 0{,}031 & 0 & 0{,}031 & 0 & 0{,}020 & 0{,}010 & 0 \\
0{,}858 & 0{,}077 & 0{,}013 & 0 & 0 & 0{,}013 & 0{,}013 & 0 & 0{,}013 & 0 & 0{,}013 & 0 & 0 \\
0{,}904 & 0{,}055 & 0{,}027 & 0 & 0 & 0 & 0 & 0 & 0 & 0 & 0{,}014 & 0 & 0 \\
0{,}810 & 0{,}070 & 0 & 0{,}010 & 0 & 0 & 0 & 0{,}010 & 0{,}090 & 0 & 0{,}010 & 0 & 0 \\
1{,}000 & 0 & 0 & 0 & 0 & 0 & 0 & 0 & 0 & 0 & 0 & 0 & 0 \\
0{,}452 & 0{,}419 & 0 & 0{,}052 & 0{,}008 & 0{,}011 & 0{,}022 & 0 & 0 & 0{,}003 & 0{,}019 & 0{,}006 & 0{,}008 \\
1{,}000 & 0 & 0 & 0 & 0 & 0 & 0 & 0 & 0 & 0 & 0 & 0 & 0 \\
0{,}654 & 0{,}131 & 0{,}004 & 0{,}004 & 0 & 0{,}021 & 0{,}076 & 0{,}004 & 0{,}105 & 0 & 0 & 0 & 0 \\
0{,}750 & 0{,}050 & 0 & 0 & 0{,}025 & 0 & 0{,}025 & 0 & 0{,}125 & 0 & 0{,}025 & 0 & 0 \\
0{,}600 & 0{,}200 & 0 & 0 & 0 & 0{,}200 & 0 & 0 & 0 & 0 & 0 & 0 & 0
\end{bmatrix}$$

Table 4: Indices of the single diagnostic service units and the total system

room	i	$E(V_{q_i})$ [min.]	$E(V_i)$ [min.]	$E(L_{q_i})$ [pat./min.]	$E(L_i)$ [pat./min.]	ξ_i [%]
FCT2	1	3,85	9,01	0,32	0,75	42,7
FCT3	2	6,82	24,01	0,11	0,40	28,4
SONO	3	1,38	10,19	0,02	0,16	13,6
ENDO	4	14,95	38,74	0,24	0,63	38,6
COMP	5	60,23	87,06	1,55	2,24	69,2
X 1	6	23,32	49,72	0,41	0,88	46,9
X 2	7	7,85	57,25	0,02	0,16	13,7
X 3	8	2,46	7,27	0,17	0,51	33,8
X 4	9	48,73	166,11	0,12	0,42	29,3
X 5.1	10	9,45	18,30	0,55	1,07	51,6
X 5.2	11	8,40	32,91	0.09	0,34	25,5
X 6	12	0,99	15,94	0,01	0,07	6,2
total system		$E(V_q)$	$E(V)$	$E(L_q)$	$E(L)$	ξ
		14,9	31,3	3,6	7,6	33,3

known dilemma of scheduling in the computerized tomography: the relatively high waiting times definitely result from the rather high load degree of nearly 70%. In the X-ray rooms 5.1 and 3 with comparatively higher load degrees only short waiting times appear because here examinations rarely last over a longer period. In the opposite sense, the dilemma of scheduling comes up in the sonography and in the X-ray room 6, too: the negligible short waiting times here solely result from the low load degrees and thus high dead times.

These weak points to be found mainly in the X-ray department can be eliminated partly by restructuring measures concerning the pooling of rooms and the shifting of staff as will be shown by the discussion of the rationalizing potential of the diagnostic system in the following chapter. The aim will be to reduce the great differences in the load degrees and to shorten the long waiting times by changing the capacity structure.

Concerning the diagnostic system as a whole the average waiting and indwelling times of the patients $E(V_q)$ and $E(V)$ can be considered as reasonable. The expected load degree ξ and thus the efficiency of the existing diagnosis system reaching 33.3% must be regarded as very low. Frequently, it is the aim of restructuring and rationalizing measures to strive for an average load degree of about 50%.

4 Possibilities of rationalization in the diagnosis system of the General Hospital in Hagen

4.1 Objectives

Generally, the object of the task to rationalize is the question: which modifying measures shall be carried out in which diagnosis rooms to which extent so that possibly high, steady load degrees and possibly low, reasonable waiting times for patients can be reached in the diagnosis system and in each diagnosis room? This limits the consideration to two system indices. There is a number of possibilities to operationalize this goal conflict of scheduling, which is a two-criteria decision problem, by formulating objective functions and constraints. In this paper the procedure to formulate the problem is as follows.

M may denote the set of all combinations m of improving measures concerning the single diagnostic service units, i.e.

$M = \{m | m = (m_1, \dots, m_{12})\}$.

From the point of view of hospital doctors and patients that alternative $m^* \in M$ would be favoured, for which the expected waiting time of patients $E(V_q)$ in the total diagnosis system becomes a minimum, i.e.

$$E(V_q(m^*)) = \min_{m \in M} \left\{ E(V_q(m)) = \frac{1}{\lambda_0^a + \lambda_0^s} \sum_{i=1}^{N(m)} \frac{\rho_i^2(m)}{1-\rho_i(m)} \right\}$$

must be fulfilled with $N(m) \leq 12$ denoting the number of diagnosis rooms possibly changed due to the pooling of rooms. This criterion tallies with the minimization of the average total time and the minimization of the expected number of patients in the diagnosis system.

On the contrary the alternative $\tilde{m}$ takes into account the objective of a possibly high load degree of the total diagnosis system usually important for the hospital management and the state. Its determination leads to the goal formulation

$$\xi(\tilde{m}) = \max_{m \in M} \left\{ \xi(m) = \frac{1}{N(m)} \sum_{i=1}^{N(m)} \rho_i(m) \right\}.$$

This is identical with the minimization of dead times and analogous to the minimization of costs, when the service spectrum is given.

Considering these criteria for the total system it must be guaranteed, however, that the patients' waiting times in front of every diagnosis room do not exceed a reasonable limit $\bar{w}$, which is ordinarily rated at $\bar{w} = 30$ minutes by the public health policy. Therefore the feasible alternatives $m \in M$ are subject to the restrictions

$$E(V_{q_i}(m)) = \frac{\rho_i(m)}{\mu_i(m)(1-\rho_i(m))} \leq \bar{w}, \quad i=1,\dots,N(m), \quad m \in M.$$

Further constraints resulting from medical needs, room situations and technical border conditions may be added. They shall not be discussed here any further, but will be implied by the definition of the measures in the following chapter for reasons of simplicity. So the problem of rationalization may be described by the decision problem or vector minimization problem respectively with

$$\underset{m \in \hat{M}}{\text{"min"}} \begin{pmatrix} E(V_q(m)) \\ -\xi(m) \end{pmatrix}$$

with

$$\hat{M} = \{m \in M \mid E(V_{q_i}(m)) \leq 30 \text{ for all } i=1,\ldots,N(m)\}.$$

Efficient compromise measures have to be taken into account as solutions not dominated by any other rationalizing measure referring to the waiting times of patients and the load degree of the total diagnosis system.

4.2 Rationalizing measures and their results

Possible rationalizing measures are the removal of examination services into other diagnostic service units, the reinstallation of equipment and the shifting of staff as well as the fusion of examination rooms, the new purchase of more powerful examination apparatus and the sacking or employment of staff. Such measures effect the number of diagnosis rooms, the arrival and examination rates of the service units, the structure of the routing matrices and, furthermore, the average waiting times and load degrees of the diagnosis rooms and the total diagnosis system. Correspondingly, it will be important to point out alternatives of the capacity structure of the diagnosis system of the General Hospital in Hagen possibly leading to more favourable constellations of the queueing theoretic indices than at present. Concerning their temporal possibilities of realization the measures of improvement to be considered must be differentiated according to their appointed times. Whereas the removal of examination services, the reinstallation of equipment, the shifting and new employment of staff can be carried out within a medium-term period, the fusion of rooms, the purchase of equipment, and the sacking of staff can only be done within a long-term period. As for the rest, attention was directed to the definition of such rationalizing measures to be mastered mainly with the present equipment and personnel and not leading to the sacking of staff within a medium-term period.

The possible measures of an organizational restructuring first concerning single diagnostic rooms, only, shall formally be described by components. A total measure m then results from the componentwise combination of single measures which can be planned for the different diagnostic service units. As the number of restructuring measures for the diagnosis system discussed is finite, the vector minimization problem, which was formulated in the last chapter, is a discrete optimizing problem. In order to make this more concrete

$$m_{ij}^{\nu} = (m_i^{\nu}, m_j^{\nu}), \ \nu \in \mathbb{N}, \ i, j \in \{1,\dots,12\}, \ i \neq j,$$

may denote a component wise single measure ν referring simultaneously to the diagnosis rooms i and j. In case of such a single measure referring to one diagnostic service unit only the notation with vector components

$$m_i^{\nu}, \ \nu \in \mathbb{N}, \ i \in \{1,\dots,12\}$$

is sufficient. It is clear that changing nothing is a single measure as well. This fact may be described by

$$m_{ij}^{0} = (m_i^{0}, m_j^{0}) \text{ or } m_i^{0} \text{ respectively.}$$

The actual state of the diagnosis system corresponds to the total measure

$$m^0 = (m_1^0,\dots,m_{12}^0).$$

The single measures of rationalization listed up in the following are - due to the preceding weak point analysis - directed to reduce the waiting times of patients at the single diagnostic service units below the reasonable level and, at the same time, not losing sight of a more equal and better load degree of the diagnosis rooms. For medical-technical reasons there are no possibilities to change anything in the function diagnostics, sonography, and endoscopy so that for these rooms every total measure is characterized by

$$m_i = m_i^0 \text{ for } i=1,\dots,4.$$

Consequently, objects for the rationalizing measures are the computerized tomography and the service units of the X-ray department. The following measures may be considered for them:

m_{67}^0: The situation in the X-ray rooms 1 and 2 (service units 6 and 7) remains unchanged.

m^1_{67}: Apart from the phlebographies and fistulographies all fluoroscopies and roentgenograms of all parts of the body as well as the examinations upper gastro-intestinal series and barium enema are carried out in the X-ray room 1. In the X-ray room 2 the diagnostic measures esophagus and ERCP are carried out as well as arthrographies and myelographies.

m^2_{67}: With the exception of fluoroscopies and roentgenographies, phlebographies and barium enema taking place in the X-ray room 1 all other diagnostics examinations are solely carried out in the X-ray room 2.

m^3_{67}: Unlike m^2_{67} the ERCP examinations are to be offered not in the X-ray room 2, but in the X-ray room 1.

m^4_{67}: Pooling of X-ray rooms 1 and 2 with the intention to purchase a more powerful fluoroscopy apparatus which will help to offer the full spectrum of the services of the both existing rooms and will be operated by one medical-technical assistant only.

m^5_{67}: Unlike m^4_{67} two medical-technical assistants will be charged with the carrying out of the diagnostic services in the new X-ray room 1/2 ([6+7]).

$m^0_{8,12}$: The situation in the X-ray rooms 3 and 6 (service units 8 and 12) remains unchanged.

$m^6_{8,12}$: The X-ray rooms 3 and 6 are merged ([8+12]) with the intention to instal the mammomat of X-ray room 6 in the X-ray room 3. The number of staff in the X-ray room 3 remains unchanged, though.

m^0_9: The situation in the X-ray room 4 (service unit 9) remains unchanged.

m^7_9: Direct preparation times needed for the examinations in the X-ray room 4 are to be transferred partially to the beginning of the examination day.

m^8_9: In addition to m^7_9 replacement of the old surgical equipment by a powerful new apparatus.

$m^0_{10,11}$: The situation in the X-ray rooms 5.1 and 5.2 (service units 10 and 11) remains unchanged.

$m^9_{10,11}$: Fusion of the X-ray rooms 5.1 and 5.2 ([10+11]) by disinvestment of the Bucky table in room 5.2 and removing the lead wall. As formerly the staff will consist of two medical-technical assistants.

$m^{10}_{10,11}$: Similar to $m^9_{10,11}$; but only one medical-technical assistant will be assigned to the combined diagnosis room [10+11].

m^0_5: The situation in the computerized tomography (service unit 5) remains unchanged.

m^{11}_5: The staff in the computerized tomography will be enlarged to three jobs for medical-technical assistants.

The single measures mentioned are compiled in table 5 as to their effects of the service units, the patients' waiting times and the load degrees. The letters mt and lt in the second column of table 5 indicate the medium-term or long-term character of the measures whereby every medium-term measure can also be realized in the long-term. It is conspicuous that the measures m^8_9 and m^{11}_5 could cause the urgently desired drastic reductions in the waiting times of patients especially in the X-ray room 4 (service unit 9) and in the computerized tomography (service unit 5). The measure $m^6_{8,12}$ causes a 100 %-increase in the load degree of the combined service unit [8+12] with the patients' waiting times being negligibly longer.

Because of the independence premises (P 4) and (P 10) a total rationalizing measure in the diagnostic system consists of a combination of single measures for the different diagnostic rooms. Thereby it is reasonable that only the combination of single measures being themselves feasible and efficient can lead to a feasible and efficient total measure. The reverse is not valid, at least not as far as efficiency is concerned! In the first column of table 5 the feasible and efficient single measures are marked by little rectangles. The destinct dominance of the medium-term measure m^2_{67} over the measures m^0_{67}, m^1_{67}, m^3_{67} is dependent on the fact that in case of the examination rooms 6 and 7 being regarded as one service unit [6+7] the total waiting time turns out the shortest while the load degree remains unchanged. At the same time this is the

Table 5: Single measures and their effects

measure	medium-term (mt) or long-term (lt)	$E(V_{q_i})$ [min.]			ξ_i [%]		
		i=6	i=7	[6+7]	i=6	i=7	[6+7]
m_{67}^{o}	mt/lt	23,32	7,85	21,37	46,9	13,7	30,3
m_{67}^{1}	mt/lt	17,86	9,72	15,93	40,5	20,0	30,3
m_{67}^{2}	mt/lt	12,95	12,68	12,92	31,9	28,6	30,3
m_{67}^{3}	mt/lt	16,18	9,99	14,02	36,6	23,9	30,3
m_{67}^{4}	lt	-	-	25,13	-	-	50,4
m_{67}^{5}	lt	-	-	17,26	-	-	44,3
		i=8	i=12	[8+12]	i=8	i=12	[8+12]
$m_{8,12}^{o}$	mt/lt	2,46	0,99	2,41	33,8	6,2	20,0
$m_{8,12}^{6}$	mt/lt	-	-	3,72	-	-	40,0
				i=9			i=9
m_{9}^{o}	mt/lt			48,73			29,3
m_{9}^{7}	mt/lt			39,39			26,8
m_{9}^{8}	lt			27,74			23,1
		i=10	i=11	[10+11]	i=10	i=11	[10+11]
$m_{10,11}^{o}$	mt/lt	9,45	8,40	9,32	51,6	25,5	38,6
$m_{10,11}^{9}$	lt	-	-	10,74	-	-	56,6
$m_{10,11}^{10}$	lt	-	-	37,98	-	-	77,2
				i=5			i=5
m_{5}^{o}	mt/lt			60,23			69,2
m_{5}^{11}	mt/lt			28,52			56,5

reason for the dominance with respect to its contribution to the total waiting time and the total load degree of the diagnostic system (cf. formulas of the indices in table 1), which are the criteria of the vector minimum problem.

The values in tables 4 and 5 elucidate at once that the actual state of the diagnosis system, i.e. the total measure m^0 is not feasible and, additionally, there exists no feasible medium-term total measure m of improvement, because in both cases the waiting times in the service unit 9 (X-ray room 4) are always above 30 minutes. Remembering that $m_i = m_i^0$ must hold for the first four service units - these single measures are all feasible - and taking into account that all single measures feasible for the other service units are listed up in table 5 one receives by the combination of the feasible and efficient single measures 3x2x1x2x1=12 feasible, alternative, long-term total measures, which have to be checked according to their efficiency and optimality. They are compiled in table 6 as the measures m^{101} through m^{112}. To make comparisons possible the actual state m^0 and a medium-term total measure $\hat{m}$ (both unfeasible) are listed up as well. One sees, that not all but five long-term measures are efficient with regard to the total waiting time of patients $E(V_q)$ and the total load degree ξ of the diagnosis system. On the other hand, there exist nine feasible long-term total measures dominating the actual state of the diagnosis system at the General Hospital in Hagen. The unfeasible medium-term total measure $\hat{m}$ also dominates the actual state and is efficient even in comparison with the long-term measures. A number of measures leads to the reduction in the number N(m) of examination rooms with the spectrum of services unchanged and - at the same time - to an improved service quality an load degree of the total diagnosis system.

Measures with the component m_{67}^2 clearly show a lower load degree of the service units 6 and 7 and a lower total load. Those with the component m_{67}^4 unsatisfactorily increase the waiting times of patients in front of the X-ray rooms 1 and 2, if they were considered as a unit, in comparison with the actual state. Therefore, the measure m^{112} seems to be the optimal compromise within the long-term period for the doctors working in the diagnosis system. Compared with the actual state this measure increases the total load of the diagnosis system by 18 % and decreases the average patients' waiting times by 20 %. It was impossible to reach a total load degree of 50 % by the measures discussed.

Table 6: Rationalizing measures, their characteristics and results

	actual state	medium-term	long-term											
	m^o	$\hat{m}$	m^{1o1}	m^{1o2}	m^{1o3}	m^{1o4}	m^{1o5}	m^{1o6}	m^{1o7}	m^{1o8}	m^{1o9}	m^{11o}	m^{111}	m^{112}
MEASURES	m_1^o	m_1^o	m_1^o	m_1^o	m_1^o	m_1^o	m_1^o	m_1^o	m_1^o	m_1^o	m_1^o	m_1^o	m_1^o	m_1^o
	m_2^o	m_2^o	m_2^o	m_2^o	m_2^o	m_2^o	m_2^o	m_2^o	m_2^o	m_2^o	m_2^o	m_2^o	m_2^o	m_2^o
	m_3^o	m_3^o	m_3^o	m_3^o	m_3^o	m_3^o	m_3^o	m_3^o	m_3^o	m_3^o	m_3^o	m_3^o	m_3^o	m_3^o
	m_4^o	m_4^o	m_4^o	m_4^o	m_4^o	m_4^o	m_4^o	m_4^o	m_4^o	m_4^o	m_4^o	m_4^o	m_4^o	m_4^o
	m_5^o	m_5^{11}	m_5^{11}	m_5^{11}	m_5^{11}	m_5^{11}	m_5^{11}	m_5^{11}	m_5^{11}	m_5^{11}	m_5^{11}	m_5^{11}	m_5^{11}	m_5^{11}
	m_6^o	m_6^2	m_6^2	m_6^2	m_6^2	m_6^2	m_6^4	m_6^4	m_6^4	m_6^4	m_6^5	m_6^5	m_6^5	m_6^5
	m_7^o	m_7^2	m_7^2	m_7^2	m_7^2	m_7^2	m_7^4	m_7^4	m_7^4	m_7^4	m_7^5	m_7^5	m_7^5	m_7^5
	m_8^o	m_8^6	m_8^o	m_8^o	m_8^6	m_8^6	m_8^o	m_8^o	m_8^6	m_8^6	m_8^o	m_8^o	m_8^6	m_8^6
	m_9^o	m_9^7	m_9^8	m_9^8	m_9^8	m_9^8	m_9^8	m_9^8	m_9^8	m_9^8	m_9^8	m_9^8	m_9^8	m_9^8
	m_{1o}^o	m_{1o}^o	m_{1o}^o	m_{1o}^9	m_{1o}^o	m_{1o}^9	m_{1o}^o	m_{1o}^9	m_{1o}^o	m_{1o}^9	m_{1o}^o	m_{1o}^9	m_{1o}^o	m_{1o}^9
	m_{11}^o	m_{11}^o	m_{11}^o	m_{11}^9	m_{11}^o	m_{11}^9	m_{11}^o	m_{11}^9	m_{11}^o	m_{11}^9	m_{11}^o	m_{11}^9	m_{11}^o	m_{11}^9
	m_{12}^o	m_{12}^6	m_{12}^o	m_{12}^o	m_{12}^6	m_{12}^6	m_{12}^o	m_{12}^o	m_{12}^6	m_{12}^6	m_{12}^o	m_{12}^o	m_{12}^6	m_{12}^6
(V_q)	14,9	11,1	1o,6	11,o	1o,9	11,4	11,6	12,1	12,o	12,4	1o,9	11,4	11,4	11,8
ξ	33,3	34,9	31,7	32,7	34,6	36,o	33,7	35,o	37,o	38,9	33,1	34,4	36,4	38,2
(m)	12	11	12	11	11	1o	11	1o	1o	9	11	1o	1o	9
ea-ible	-	-	+	+	+	+	+	+	+	+	+	+	+	+
ffi-ient	-	+	+	-	+	-	-	-	-	+	-	-	+	+

Literature:

Bailey, N. T. J.: Queueing for Medical Care, in: Journal of the Royal Statistical Society 3, 1954, series C, pp. 137-145.

Burke, P. J.: The Output of a Queueing System, in: Operations Research 4, 1956, pp. 699-704.

Burke, P. J.: Output Processes and Tandem Queues, in: Proceedings of the Symposium on Computer-Communications Networks and Teletraffic, New York 1972, pp. 419-428.

Carruthers, M. E.: Computer Analysis of Routine Pathology Work Schedules Using a Simulation Programme, in: Journal of Clinical Pathology 23, 1970, pp. 269-272.

Eichhorn, S.: Krankenhausbetriebslehre, vol. II, 3rd edition, Köln 1976.

Ferschl, F.: Zufallsabhängige Wirtschaftsprozesse, Wien/Würzburg 1964.

Fleck, H.: Analyse der Ablauforganisation in einem medizinischen Untersuchungszentrum mit Hilfe der Netzwerktechnik, in: Methods of Information in Medicine 16, 1977, pp. 81-88.

Gierl, L.: Partialmodelle der Ablaufplanung im Krankenhaus auf empirischer Grundlage, Ph. D. thesis, Nürnberg 1976.

Gross, D., and Harris, C. M.: Fundamentals of Queueing Theory, New York/London/Sydney/Toronto 1974.

Hegemann, H.: Zur Kapazitäts- und Prozeßplanung in der klinischen Diagnostik, Berlin/Heidelberg/New York/Tokyo 1985.

Jackson, J. R.: Jobshop-like Queueing Systems, in: Management Science 10, 1963, pp. 131-142.

Kendall, D. G.: Stochastic Processes Occuring in the Theory of Queues and their Analysis by the Method of the Imbedded Markov Chain, in: The Annals of Mathematical Statistics 24, 1953, pp. 338-354.

Klimow, G. P.: Bedienungsprozesse, Basel/Stuttgart 1979.

Lemoine, A.J.: Networks of Queues - A Survey of Equilibrium Analysis, in: Management Science 24, 1977, pp. 464-481.

Little, J. D. C.: A Proof of the Queueing Formula L = λ W, Operations Research 9, 1961, pp. 383-387.

Melamed, B.: On Poisson Traffic Processes in Discrete-State Markovian Systems with Applications to Queueing Theory, in: Advances in Applied Probability 11, 1979, pp. 218-239, (1979a).

Melamed, B.: Characterizations of Poisson Traffic Streams in Jackson Queueing Networks, in: Advances in Applied Probability 11, 1979, pp. 422-438, (1979b).

Neumann, K., and Steinhardt, U.: GERT Networks and the Time-Oriented Evaluation of Projects, in: Lecture Notes in Economics and Mathematical Systems, vol. 172, Berlin/Heidelberg/New York 1979.

O'Kane, P. C.: A Simulation Model of a Diagnostic Radiology Department, in: European Journal of Operational Research 6, 1981, pp. 38-45.

Pritsker, A. A. B., and Happ, W. W.: GERT: Graphical Evaluation and Review Technique, in: Journal of Industrial Engineering 17, 1966, pp. 267-274 and pp. 293-301.

Revesz, G., Shea, F. J., and Ziskin, M. C.: Patient Flow and Utilization of Resources in a Diagnostic Radiology Department, in: Radiology 102, 1972, pp. 21-30.

Taylor, B. W., and Keown, A. J.: A Network Analysis of an Inpatient-Outpatient Department, in: Journal of the Operational Research Society 31, 1980, pp. 169-179.

Taylor, I. D. S., and Templeton, J. G. C.: Waiting Time in a Multi-Server Cutoff-Priority Queue, and its Application to an Urban Ambulance Service, in: Operations Research 28, 1980, pp. 1168-1188.

Walrand, J.: On the Equivalence of Flows in Networks of Queues, in: Journal of Applied Probability 19, 1982, pp. 195-203.

Simulation Models for the Analysis of Hospitals with Regard to their Emergency Infrastructure

Paul Stähly

1 Summary

A model of hospitals is presented which simulates the real behaviour of a hospital in extreme situations. The generally designed hospital model can, by entering parametric values, be adapted to real hospitals (small, medium and big hospitals with the exception of huge hospitals with decentralized clinical hospitals). The model can be confronted with freely compilable scenarios (technical and natural catastrophes of any period of time). The simulation model is able to show process and success of the patients treatment for a given scenario in the modelled hospital. It helps us to discover potential capacity bottle-necks, to verify the effects of measures to improve the efficiency and the elimination of bottle-necks and to estimate the limits of all capacity reserves. Furthermore the model issues critical values (throughputs/capacities) of attending patients. These values define the limits of a regular attention.

This Project was developed at the Institute of Operations Research at the University of St. Gallen for Business Administration, Economics and Social Sciences in cooperation with the Institute for Hospitals and Public Health in Aarau and the Swiss Department of Defence. It was supported from the Research Fund of the University of St. Gallen and from the Swiss National Fund. This paper represents a part of several years of research effort. Many people of the three Institutes mentioned contributed to its success. In particular I want to recognize the participation of R. Fischer, P. Frick, A. Stäger and especially of J. Sperry. I also be indebted to M. Freiburghaus, Th. Kirchhofer, A. Pleninger, R. Renz, D.Salamin and I. Salaorni for their contributions.

This hospital model can also be used to check the alarm organization of a hospital and also to train hospital management. Under this aspect, the main goal is to train the management in a way, that in an extreme situation no capacity of the hospital is lost because of wrong decisions.

To be able to master the organizational limits of large hospitals on the one hand and to model whole hospitalization areas on the other hand, we started a successor project in fall 1985.

This project, titled "Simulation of Emergency-Infrastructures (management, transportation facilities and structure of hospitalization area) in Hospitalization Areas" is discussed in the last chapter. This general model is able to simulate the behaviour of any hospitalization area (controlled through parameters) as a consequence of chosen scenarios. Thus it enables to examine the progress and success of patient treatment and care. The analysis of simulation results builds the base for preventive decisions regarding the mastering of large catastrophies.

Furthermore the model should serve as an analytical tool to prepare emergency plans for predefined scenarios as well as for training management staff of hospitalization areas.

2 Problem

The capacity of hospitals for taking up patients is limited. For the usual flow of patients, if the arrival of patients is limited in number, time and place, capacity is sufficiently available. Furthermore it is possible to free additional short-term capacity by organizational decisions.

In case of other assumptions problems will arise. From the hospitals's viewpoint we are faced with one of the following types of scenario:

- Measured by the capacity of the hospital, a quite large number of patients arrive (as a result of one or several events).
- A substantial increase of patients conitinues for a longer period.

With respect for getting such extreme problems under control, the managers of the hospital are faced with the problem to preventively analyse possible increases of capacity (changing the level of alarm, additional staff, changing organisation plans, simplifying administration of patients, additional rooms, etc.), to improve their emergency plans and to realize them without delay. Another problem is to define the moment, when the managers are forced to set additional actions, as to change the level of care or to start the operating of a triage hospital (triage means setting medical priorities).

3 Goals of the project

There are two main goals for the model's use:

1. The model can serve as an analysis tool for the examination of hospitals. In dependence on free chosen scenarios every hospital (except large hospitals with decentralized clinics) can be analysed. Analysis covers the detection of passes in several functions (e.g. reception, triage, x-ray, operation, also see chapter 6), the estimation of threshold values depending on the grade of treatment and the examination of decisions in order to remove passes.

2. The model should be used for the training of hospital management. The managers should be able to detect and realize the best decisions for the maximization of the hospital's throughput. Thus it is possible to check real emergency plans on weaknesses.

To a great extent these goals have been reached with the model which currently exists. We proved it to be an excellent tool for analysis more than once. To enlarge the motivation for using the model as a training instrument, we are currently developing a brandnew user interface which enables to run the whole simulation interactively. Therefore we are forced to implement the whole model on a VAXStation 2000 (for actual data see chapter 6.4).

4 Procedure

The project had to be tackled in an interdisciplinar way. Under the aspect of medicine on the one hand and under the aspect of operations research and informatics on the other hand. Especially important were the needs of use. To make sure that all these aspects were taken into consideration, a advisory board was founded. The members of this board came from the Swiss Institute for Health Service and Hospitals in Aarau, the VESKA, the Institute for Operations Research of the University of St. Gallen for Business Administration, Economics and Social Sciences, a district hospital, the Swiss Department of Defence and district authorities. On this board the project and the practical usefullness was discussed in periodical meetings.

5 Concept of the model

5.1 Method

The model building process is used to create a sufficient detailed image of reality in order to examine critical aspects of reality in models.

Since the model contains only those components of reality, which are relevant to the desired evaluations, it is an abstraction of reality. Consequently, all other components are not part of the model. As far as the logic of all transactions is not concerned, the model composes sub-models from more detailed functions and events.

The realization of the basic idea has been completed with a simulation model. The simulation especially includes the aspect of uncertainty. As a consequence random details of events (showing up in random deviations from a mean (transportation time, treatment time and the like)) are a principle of the model.

Although the model has been simplified to a great extent, the use of a computer and an implementation using a special simulation language is indispensable. Operating with behaviour and interactions of real objects and due to former experience we decided to use an object-oriented programming language.

The rules of the object's behaviour - comprised in classes and subclasses of the same structure - have been implemented in SIMULA 67, which was the programming language to realize our model.

The simulation also included the dynamic aspects of the model, thus it should be higly valid for reality.

Generally based on basic decisions (if-then-else) the model should show the results of former decisions. Picking the best solution from a lot of various single simulation results proved to be the only way to get good solutions based on simulation.

The possibility to examine the results of the variation of parameters (capacity, scenario etc.) tassed out to be a helpful and important way to come to conclusions. It is possible for example, to examine the change in patient service times as a consequence of capacity increase or as a consequence of a lower treatment level.

5.2 Stochastical aspects

The goal of the simulation model is to show up the possible sequence of transactions - as a consequence of a catastrophe - in a hospital in an advanced abstracted way.

Thus all random parameters (like service times or arrival time) are not given as fixed values but as distributions. This does not include parameters like number of doctors, rooms, hospitals, beds and other "naturally fixed" numbers.

The model uses the following types of distributions:
- normal distribution
- poisson distribution
- exponential distribution
- triangle distribution.

Poisson and exponential distributions are used for generating arrival times of patients.

Normal and triangle distributions are used for stochastical change of parameters that describe the duration of activities, changes in place e.g. the duration of an operation or the transport of patients. The generation is traced from random number generators.

The sequence of random numbers depends on the start value. We had used this fact for the possibility to get various simulation results under equal conditions. So we could master the variance of results.

5.3 Benefit of the project

The complexity of the model has reached a degree, where it is impossible to get results analytically. Simulation here serves as a tool, which allows experiments, which cannot be implemented in reality (only with unresponsible consequences like endangering human life).

Furthermore, processes which last days and months in reality, can be simulated in a few seconds on a computer. Thus a lot of combinations of scenarios and decisions can be realized in quite small amount of time.

As - to our knowledge - no such detailed model has existed until today, it is the first time that we can determine the threshold values of a hospital's capacity for patients.

Analysis of the model enables the hospitals management staff to examine changes in capacity, internal patient transports and treatment level and its effects on the hospitals performance (measured in patient throughput and effects of treatment).

Based on the goal of the simulation model - to be able to answer all questions mentioned in the problem definition - all Swiss hospitals (some 600) and almost all hospitals all over the world can be analysed with our model.

The analysis and the planning covers both the estimation of threshold values and the development and improvment of emergency plans.

6 The structure of the model

6.1 Introduction

The model consists of two independent parts, the szenario-model and the model of the hospital; both are decomposed in modules. The output of the szenario-model is the input of the hospital-model (see figure 6.1).

After model-simulation, log-files and patient-flows are analysed, evaluated and reports are generated.

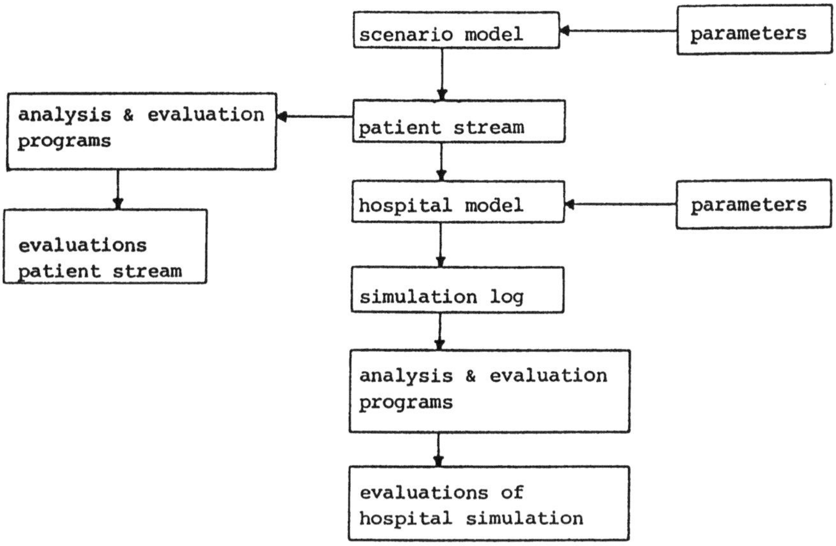

Figure 6.1: Architecture of the model

6.2 The scenario-model

This model generates the flow of patients arriving at the hospital's entrance.

The flow consists of several, different patient-types, taken from a "standard patient catalogue", which contains the most frequent types of patients. The catalogue has been developed under the guidance of several physicians of the Swiss Army. It contains more than 100 types of patients with different injuries and illnesses. The catalogue is reviewed and improved permanently.

Each patient has its own attributes, either taken from the patient catalogue or based on probability distributions.

The result (flow of patients) is the picture of one or several real disasters and the basis of the model simulation. Furthermore, the scenario-model generates the patients to fill up the hospital.

Each part of the disaster is defined as a sub-scenario. A sub-scenario consists of at least one patient-component and at least one transport-component. The components can start and end at any time, they can run in sequence or simultaneously.

The scenario-model can generate various sub-scenarios. Each sub-scenario has its own transport resources. The central coordination of all resources like vehicles or staff is considered in the successor of this research-project, "Simulation of emergency-structures in hospital-regions". The centralization is a consequence of centralized management structures.

The transport resources are random-generated, the user can determine rate and distribution of vehicle's capacity (how many percent of cars with 1 seat, 2 seats, etc.). Furthermore he can choose between two strategies of patient-transportation sequence: FIFO (first come, first served) and RANDOM. The waiting strategies of the transport resources include a fill-up-strategy (wait, until a vehicle is totally full with patients) and a fast-serve-strategy (load patients as long as available, then drive, even when seats are free; see figure 6.2).

Data collection is realized by filling predefined forms.

Thus the total flow of patients depends on

- the number of patients generated by sub-scenarios
- the start-time and parameters of the sub-scenarios
- the distance between the sub-scenario and the hospital
- the number and capacity of transport resources
- the patient-transportation strategy
- the vehicle-fill-up-strategy.

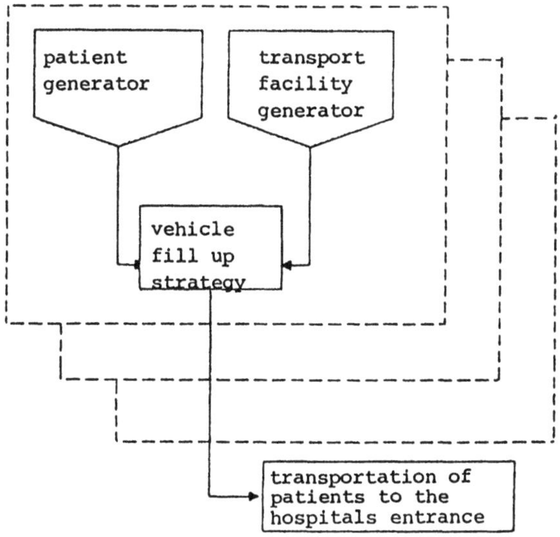

Figure 6.2: Scenario Model: Architecture

6.3 Hospital

6.3.1 Notes about the formulation of the problem

The hospital as a complex system of relations must in this model be abstracted to the relevant aspects of the problem. Only the actions directly related to patients or medical attendance are being treated (e.g. backup services were omitted) and these processes were only examined in their temporary dimension. We were not looking at the surgical side of an operation thus we were only interested in the amount of time in which the capacity of personnel, rooms and so on, was needed.

The problem to figure the amount of material needed was treated exceptionally. It gives a quantitative dimension to the whole simulation. Nevertheless the effects on the model are marginal because only calculations in the sense of a book-keeping of stock and consumption are done.

The complexity of a hospital in this model had to be limited, because this model must run on a computer system. This process of simplification was done in a way that the elements that were important for the simulation were modelled in quite a detailed way, the less important ones were also modelled less detailed and all the insignificant elements were left out. These restrictions were necessary condidering memory and performance limitations.

For an easy adaption of the model to real hospitals all data which are common to all the hospitals are already included in the model. To analyse an existing hospital, only the specific data have to be entered.

The partial model "hospital" can be divided into the following sub-models:

- one sub-model per treatment-function
- one sub-model per transportation-function
- one sub-model for decisions of the management of the hospital
- one sub-model for the analysis of certain points of time.

For all sub-models it is necessary to enter specific parameters. Through these sub-models, which were internally designed as processes, several object-types are connected with

- patients
- hospital staff
- beds
- material
- mobile installations.

The treatment-functions represent simplified structures of the wards of the hospital (e.g. surgical function). The general design required the definition of the smallest still autonomously working unit (e.g. for the surgical function 1: an operating table including the necessary equipment for the care for a single patient for the time of a operation). The supposition for the starting of the units is the availability of the necessary staff. The adaption to the capacity of a real hospital can be achieved by defining the same number of units equal to the number of patients.

These units are able to:

- exist simultaneously in the model,
- cooperate or
- compete with each other.

Each unit has a certain structure, in which the data for its behaviour, among other things, is contained. The simulation model is constructed in a way that the single units can act independently in regard to their competence. For instance a surgical function gives the order to prepare the next patient a certain time before the expected end of an operation that is taking place in a surgical unit. The limit in which the units can act independently is given by the conditions that are defined globaly and/or by the hospital management. Overall restrictions for hospital staff units are for example the maximum working hours and minimum leisure time. By decisions of the hospital management shifts can be forced to exceed the overall working hours.

The hospital model is designed in a way that "reasonable" system decisions replace missing decisions of the hospital management. For example units in which the shifts do not change after the maxium working time are automatically closed (with a corresponding message in the simulation report) and their personnel are sent to their rest billets.

Parallel to the acting units in the model all the relevant events for the analysis are taken down to the report. These event messages can be analysed after the model simulation from different points of view. For example under the aspect of the patients, the hospital personnel or the treatment functions (temporary flow, capacity utilization of personnel and treatment function units, waiting and idle time, queues, consecutive working time, analysis of situations and points in time).

6.3.2 The basic components

6.3.2.1 The patients

The patients are brought to the entrance of the hospital by the model. They are designed as independent objects of a class and have the following attributes:

- running number for identification
- time of damage
- remaining time until stable condition gets unstable (urgency)
- assigned personal diagnosis in descending treatment priority
- momentary location
- remarks about provisional treatment and complications
- degree of ability of transportability (e.g. patient's ability to walk without support)
- time registration for statistical analysis.

The following attributes are not considered in the proposed model:

- blood-group
- sex
- age.

The blood-groop could, together with the treatment (adequate to the diagnosis), be the basis for the rationing of the blood-bank.

The sex would be important if the diagnosis had to be different by sexes or male and female patients had to be brought to different rooms in the ward.

But these three attributes don't influence the treatment in such a way that the duration of the treatment would be affected. The analysis of the emergency infrastructure of a hospital doesn't change regarding these three parameters.

A diagnosis defines for each of five different aspects (= diagnostic aspects) a certain assumption (= characteristic). Every single diagnosis of an emergency patient suits the determination of a characteristic per attribute out of the following list of diagnosis:

Attr. Nr.	attribute	characteristic
1	place of treatment	ambulant
		stationary
		separate
		lay out
2	kind of treatment	surgical
		medical
3	urgency	urgent operation necessary
		condition stable
4	topography	head, throat
		thorax
		abdomen
		extremities
		burns
		other injury
		sick patients
5	seriousness of injury	slight
		medium
		serious
		hopeless.

As already said the diagnosis of a patient is computed out of the information entered at the beginning of the simulation run. For example for the attribute "seriousness of injury" the following distribution has been entered.

Attribute	characteristic	probability
seriousness of injury	slight	40 %
	medium	40 %
	serious	15 %
	hopeless	5 %

For every patient, corresponding to the distribution, a characteristic is randomly assigned, the matching process in the hospital computed and stored as a present parameter.

At the time, more than 100 standard patients (patient types) are already defined in an open patient's catalogue. These exogeneously defined patient types represent certain damages with different degrees of seriousness of injury and define the corresponding treatment requirement up to three treatment qualities and, partly, with different degrees of rehabilitation. In each of these three main variants, patients can go detours instead of the direct way, depending on the capacity utilization of the units. Every need of a patient is modelled after the statistical distribution. The characteristic of every patient is determined randomly corresponding to the given distributions.

To avoid potential medical objections about the patient types it must be said, that the model supplies only a basic structure, so that the concrete realization of the medical care of the standard patient can be altered by the user of the model at any time.

6.3.2.2 The hospital staff

For the hospital personnel units only one class of units is defined. But this class can be differed by the value of the attribute "personnel category" in medical personnel, nursing staff, assistent personnel and so on.

The personnel object (= the single person) posesses the following attributes:
- running number for identification

- 1st engagement priority (=primarily intended engagement)
- 2nd engagement priority (=alternative possible engagement)
- 3rd engagement priority (=alternative possible engagement)
- alarm time (time until the readiness to act)
- momentary location
- time of changing the location
- maximal consecutive engagement under normal conditions
- maximal consecutive engagement under extreme conditions
- minimal time of rest under normal conditions
- minimal time of rest under extreme conditions
- time registration for statistical analysis.

To every single person or group of people therefore three engagement priorities can be associated with. The model tries with the help of a personnel association algorithm to engage the staff - as far as possible - corresponding to the defined priorities. The algorithm changes only to lower level of priority, if there is no personnel left on the higher one.

For example the priorities for a surgeon can be defined in the following way:

- 1st priority: thorax surgeon
- 2nd priority: general surgeon
- 3nd priority: surgical assistant.

This means, that this surgeon works - whenever possible - on his special subject. If there is no work for him to do as a thorax surgeon he will be used as a general surgeon or as a surgical assistant. If a specialist only should work on his special subject, this subject must be defined in all three priorities.

6.3.2.3 Treatment and transportation functions

The caretaking of patients is done in special treatment functions, where each one represents a basic medical treatment. When the model is adapted to an existing hospital, these treatment functions are defined locally and temporally. The following treatment functions are defined in the model:

- treatment function units for only one patient at the time
  - entrance function type
  - triage function type (to set medical priorities)
  - surgical function type
  - emergency operation function type
  - ambulant function type
  - X-ray function type
  - plaster function type
  - release function type

- treatment function units for several patients simultanously
  - caretaking function type (normal care)
  - seperation function type
  - lay out function type
  - monitoring function type
  - intensive caretaking function type

- transportation functions
  - transportation function type for patients unable to walk
  - transportation function type for patients able to walk

Each function contains the rules for the service and the rules for the necessary coordination with the other functions. They can be generated in any number, depending on the chosen hospital. Assigned to the functions are the individual personnel assignments on the different stand-by and operating levels. In certain cases, important installations and equipment that are used by different functions, can be defined.

The treatment function objects have the following capacity parameters:

- personnel dowry per operation level (e.g. night, day, extreme situation), differed by personnel categories and sub-categories

- maximal number of patients that can wait for the treatment in the waiting-room in front of the treatment function

- amount of time for re-establishment between two treatments

- function utility registrations for statistical analysis.

As a result of the team's discussion it is possible to define the concrete patient's way in the treatment function. This has the advantage that for a patient with a distinct diagnosis several potential treatments are possible, not only depending on the diagnosis but also on other criteria, such as:

- hospital function (triage hospital, non-triage hospital)
- momentary stress of the possible following treatment functions
- stability of the patient

Figure 6.3 shows the units of the partial model "hospital". The number of units must be determined corresponding to the number in the modelled hospital.

Symbols used:

- drawn squares: units of treatment functions that can handle only one patient at the time

- squares open on the sides: units of treatment functions that can handle several patients simultanously

- bridge symbol: area with possible queues.

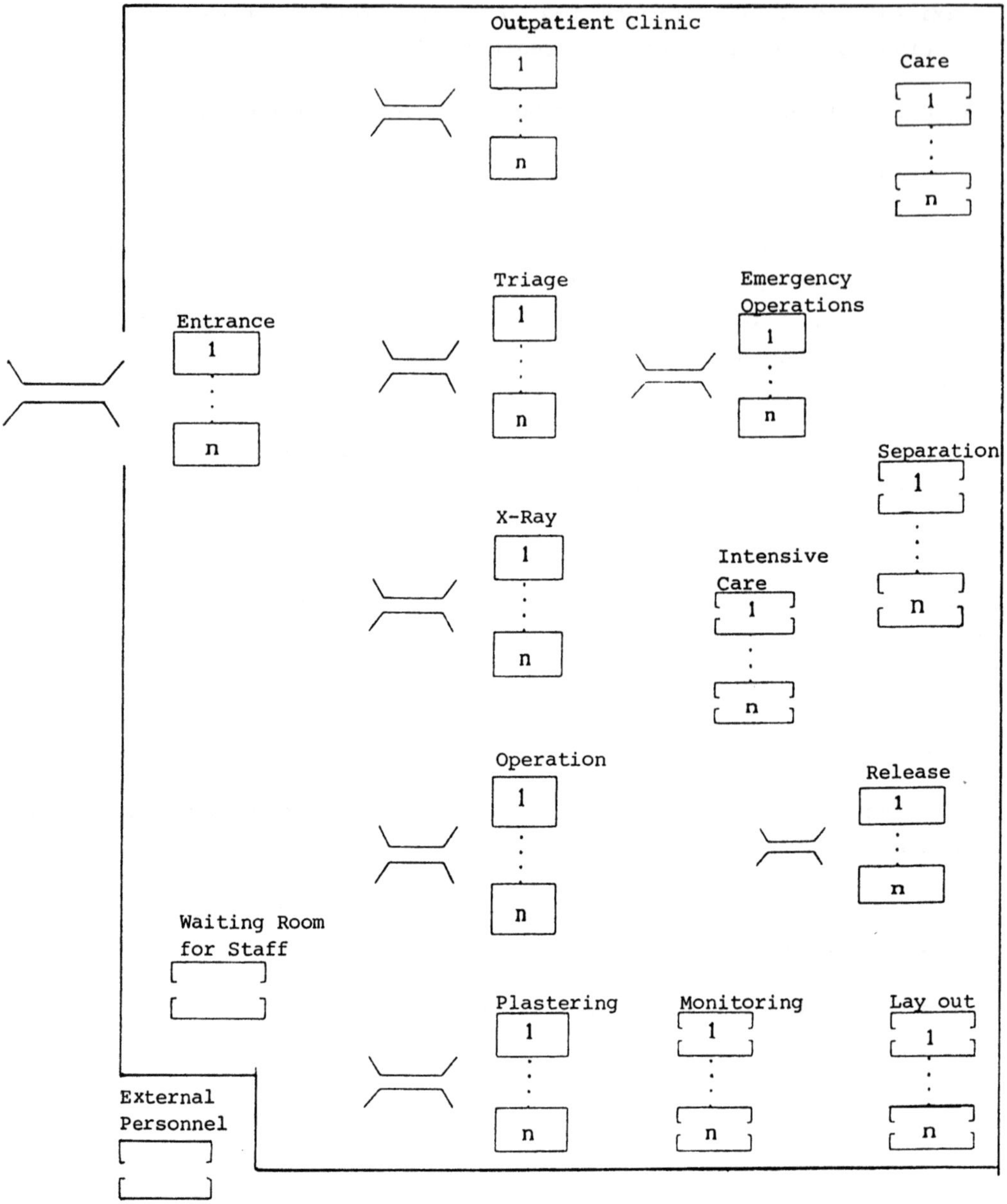

Figure 6.3: Partial Model "Hospital"

6.3.3 Transportation of patients and personnel

Inside the hospital no rationing in means of transport is simulated but the temporal aspect of transportation is regarded. With that it is possible to take the location of the treatment functions into consideration.

Two transportation tables are provided:

- a patients transportation table and
- a staff transportation table.

The patients transportation table contains the transportation times between two treatment functions. The transportation times can be either fixed deterministic or stochastic in relation with a distribution and the necessary parameter (e.g. normal distribution with mean and variance).

Transportation times for the personnel are represented in a similar way, but the staff transportation table contains in addition a row or a column for the recreation room and the elements in this row or column represent the transportation times between the recreation room and the treatment functions. Eventual time needed for preperation or changing clothes can be contained in there. The alarm time, i.e. the time needed from the alarm until the arrival in hospital for absent personnel is contained in the parameter list of every single person (refer class personnel). The case of bottle-necks in the transportation system (e.g. number of elevators between operation room and ward or the number of vehicles or the number of aids between two treatment functions) can be taken into consideration with the help of an additional class "transportation bottle-necks". Every possible bottle-neck is modelled by a transportation bottle-neck object. With this object patients are moved out of the queue in front of the bottle-neck in regard to the capacity of the transportation system between the two treatment functions.

6.3.4 Coordination and control of the model

All classes and their objects were as far as possible self-coordinating programmed. The actual model command is performed from the outside with the help of general command parameters and starting data.

A first group of data to be entered contains all information that is identical with the simulation in connection with a hospital. This is the determination of the hospital's configuration. For an example the number of operating tables, X-ray equipment etc. Each determination contains different treatment functions and equipment. Furtheron the personnel is described by its category, its primary engagement priority, its priority for other treatment functions and sub-functions.

A second group of data to be entered must be produced separately for every new simulation run. The simulation to run is characterized by this group, e.g.:

a) The scenario for the simulation run

This scenario is described with regard to the effects of the arrival of patients at the entrance of the hospital and with regard to the adequate diagnosis of every patient. The control of the temporal distances between the arrival of the patients, their diagnosis, the individual times for the treatment functions is indirectly determined. Not individual values per patient or treatment function are given, but statistical distributions for all patients, diagnosis and treatment functions in connection with the necessary parameters.

During the simulation the treatment or transportation times for every single patient are computed according to the entered distribution with the help of random number generators. They are used to control the processes in the hospital.

b) Starting data for the simulation

The starting data define the state of the hospital at the beginning of the simulation. Examples are: working condition of the hospital, starting state of the personnel, possible modifications of the infrastructure and so on.

c) Decisions of the game management

The simulation run is controlled by the decisions of the game management. Some outside conditions can be altered. With the help of the automatic command repetition tool simple decision programs can be developed e.g. a program for regular shift-changes in treatment functions. Examples are: alarming the personnel, setting to work, increase or closing of treatment functions, disposition of aids for the transportation of patients etc. Furthermore decisions can be made on the transfer of patients and on treatment variances (normal, reduced or war medicine). The simulation can be interrupted for analysis at any time.

6.4 Technical data of the model

The model system consists now of the scenario model, the hospital model, 18 different analysis programs and a user system for the model user. Altogether 5500 program lines were coded for the scenario model and the hospital model (both in SIMULA 67) and 1600 program lines for the analysis programs (in SAS (Statistical Analysis System)). The scenario and the hospital model are adjusted and controlled with the help of over 140 different paramters (about 10000 parameter values per model simulation). 18 forms were designed for the data inquiry. The program presents default values for most parameters, that can be changed if necessary. The execution of the model simulation is supported by the menu-guided user system, which guides the user through all necessary activities, including database management. Furthermore the user system makes simultaneous work on models of different hospitals possible. The simulation models and the user system are implemented on a IBM 3033 wheras the analysis programs are run on a VAX 8500, which is connected with the IBM 3033 by a telephone line. The user does not realize that he works with two mainframes, all actions between the IBM and the VAX are handled by the user-interface. As already mentioned in chapter 3, the necessary programs will be implemented on a VAXStation 2000. Thus the whole model system, implemented on hardware, can be carried around. Meanwhile the user interface is going to be easier to handle and the exploitations possibilities are going to be more refined.

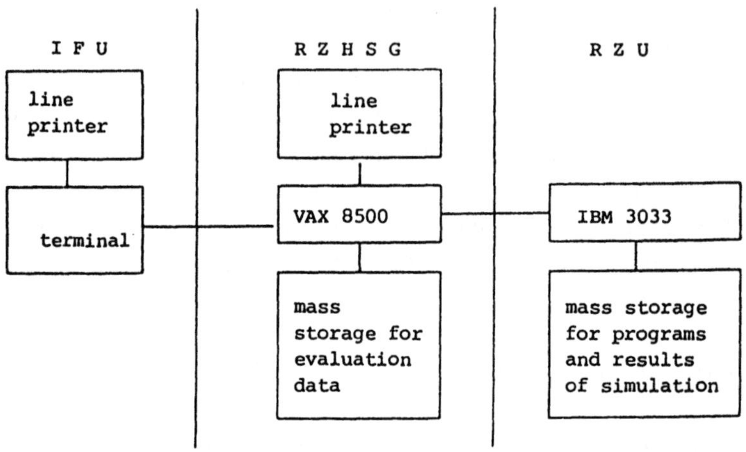

IFU = Institut für Unternehmensforschung (Operations Research) and RZHSG = Computing Center of the University of St. Gallen for Business Administration, Economics and Social Sciences; RZU = Computing Center of the University of Zurich

Figure 6.4: The System's Network

7 Model-simulation and -evaluation

Using a set of aids (forms, checklists) for the data collection of infrastructures, the data of seven different hospitals has been collected.

In the same way the data for more than 100 types of patients has been defined and collected under the scientific guidance of specialists of the Swiss Federal Office for Medical Affairs.

Thus the model has been tested for seven hospitals. The tests comprised two scenarios for each hospital and a subsequent evaluation.

7.1 Simulation of a small civil hospital

The test runs of a small civil hospital ran in spring 1985. Figure 7.1 shows the patient flow inside the hospital. The basic data of the hospital were given as follows :

number of beds	64
number of operation tables	2
average number of personnel	84
equipment	X-ray-room
	physiotherapeutical room
	lab
	plaster room
	others

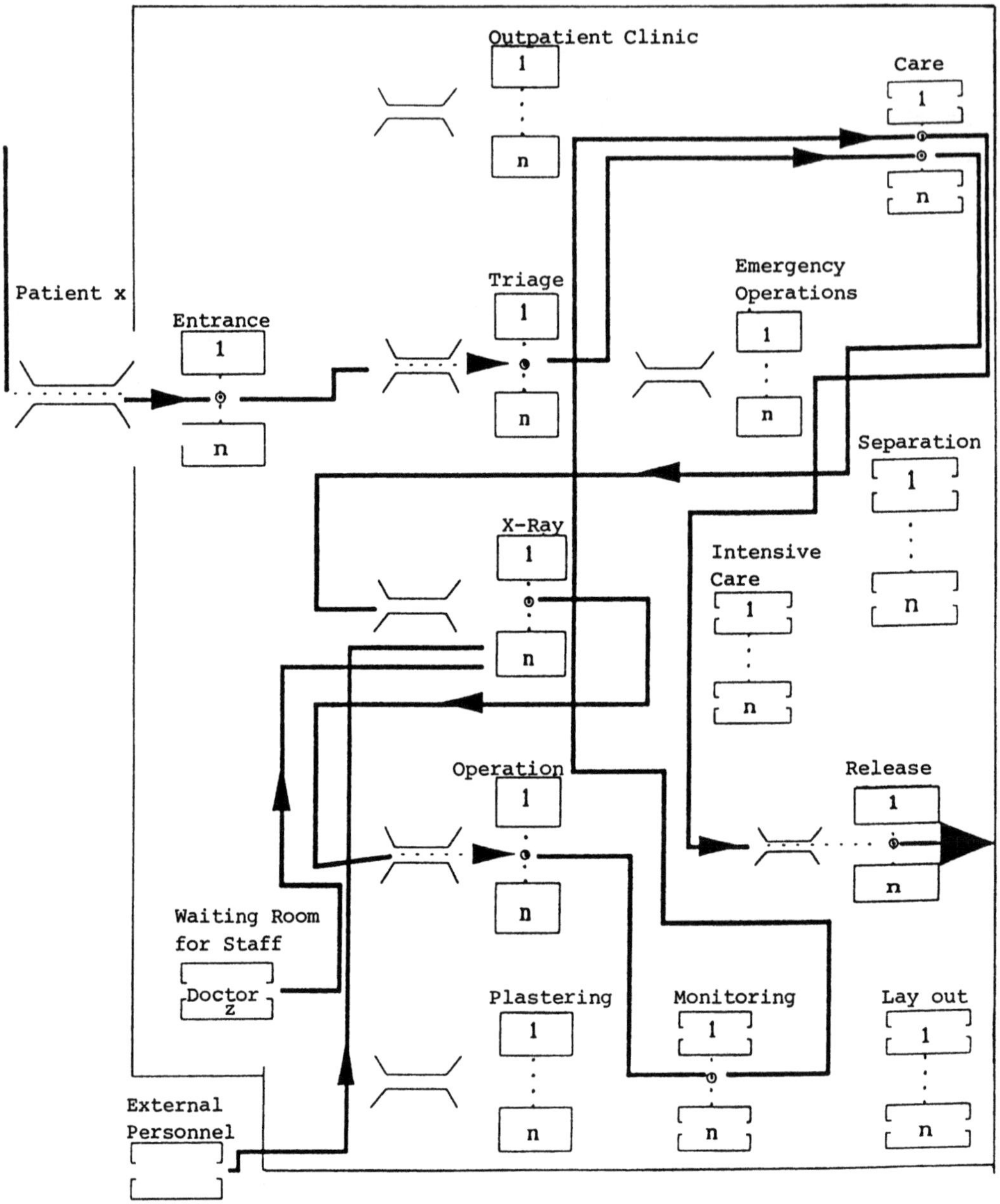

Figure 7.1: Patients flow in the simulation model

The first scenario was taken from the data of the hospital in Thusis, Graubuenden, Switzerland and was tested in the simulation-model.

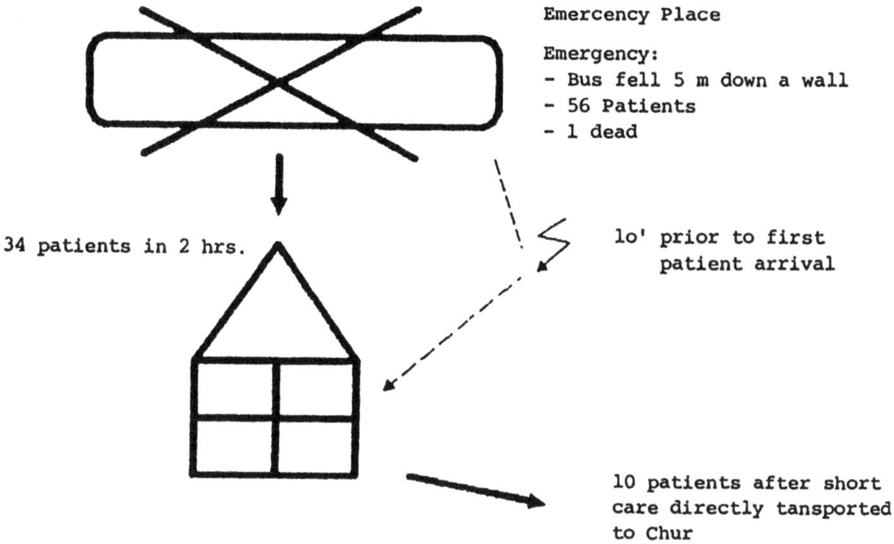

Figure 7.2: Thusis Scenario No. 1

Thus it was possible to compare the behaviour of the model with reality. As we found out, the model simulated reality quite well.

The second scenario was based on an imaginary desaster: We assumed a mass collision at the San Bernardino-Route. Number of vehicles being involved :

1 bus	32 passengers
1 bus	26 passengers
1 truck	2 persons
1 car	6 persons
1 car	4 persons
1 car	3 persons
3 cars	2 persons
9 vehicles,	79 persons

Number of injuries being involved :

13 persons uninjured
62 persons injured
4 persons dead.

4 of the 62 injured persons were brought to the hospital in Chur, thus the hospital of Thusis had to take up 58 patients.

Time	Event
07:00	moment of accident
07:20	the police was alarmed
07:28	the hospital in Thusis was alarmed
07:29	police arrives at the collision
07:34	ambulance arrives at the collision
07:36	first patient delivered to the hospital in Thusis
07:54	first organized transport of patient arrives at the hospital
09:38	Last patient arrives at the hospital.

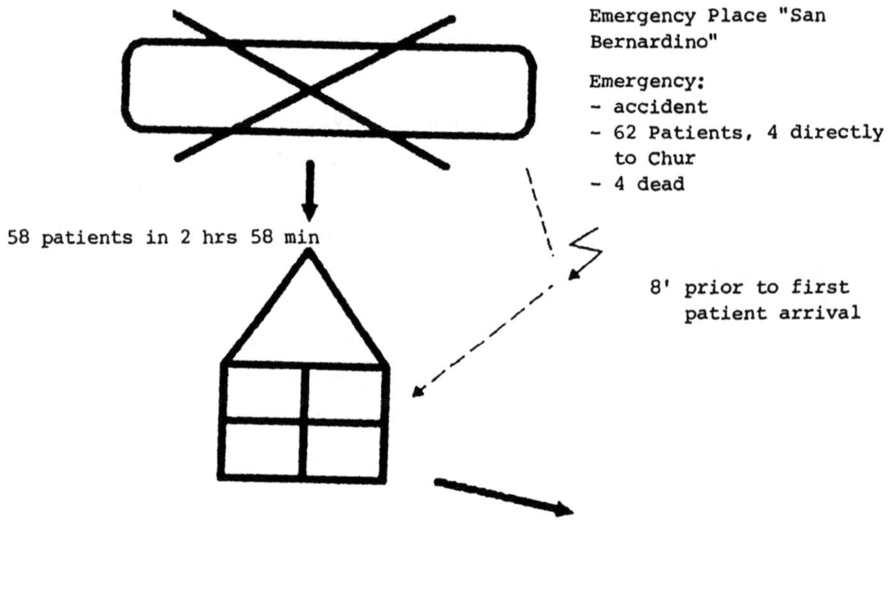

Figure 7.3: Thusis Scenario No. 2

7.2 Simulation of a military hospital

There was also a military hospital under the seven hospitals on which data was collected, because

1) the problems are similar for both types of hospitals
2) the data were also of interest with respect to the successor of this project, "Simulation of emergency-structures in hospital-regions".

The military hospital was simulated to be used as a training instrument for the staff of the hospital on the one hand and in officers' schools on the other hand. Two scenarios were selected. The data of the military hospital were the following:

type of the hospital	military base hospital
number of beds	500 (358 overground)
number of GOPS beds	142 (underground)
number of GOPS operation tables	4 (underground)
equipment	X-ray-room
	physiotherapeutical room
	lab
	plastering room
	others.

The scenario was a sabotage actions on a troop barracks. The data of the scenario were the following:

Time	Event
01:07:00	activation of the hospital with a standard reception of 2-4 patients/hour.
02:05:00	sabotage action on a troop barracks (about 250 men involved)
02:06:00	the military hospital was alarmed
02:09:50	reception of 61 patients with need for care from primary transports (simultaneously standard patients arrive)

Conditions: no secondary transports (from this hospital to another) are possible.

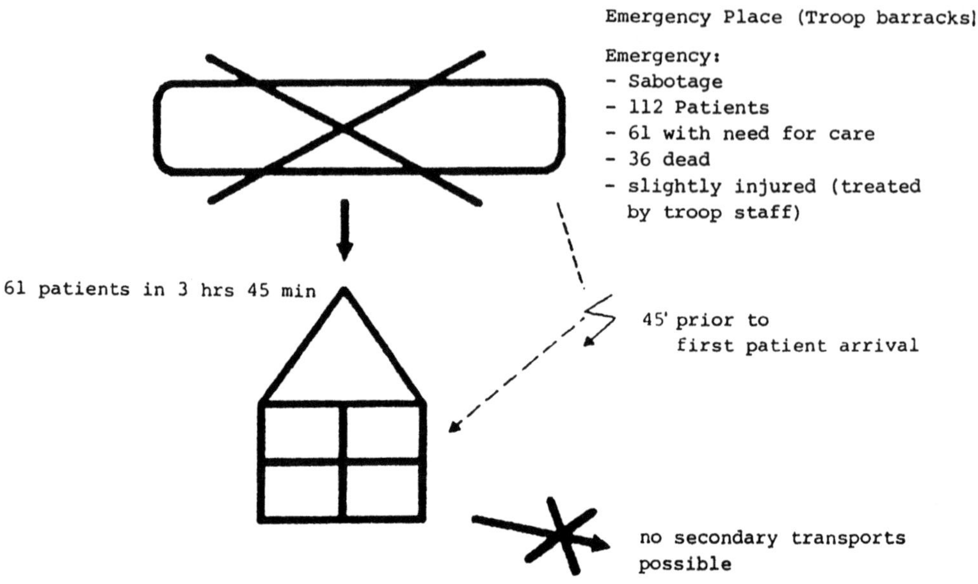

Figure 7.4: Military Hospital Scenario

7.3 First results

In all cases the validity of the model was sufficient. By comparing the threshold values estimated by the hospital managers and those brought up from the model we found that the model was able to prove, that the possible throughput was greater than estimated by the managers. Furthermore we found out, that patients with high demand of care lowered the throughput substantially, because they consume quite high capacities in critical functions. Consequently, sequencing and scheduling planning enables the prevention, avoidance or at least the delay of those bottle-necks. In addition to that we found out that in long-term scenarios the hospital's management demanded too much from the personnel. Thus the effort of the staff over a longer time period was defeated by the workload.

8 The hospital model as a concept for coordinated medicine services

8.1 Outlook

It is possible to form hospital models of most of the Swiss hospitals (Some 600). The model can be used for analysing hospitals as well as for training hospital managers. The patient catalogue shall be extended to about 100 types of patients to be able to define a wide range of scenarios better than it is possible now.

The underlying model is a part of the next project, which deals with desasters too large to be mastered by one single hospital. Regions of hospitals are necessary to guarantee sufficient treatment for all patients. In addition to different hospitals the model comprises transport facilities and management structures. The goal of this model is to analyse and test different types of management principles and organisation structures in such regions. The model is going to be enlarged and improved to be able to model all kinds of hospitals in Switzerland.

Depending on the size of the disaster a hospitalization region has- due to the transport-restricted number of hospitals in a region - a natural limit in treatment capacity. Exceeding that limit means that the patient's grade of rehabilitation decreases naturally. Consequently, some of the patients will die because they cannot be treated in time.

The treatment capacity of a hospitalization region thus depends on:

- the treatment capacity of each hospital
- the transport capacity for
  - transports from the disaster to a treatment
  - transports between hospitals (transport after first treatment)

- organization structures
  - build up triages at the disaster's location
  - build up triage-hospitals
  - management of transportation facilities
- decrease of grade of treatment.

8.2 Problem

The basic idea is to create an instrument to find the threshold values of treatment capacities of the hospitalization region investigated theoretically. This calculation has to be done with respect to different types of patients, transport facilities, grade of treatment and organisation structure. Finally the model should find out the circumstances under which large disasters (both technical and natural) can be mastered.

8.3 Goal of the project

The goal of this research-project is the formulation and implementation of computer-based simulation models in SIMULA 67. With respect to the parameters (hospital-capacity, transport-capacity, grade of treatment) the model should be able to simulate the catastrophe and its mastering (success). The simulation should show up free capacity, test the efficiency of organisation structures and to improve and test emergency plans as well as to examine increases in capacity.

8.4 The state of the project

The underlying project includes the development of a system of simulation models, decomposed in the following parts:

- a hospital model
- a transportation model
- a scenario model
- an organizational model

The models should be able to work - depending on the parameters - in various variants as a part of the system.

8.4.1 The hospital model

The hospital model described earlier is constructed to be open for expansion and adaptation. Adaptations mostly mean a reduction to simplify the model in order to restrict memory and CPU time. Nevertheless some new features have been added to the model (transportation of patients, request of transportation facilities).

8.4.2 The transportation model

The transportation model had to be newly developed, based on research done earlier. The model can perform several tasks, including

- management of all transportation activities
- manage different paths between two points
- manage different facilities (cars, trains, helicopters)
- manage different transportation strategies.

For the construction of this model a lot of analytical work - regarding catastrophe management - is indispensable. The analysis covers all issues of transportation problems and transportation strategy. After checking the model's validation, it has to be realized by stepwise refinement.

8.4.3 The scenario model

For the generation of the systems's total patient flow a parameter-controlled model was implemented. It is able to realize a wide range of catastrophes and disasters. Both patient-types and flow rates can be varied. Thus the model is able to realize sudden catastrophes (such as many patients in a short time) and long-term disasters (like epidemic deseases) and combination of the two.

8.4.4 The organization model

The organization model builds the frame of the three models yet described (hospital-, transportation- and scenario-model, see figure 8.1). The organization structure described here controls all primary and secondary transports. It comprises the competences of management, the possibilty to introduce a triage on the place of disaster or to guarantee primary treatment with mobile ambulant stations.

Furthermore the whole simulation (time frame, management of single hospitals, transportation management) is controlled by this module.

The competence to lower the grade of treatment and other competences, which are assigned to local administrative authorities, become part of the model. The control in this model should be able to realize all decisions, that were taken by these authorities.

The characteristic of this model is its dynamic behaviour, as its structure changes in time (during simulation). The way to master a catastrophe can be described in three phases. The phases need not to run a sequence, they can overlap in time i.e. they can run simultaneously. Thus the sequence varies in dependence on the disaster. The three phases are:

Phase	Time	Characteristics
1	minutes	disaster starts, isolation, uncertainty, chaos, without orientation
2	hours	first rescues, salvation, alarms, building a catastrophe management
3	days	recovery, aid, well organized

The overall model

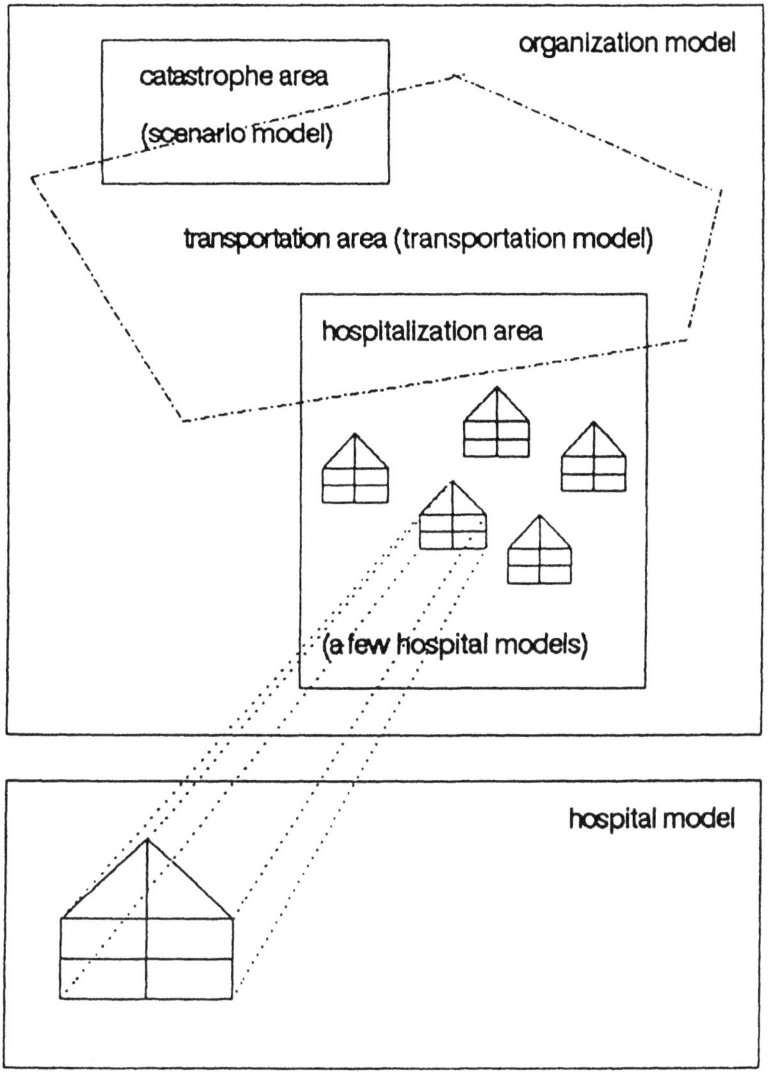

The hospital model

Figure 8.1: Controlled use of medical infrastructures in special cases

Literature:

Ahnefeld, F.W., and Gorgass, B.: Der Rettungssanitäter - Ausbildung und Fortbildung, Berlin/Heidelberg/New York 1980.

Ärztekammer Niedersachsen (ed.): Wegweiser Medizinische Katastrophenhilfe, Hannover 1982.

Bundesminister des Innern (ed.): Katastrophenmedizin, Leitfaden für die ärztliche Versorgung im Katastrophenfall, 2nd edition, Bonn 1982.

Bütikofer, H.: Zivile Führung in außerordentlichen Lagen, Frauenfeld 1979.

Häfeli, M.: Das Notfallwesen einer Region, Schlußbericht zum Nationalfondsforschungsprojekt, 4.14.70 FKG, St. Gallen 1974.

Nussbaumer, S. (ed.): Katastrophe: Was tun?, Lugano/Massagno 1983.

Sefrin, P., and Skrobek, W.: Notfallmedizin, Praxis und Tendenzen, Hannover 1981.

Sperry, J., and Stähly, P.: Im Extremfall bereit? Computergestützte Analyse von Spitälern hinsichtlich der Bewältigung von Katastrophen, in: Schweizer Spital 9/1985, pp. 11.

Sperry, J., and Stähly, P.: Analyse der Infrastruktur von Krankenhäusern hinsichtlich ihres Patienten-Throughputs unter Extrembedingungen mit Hilfe der Simulation, in: Streitferdt, L., Hauptmann, H., Marusev, A.W., Ohse, D., and Pape, U. (eds.): Operations Research Proceedings 1985, Berlin/Heidelberg/New York/Tokyo 1986, pp. 178.

List of Contributors

Lüder Bach
Universität Bayreuth
Postfach 3008
D-8580 Bayreuth

Günter Fandel
FernUniversität
Postfach 940
D-5800 Hagen

Hildegard Feucht
Industrieanlagen-Betriebs-
gesellschaft mbH
Einsteinstr. 20
D-8012 Ottobrunn

Klaus Hansen
Universität Hamburg
Von-Melle-Park 5
D-2000 Hamburg 13

Holger Hegemann
Weltistr. 79
D-8000 München 71

Kurt Heidenberger
Universität Erlangen-Nürnberg
Lange Gasse 20
D-8500 Nürnberg 1

Ernst Ostheimer
Industrieanlagen-Betriebs-
gesellschaft mbH
Einsteinstr. 20
D-8012 Ottobrunn

Antonius Prasiswa
Hoechst AG
Postfach
D-6230 Frankfurt am Main 80

Erhard Schmidt
Bundesministerium für
Arbeit und Sozialordnung
Rochusstr. 1
D-5300 Bonn 1

Paul Stähly
Hochschule St. Gallen für
Wirtschafts- und Sozialwissenschaften
Bodanstr. 6
CH-9000 St. Gallen

MIX
Papier aus verantwortungsvollen Quellen
Paper from responsible sources
FSC® C105338

If you have any concerns about our products,
you can contact us on
ProductSafety@springernature.com

In case Publisher is established outside the EU,
the EU authorized representative is:
Springer Nature Customer Service Center GmbH
Europaplatz 3, 69115 Heidelberg, Germany

Printed by Libri Plureos GmbH
in Hamburg, Germany